Management and Cost Accounting

Student's Manual

COLIN DRURY

Management and Cost Accounting

SIXTH EDITION

Student's Manual

THOMSON
™

Australia • Canada • Mexico • Singapore • Spain • United Kingdom • United States

Management and Cost Accounting, 6th edition: Student's Manual

Copyright © 2004 Colin Drury

The Thomson logo is a registered trademark used herein under licence.

For more information, contact Thomson Learning, High Holborn House,
50-51 Bedford Row, London WC1R 4LR or visit us on the World Wide Web at:
http://www.thomsonlearning.co.uk

British Library Cataloguing-in-Publication Data
A catalogue record for this book is available from the British Library

ISBN-13: 978-1-84480-030-8
ISBN-10: 1-84480-030-X

First edition published by Chapman & Hall 1985
Second edition published by Chapman & Hall 1988
Third edition published by Chapman & Hall 1992
Fourth edition published by International Thomson Business Press 1996
Fourth edition (revised) published by International Thomson Business Press 1999
Fifth edition published by Thomson Learning 2000
Sixth edition published by Thomson Learning 2004
Reprinted by Thomson Learning 2004, 2005 and 2006

Typeset by Saxon Graphics Ltd, Derby
Printed in Singapore by Seng Lee Press

Contents

Preface

This manual is complementary to the main textbook, *Management and Cost Accounting*. Throughout the main book I have kept the illustrations simple to enable the reader to understand the principles involved in designing and evaluating management and cost accounting systems. More complex problems are provided at the end of each chapter so that the student can pursue certain topics in more depth, and concentrate on the application of principles. The objective of this manual is to provide solutions to those additional problems contained in the white boxes within the main text and, where necessary, to supplement the main text with a discussion of the additional issues raised by the questions.

The solutions given in this manual are my own and not the approved solutions of the professional body setting the question. Where an essay question is asked and a full answer requires undue repetition of the book, either references are made to the appropriate sections of the main book, or an answer guide or outline is provided. You should note that there will be no 'ideal' answer to questions which are not strictly numerical. Answers are provided which, it is felt, would be generally acceptable in most contexts.

Where possible the questions are arranged in ascending order of difficulty. The reader should select questions which are appropriate to the course which is being pursued. As a general rule questions titled 'Intermediate' and designated as ACCA Level 1, ACCA Foundation, CIMA Foundation, CIMA Cost Accounting 1 and 2 (or stages 1 and 2) and AAT are appropriate for a first year course. These questions are mainly concerned with cost accounting which is covered in Part II of the main text. Questions titled 'Advanced' and designated as CIMA Management Accounting, ICAEW Management Accounting, ACCA Level II Management Accounting and ACCA Professional Two Management Accounting are appropriate for a second year course.

Finally I would like to thank, once again, the Association of Accounting Technicians, the Institute of Chartered Accountants in England and Wales, the Chartered Association of Certified Accountants and the Chartered Institute of Management Accountants for permission to reproduce questions which have appeared in past examinations.

An introduction to cost terms and concepts

Solutions to Chapter 2 questions

In Chapters 1 and 2 it was pointed out that a management accounting system should generate information to meet the following requirements:

1. to allocate costs between cost of goods sold and inventories for internal and external profit measurement and inventory valuation;
2. to provide relevant information to help managers to make better decisions;
3. to provide information for planning, control and performance measurement.

The question relates to how costs can be classified for meeting the planning, control and decision-making requirements.

Planning relates to the annual budgeting and long-term processes described in Chapter 15. Within these processes costs can be classified by:

- *Behaviour* – By classifying costs into fixed, variable, semi-fixed and semi-variable categories the outcomes from different activity levels can be examined.
- *Function* – Functions are the different responsibility centres within the organization. The budget is built up by the functional levels so that everyone in the organization has a clear understanding of the role that their responsibility centre has in achieving the annual budget.
- *Expense type* – Classifying by expense types provides useful information on the nature, content and trend of different expense categories that is useful for planning how much should be authorized on spending within the different categories.
- *Controllability* – Classifying expenses by responsibility centres determines the individuals who are accountable for achieving the budget and who should thus be involved in setting the budget for the specific responsibility centres.

The management function of control consists of the measurement, reporting and the subsequent correction of performance in an attempt to ensure that a firm's objectives and plans are achieved. Within the control process costs can be classified by:

- *Behaviour* – Costs must be classified by behaviour for comparing actual and budgeted performance using flexible budgets. You should refer to Chapter 16 for a description of flexible budgeting.
- *Function* – For control, cost and revenues should be traced to the heads of the responsibility centres who are responsible for incurring them. For a description of this process you should refer to 'Responsibility Accounting' in Chapter 2.
- *Expense type* – This will ensure that like items are compared with one another when budget and actual performance are compared and trends in revenues and different expense categories are monitored.
- *Controllability* – Costs and revenues must be assigned to the responsibility heads who are made accountable for them so that effective control can be exercised.
- *Relevance* – Attention should only be focused on those expense categories where there are significant deviations from the budget. Insignificant deviations are not relevant for cost control. See 'Management by Exception' in Chapter 1 for a more detailed explanation of this point.

Decision-making involves choosing between alternative courses of actions. The following classifications are important for decision-making:

- *By behaviour* – Classification of costs by fixed, variable, semi-fixed and semi-variable is necessary for predicting future costs for alternative courses of action. In particular, classification is necessary for cost–volume–profit analysis and identifying break-even levels. You should refer to Chapter 8 for a more detailed discussion of these topics.
- *By expense type* – This is necessary to identify how different cost categories will change as a result of pursuing alternative courses of action.
- *By relevance* – For decision-making it is necessary to distinguish between relevant and irrelevant costs and revenues for alternative courses of action. For a more detailed explanation you should refer to 'Relevant and Irrelevant Costs and Revenues' in Chapter 2.

It is apparent from the above discussion that costs should be classified in different ways for different purposes. This is explained in more detail in the section entitled 'Maintaining a cost database' in Chapter 2.

Question 2.35 (a) A large proportion of non-manufacturing costs are of a discretionary nature. In respect of such costs, management has some significant range of discretion as to the amount it will budget for the particular activity in question. Examples of discretionary costs (sometimes called *managed* or *programmed costs*) include advertising, research and development, and training costs. There is no optimum relationship between inputs (as measured by the costs) and outputs (as measured by revenues or some other objective function) for these costs. Furthermore, they are not predetermined by some previous commitment. In effect, management can determine what quantity of service it wishes to purchase. For example, it can choose to spend small or large amounts on research and development or advertising. The great difficulty in controlling such costs is that there is no established method for determining the appropriate amount to be spent in particular periods.

For a description of fixed and variable costs see Chapter 2. Examples of fixed costs include depreciation of the factory building, supervisors' salaries and leasing charges. Examples of variable costs include direct materials, power and sales commissions.

(b) The £500 000 is a sunk cost and cannot be avoided. It is therefore not a relevant cost for decision-making purposes. The project should be continued because the incremented/relevant benefits exceed the incremental/relevant costs:

	(£000)
Incremental benefits	350
Incremental costs	200
Net incremental benefit	150

(c) An opportunity cost is a cost that measures the opportunity lost or sacrificed when the choice of one course of action requires that an alternative course of action be given up. The following are examples of opportunity costs:

(i) If scarce resources such as machine hours are required for a special contract then the opportunity cost represents the lost profit that would have been earned from the alternative use of the machine hours.

(ii) If an employee is paid £5 per hour and is charged out at £11 per hour for committed work then, if that employee is redirected to other work, the lost contribution of £6 per hour represents the opportunity cost of the employee's time.

The CIMA terminology defines a notional cost as: 'A hypothetical cost taken into account in a particular situation to represent a benefit enjoyed by an entity in respect of which no actual cost is incurred.' The following are examples of notional costs:

(i) interest on capital to represent the notional cost of using an asset rather than investing the capital elsewhere;

(ii) including rent as a cost for premises owned by the company so as to represent the lost rent income resulting from using the premises for business purposes.

Question 2.36

(a) See Chapter 2 for a description of opportunity costs. Out of pocket cost can be viewed as being equivalent to incremental or relevant costs as described in Chapter 2.

(b) Depreciation is not a relevant cost since it will be the same for both alternatives. It is assumed that tyres and miscellaneous represent the additional costs incurred in travelling to work. The relevant costs are:

Using the car to travel to work:

	(£)
Petrol	128
Tyres and miscellaneous	52
	180
Contribution from passenger	120
Relevant cost	60

Using the train:

Relevant cost	£188

(c)

	(£000)	(£000)	(%)
Sales		2560.0	100
Direct materials	819.2		32
Direct wages	460.8		18
Variable production overhead	153.6		6
Variable administration/selling	76.8		3
Total variable cost		1510.4	59
Contribution		1049.6	41
Fixed production overhead[a]	768		30
Fixed administration/selling[b]	224		8.75
		992	
Profit		57.6	2.25

Notes

[a] $100/80 \times £2\,560\,000 \times 0.24$

[b] $100/80 \times £2\,560\,000 \times 0.07$

Cost assignment

Solutions to Chapter 3 questions

Question 3.30

(a) Calculation of department overhead rates

	Department P (£)	Department Q (£)	Department R (£)
Repairs and maintenance	42 000	10 000	10 000
Depreciation	17 000[a]	14 000	9 000
Consumable supplies	4 500[b]	2 700	1 800
Wage related costs	48 250	26 250	12 500
Indirect labour	45 000	27 000	18 000
Canteen/rest/smoke room	15 000[c]	9 000	6 000
Business rates and insurance	13 000[d]	10 400	2 600
	184 750	99 350	55 900
Direct labour hours	50 000	30 000	20 000
Overhead absorption rate	£3.70	£3.31	£3.00

Notes:
The calculations for Department P are:
[a]Depreciation = £170 000/£400 000 × £40 000.
[b]Consumable supplies = 50 000/100 000 × £9000.
[c]Canteen = 25/50 × £30 000.
[d]Business rates insurance = 5000/10 000 × £26 000.

(b) Job 976: Sample quotation

		(£)	(£)
Direct materials			800.00
Direct labour	P (30 × £7.72[a])	231.60	
	Q (10 × £7.00[b])	70.00	
	R (5 × £5.00[c])	25.00	326.60
Overhead absorbed	P (30 × £3.70)	111.00	
	Q (10 × £3.31)	33.10	
	R (5 × £3.00)	15.00	159.10
Production cost			1285.70
Selling, distribution and administration costs (20% × £1285.70)			257.14
Total cost			1542.84
Profit margin (20% of selling price)			385.71
Selling price (£1542.84 × 100/800)			1928.55

Notes:
[a]£386 000/50 000.
[b]£210 000/30 000.
[c]£100 000/20 000.

(c)

	(£)
Direct materials	800.00
Direct labour	326.60
Prime cost	1126.60
Overhead applied (125%)	1408.25
Total cost	2534.85

The auditor's system results in a higher cost for this quotation. However, other jobs will be overcosted with the previous system. The auditor's system will result in the reporting of more accurate job costs with some job costs being higher, and others being lower, than the present system. For a more detailed answer see the section on plant-wide (blanket) overhead rates in Chapter 3.

Question 3.31

(a)

Calculation of overhead absorption rates

	Machining (£000)	Assembly (£000)	Finishing (£000)	Stores (£000)	Maintenance (£000)
Allocated costs	600.00	250.00	150.00	100.00	80.00
Stores apportionment	40.00 (40%)	30.00 (30%)	20.00 (20%)	(100.00)	10.00 (10%)
Maintenance apportionment	49.50 (55%)	18.00 (20%)	18.00 (20%)	4.50 (5%)	(90.00)
Stores apportionment[a]	2.00 (4/9)	1.50 (3/9)	1.00 (2/9)	(4.50)	
Total	691.50	299.50	189.00	—	—
Machine hours	50 000				
Labour hours		30 000	20 000		
Overhead absorption rates[b]	13.83	9.98	9.45		

Notes

[a] Costs have become too small at this stage to justify apportioning 10% of the costs to the maintenance department. Therefore stores costs are apportioned in the ratio 40: 30: 20.

[b] Machine hours are the predominant activity in the machine department whereas labour hours are the predominant activity in the assembly and finishing departments. Therefore machine hours are used as the allocation base in the machining department and direct labour hours are used for the assembly and finishing departments.

(b)

Quotation for Job XX 34

	(£)	(£)
Direct material		2400.00
Direct labour		1500.00
Overhead cost:		
Machining (45 machine hours at £13.83)	622.35	
Assembly (15 labour hours at £9.98)	149.70	
Finishing (12 labour hours at £9.45	113.40	885.45
Total cost		4785.45

Selling price (Profit margin = 20% of selling price
∴ selling price = £4785.45/0.8) 5981.81

(c)

Overhead control account

	(£)		(£)
Overhead incurred	300 000	WIP control (30 700 hrs at £9.98)	306 386
Balance – over-recovery transferred to costing profit and loss account	6 386		
	306 386		306 386

(d) For the answer to this question see 'An illustration of the two-stage process for an ABC system' in Chapter 3. In particular, the answer should stress that cost centres will consist of activity cost centres rather than departmental centres. Separate cost driver rates would also be established for the service departments and the costs would be allocated to cost objects via cost driver rates rather than being reallocated to production departments and assigned within the production department rates. The answer should also stress that instead of using just two volume-based cost drivers (e.g. direct labour and machine hours) a variety of cost drivers would be used, including non-volume-based drivers such as number of set-ups and number of material issues. The answer could also stress that within the machining department a separate set-up activity centre might be established with costs being assigned using the number of set-ups as the cost driver. The current system includes the set-up costs within the machine hour overhead rate.

Question 3.32

(a)

	Department A	Department B
Allocated costs	£217 860	£374 450
Apportioned costs	45 150	58 820
Total departmental overheads	263 010	433 270
Overhead absorption rate	£19.16 (£263 010/13 730)	£26.89 (£433 270/16 110)

(b)

	Department A (£)	Department B (£)	Department C (£)
Allocated costs	219 917	387 181	103 254
Apportionment of 70% of Department C costs [a]	32 267	40 011	(72 278)
Apportionment of 30% of Department C costs [b]	11 555	19 421	(30 976)
Total departmental overheads	263 739	446 613	
Overheads charged to production	261 956 [c]	455 866 [d]	
Under/(over-recovery)	1 783	(9 253)	

Notes:
[a] Allocated on the basis of actual machine hours
[b] Allocated on the basis of actual direct labour hours
[c] £19.16 × 13 672 actual machine hours
[d] £26.89 × 16 953 actual direct labour hours

(c)

See Appendix 3.1 (Chapter 3) for the answer to this question.

Question 3.33

(a) *Year 1*
  (1) Budgeted machine hours   132 500
  (2) Budgeted fixed overheads   £2 411 500 (132 500 × £18.20)
  (3) Actual machine hours   134 200 (£2 442 440/£18.20)
  (4) Fixed overheads absorbed   £2 442 440
  (5) Actual fixed overheads incurred   £2 317 461

  Over-absorption of fixed overheads   £124 979 (5 − 4)

The section on 'Under- and over-recovery of fixed overheads' in Chapter 3 indicates that an under- or over-recovery will arise whenever actual activity or expenditure differs from budgeted activity or expenditure. Actual activity was 1700 hours in excess of budget and this will result in an over-recovery of fixed overheads of £30 940. Actual overheads incurred were £94 039 (£2 317 461 – £2 411 500) less than budget and this is the second factor explaining the over-absorption of fixed overheads.

Summary	(£)
Over-recovery due to actual expenditure being less than budgeted expenditure	94 039
Over-recovery due to actual activity exceeding budgeted activity	30 940
Total over-recovery of overhead for year 1	124 979

Year 2

(1) Budgeted machine hours (134 200 × 1.05)	140 910
(2) Budgeted fixed overheads	£2 620 926
(3) Fixed overhead rate (£2 620 926/140 900 hours)	£18.60
(4) Actual fixed overheads incurred	£2 695 721
(5) Fixed overheads absorbed (139 260 × £18.60)	£2 590 236
(6) Under-recovery of overhead for year 2 (4 – 5)	£105 485

Analysis of under-recovery of overhead	(£)
Under-recovery due to actual activity being less than budgeted activity (139 260 – 140 910) × £18.60	30 690
Under-recovery due to actual expenditure being greater than budgeted expenditure (£2 695 721 – £2 620 926	74 795
Total under-recovery for the year	105 485

Change in the overhead rate

Change in the rate (£18.60 – £18.20)/£18.20	=	+ 2.198%
This can be analysed as follows:		
Increase in budgeted expenditure (£2 620 926 – £2 411 500)/£2 411 500	=	+ 8.684%
Increase in budgeted activity (140 910 hours – 132 500 hrs)/132 500	=	+ 6.347%

The increase of 2.198% in the absorption rate is due to an expenditure increase of 8.684% in budgeted expenditure partly offset by an increase in budgeted activity of 6.347% over the 2 years.

Proof
(1.08684/1.06347) – 1 = 0.02198 (2.198%)

(b) See 'Plant-wide (blanket) overhead rates' and 'Budgeted overhead rates' in Chapter 3 for the answers to these questions.

(a) (i) and (ii) An activity increase of 150 hours (1650 – 1500) results in an increase **Question 3.34** in total overheads of £675. It is assumed that the increase in total overheads is due entirely to the increase in variable overheads arising from an increase in activity. Therefore the variable overhead rate is £4.50 (£675/150 hours) per machine hour. The cost structure is as follows:

1. Activity level (hours)	1 500	1 650	2 000
2. Variable overheads at £4.50 per hour	£6 750	£7 425	£9 000
3. Total overheads	£25 650	£26 325	£27 900
4. Fixed overheads (3 – 2)	£18 900	£18 900	£18 900

(iii) The fixed overhead rate is £10.50 (£15 − £4.50 variable rate)

$$\text{normal activity} = \text{fixed overheads (£18 900)/fixed overhead rate (£10.50)}$$
$$= 1800 \text{ machine hours}$$

(iv) Under-absorption = 100 machine hours (1800 − 1700) at £10.50 = £1050

(b) (i) A machine hour rate is recommended for the machine department because most of the overheads (e.g. depreciation and maintenance) are likely to be related to machine hours. For non-machine labour-intensive departments, such as the finishing department, overheads are likely to be related to direct labour hours rather than machine hours. Overheads are therefore charged to jobs performed in the finishing department using the direct labour hour method of recovery.

Calculation of overhead rates

	Machining department	Finishing department
Production overhead	£35 280	£12 480
Machine hours	11 200	
Direct labour hours		7800
Machine hour overhead rate	£3.15	
Direct labour hour overhead rate		£1.60

(ii)

	Machining department (£)	Finishing department (£)
Direct materials		
(189 × 1.1 × £2.35/0.9)	542.85	—
Direct labour[a]		
25 hours × £4	100.00	
28 hours × £4		112.00
Production overhead		
46 machine hours at £3.15	144.90	
28 direct labour hours at £1.60		44.80
	787.75	156.80

Total cost of job = £944.55 (£787.75 + £156.80)

Note
[a]Overtime premiums are charged to overheads, and are therefore not included in the above job cost.

Question 3.35

(a) To calculate product cost, we must calculate overhead absorption rates for the production departments. You can see from the question that the service departments serve each other, and it is therefore necessary to use the repeated distribution method or the simultaneous equation method to reallocate the service department costs. Both methods are illustrated below:

	Cutting (£)	Machining (£)	Pressing (£)	Engineering (£)	Personnel (£)
Allocation per question	154 482	64 316	58 452	56 000	34 000
Engineering reallocation	11 200 (20%)	25 200 (45%)	14 000 (25%)	(56 000)	5 600 (10%)
Personnel reallocation	21 780 (55%)	3 960 (10%)	7 920 (20%)	5 940 (15%)	(39 600)
Engineering reallocation	1 188 (20%)	2 673 (45%)	1 485 (25%)	(5 940)	594 (10%)

Personnel reallocation	327 (55%)	59 (10%)	119 (20%)	89 (15%)	(594)
Engineering reallocation[a]	20	44	25	(89)	
	188 997	96 252	82 001	—	—

Note

[a]The costs are so small that any further apportionments are not justified. Consequently a return charge of 15% is not made to the engineering department and the costs are apportioned in the ratio 55:10:20.

Simultaneous equation method

Let

E = total overhead allocated to engineering department

and

P = total overhead allocated to personnel department

Then

$E = 56\,000 + 0.15P$

$P = 34\,000 + 0.10E$

Rearranging the above equations,

$$E - 0.15P = 56\,000 \qquad (1)$$
$$-0.10E + P = 34\,000 \qquad (2)$$

Multiplying equation (2) by 0.15 and equation (1) by 1,

$$E - 0.15P = 56\,000$$
$$-0.015E + 0.15P = 5\,100$$

Adding these equations,

$$0.985E = 61\,100$$

and so $\qquad E = £62\,030$

Substituting for E in equation (1),

$$62\,030 - 0.15P = 56\,000$$
$$6030 = 0.15P$$

and so $\qquad P = 40\,200$

We now apportion the values of E and P to the production departments in the agreed percentages:

	Cutting (£)	Machining (£)	Pressing (£)
Allocation per question	154 482	64 316	58 452
Allocation of engineering	12 408(20%)	27 914(45%)	15 508(25%)
Allocation of personnel	22 110(55%)	4 020(10%)	8 040(20%)
	189 000	96 250	82 000

Overhead absorption rates

A comparison of the machine and direct labour hours in the machine department indicates that machine hours are the dominant activity. Therefore a machine hour rate should be used. A direct labour hour rate is appropriate for the cutting and pressing departments. Note that unequal wage rates apply in the cutting department, but equal wage rates apply in the pressing department. The direct wages percentage and the direct labour hour methods will therefore result in identical overhead charges to products passing through the pressing department, and either method can be used. Because of the unequal wage rates in the cutting department, the direct wages percentage method is inappropriate.

The calculation of the overhead absorption rates are as follows:

		(hours)
Cutting:	Product A (4000 × 9 hours)	36 000
	Product B (3000 × 6 hours)	18 000
	Product C (6000 × 5 hours)	30 000
	Total	84 000

$$\text{Absorption rate} = \frac{£189\,000}{84\,000} = £2.25 \text{ per direct labour hour}$$

Machining:	Product A (4000 × 2)	8 000
	Product B (3000 × $1\frac{1}{2}$)	4 500
	Product C (6000 × $2\frac{1}{2}$)	15 000
		27 500

$$\text{Absorption rate} = \frac{£96\,250}{27\,500} = £3.50 \text{ per machine hour}$$

Pressing:	Product A (4000 × 2)	8 000
	Product B (3000 × 3)	9 000
	Product C (6000 × 4)	24 000
		41 000

$$\text{Absorption rate} = \frac{£82\,000}{41\,000} = £2 \text{ per direct labour hour}$$

Product cost calculations

		A (fully complete) (£)	B (partly complete) (£)
Direct materials		7.00	4.00
Direct labour: Cutting	(Skilled)	12.00 (3 × £4)	20.00 (5 × £4)
	(Unskilled)	15.00 (6 × £2.50)	2.50 (1 × £2.50)
Machining		1.50 ($\frac{1}{2}$ × £3)	0.75 ($\frac{1}{4}$ × £3)
Pressing		6.00 (2 × £3)	—
Prime cost		41.50	27.25
Overhead:	Cutting	20.25 (9 × £2.25)	13.50 (6 × £2.25)
	Machining	7.00 (2 × £3.50)	5.25 ($1\frac{1}{2}$ × £3.50)
	Pressing	4.00 (2 × £2)	—
		72.75	46.00
		a(i)	a(ii)

(b) The accounting entries for overheads are presented in Chapter 4. You will find when you read this chapter that a credit balance in the overhead control account represents an over recovery of overheads. Possible reasons for this include:

(i) actual overhead expenditure was less than budgeted expenditure;
(ii) actual production activity was greater than budgeted production activity.

(a) (i) *Direct apportionment*

	Heat (£000)	Maintenance (£000)	Steam (£000)	Processing (£000)	Assembly (£000)	Total (£000)
Allocation	90	300	240			630
Heat (4 : 5)	(90)			40	50	—
Maintenance (1 : 2)		(300)		100	200	—
Steam (2 : 1)			(240)	160	80	—
				300	330	630

With the direct method of allocation, inter-service department apportionments are ignored; service department costs are reapportioned to *production* departments only.

(ii) *Step-down method*

This method is the specified order of closing described in Appendix 3.1. There the service department that provided the largest proportion of services for other services was closed first. In this answer the service department providing the largest value of cost inputs to other service departments (namely the maintenance department) is closed first, and the department providing the second largest value of cost input to other service departments (namely steam) is closed next. Return charges are not made.

	Heat (£000)	Maintenance (£000)	Steam (£000)	Processing (£000)	Assembly (£000)	Total (£000)
Allocation	90	300	240			630
Maintenance[a]	30	(300)	45	75	150	
Steam[a]	60		(285)	150	75	
Heat[a]	(180)			80	100	
				305	325	630

Note

[a]Proportions allocated to each department:
 Maintenance = 3/30, 4.5/30, 7.5/30, 15/30
 Steam = 192/912, 480/912, 240/912
 Heat = 4/9, 5/9.

(iii) *Reciprocal method*

Either the algebraic method or the repeated distribution method can be used to take account of reciprocal service arrangements. Both are illustrated in this answer.

Algebraic method
Let
h = total cost of heating
m = total cost of maintenance
s = total cost of steam
Then
h = 90 + (3/30)m + (192/960)s
m = 300 + (5/100)h + (48/960)s
s = 240 + (5/100)h + (4.5/30)m

Expressing these equations in decimal form, we get:

$$h = 90 + 0.10m + 0.2s \qquad (1)$$
$$m = 300 + 0.05h + 0.05s \qquad (2)$$
$$s = 240 + 0.05h + 0.15m \qquad (3)$$

Substituting for s,

$$h = 90 + 0.10m + 0.2(240 + 0.05h + 0.15m)$$
$$m = 300 + 0.05h + 0.05(240 + 0.05h + 0.15m)$$

Expanding these equations gives:

$$h = 90 + 0.10m + 48 + 0.01h + 0.03m$$
$$m = 300 + 0.05h + 12 + 0.0025h + 0.0075m$$

Rearranging,

$$0.99h = 138 + 0.13m \qquad (4)$$
$$0.9925m = 312 + 0.0525h \qquad (5)$$

Substituting in equation (4) for m,

$$0.99h = 138 + 0.13 \frac{(312 + 0.0525h)}{0.9925}$$

$$0.99h = 138 + 40.866 + 0.0069h$$

$$h = \frac{138 + 40.866}{0.99 - 0.0069} = 181.941$$

Substituting for h in equation (5),

$$0.9925m = 312 + 0.0525(181.941)$$

$$m = \frac{312 + 0.0525(181.941)}{0.9925} = 324.165$$

Substituting into equation (3),

$$s = 240 + 0.05(181.941) + 0.15(324.165) = 297.722$$

We now apportion the values of h, m and s to the production departments according to the basis of allocation specified:

	Processing (£000)	Assembly (£000)
Heat (181.941)	72.776 (40/100)	90.970 (50/100)
Maintenance (324.165)	81.041 (7.5/30)	162.082 (15/30)
Steam (297.722)	148.861 (480/960)	74.431 (240/960)
	302.678	327.483

Repeated distribution method

	Heat (£000)	Maintenance (£000)	Steam (£000)	Processing (£000)	Assembly (£000)
Allocation per question	90.00	300.00	240.00		
Heat reallocation	(90.00)	4.50(5%)	4.50(5%)	36.00(40%)	45.00(50%)
Maintenance reallocation	30.45(10%)	(304.50)	45.67(15%)	76.13(25%)	152.25(50%)
Steam reallocation	58.03(20%)	14.51(5%)	(290.17)	145.09(50%)	72.54(25%)
Heat reallocation	(88.48)	4.42(5%)	4.42(5%)	35.40(40%)	44.24(50%)
Maintenance reallocation	1.89(10%)	(18.93)	2.84(15%)	4.73(25%)	9.47(50%)
Steam reallocation	1.45(20%)	0.36(5%)	(7.26)	3.63(50%)	1.82(25%)
Heat reallocation	(3.34)	0.16(5%)	0.17(5%)	1.34(40%)	1.67(50%)

Maintenance reallocation[a]	(0.52)		0.17	0.35
Steam[a]		(0.17)	0.11	0.06
			302.6	327.4

Note

[a]At this stage the costs are so small that no further reallocations between service departments are justified. The costs of the maintenance department are reapportioned in the ratio 7.5:15, while those of the steam department are reapportioned in the ratio 480:240.

(b) The main problems encountered are as follows:

   (i) The costs allocated to the service departments are the result of arbitrary apportionments. The costs are then reallocated from the service to production departments using further arbitrary allocations. Consequently, the associated costs attached to products will be arbitrary and dependent upon the selected apportionment methods.

   (ii) If a substantial part of the service department costs are fixed and costs are allocated to production departments on the basis of usage, there is a danger that the resulting unit product costs will fail to distinguish between the fixed and variable cost categories. This could result in misleading information being used for short-term decisions.

   (iii) If the responsibility accounting system allocates the actual costs of the service departments to the production departments, the production departments will be accountable for the inefficiencies arising in the service departments. Consequently, the production managers will be demotivated and the service department managers will not be motivated to be efficient because they will always be able to recover their costs.

   Possible solutions include the following:

   (i) Avoid the use of arbitrary apportionments and identify appropriate cost drivers for the main activities undertaken by the service/support departments using an activity-based costing (ABC) system. See Chapters 3 and 10 for an explanation of an ABC system.

   (ii) Separate fixed and variable costs when reallocating service department costs to production departments.

   (iii) Charge service department costs to production departments on the basis of actual usage at standard cost. If the production managers have no control over the usage of the service, the service department costs should be regarded as uncontrollable (see 'Guidelines for applying the controllability principle in Chapter 16 for a discussion of this point). The service department managers will be motivated to control costs if they are accountable for the difference between actual and standard usage multiplied by the standard cost.

(c) The answer should include a discussion of the following points:

   (i) In today's production environment an increasing proportion of total costs are fixed, and short-term variable costs do not provide a useful measure of the cost of producing a product. Managers require an estimate of long-run product costs. The allocation of fixed costs to products provides a rough guide of a product's long-run cost. The answer should draw attention to the criticisms that Kaplan and Cooper (see Chapter 10) have made of traditional cost allocation methods and explain that an ABC system is an approach that has been recommended to overcome the problems of arbitrary overhead allocations.

   (ii) It is a tradition in some industries (e.g. Government contracts) for selling prices to be based on full product costs plus a percentage profit margin.

   (iii) Total manufacturing costs are required for stock valuation for external reporting. However, it is questionable whether costs computed for stock valuation ought to be used for decision-making.

(iv) It is sometimes claimed that fixed costs should be allocated to managers in order to draw their attention to those costs that the company incurs to support their activities. This is because the manager may be able to indirectly influence these costs, and should therefore be made aware of the sums which are involved. If this approach is adopted, controllable and non-controllable costs ought to be distinguished in the performance reports.

Question 3.37

(a) *Cost of Job 123*

	(£)	(£)
Direct materials:		
Y (*W1*) (400 kg × £0.505)	202.00	
Z (*W2*) (265 kg × £1.45)	384.25	586.25
Direct labour:		
Department A (*W3*) (76 hrs × £4.50)	342.00	
Department B (*W4*) (110 hrs × £4)	440.00	782.00
Overhead (*W5*):		
Department A (76 hrs × £2.70)	205.20	
Department B (110 hrs × £2.25)	247.50	452.70
		1820.95

Workings and comments

(*W1*) $\dfrac{(£529.75) + (600 \times £0.50)}{} $
$+\dfrac{(500 \times £0.50) + (400 \times £0.52)}{1050 + 600 + 500 + 400} = £0.505$ weighted average price

400 kg issued to job 123 is a direct cost

(*W2*) $\dfrac{£9946.50 + (16\,000 \times £1.46)}{6970 + 16\,000} = £1.45$ weighted average price.

Direct issues to the job are 270 kg (300 − 30), but 5 kg were damaged and destroyed. It is unlikely that the materials are a direct consequence of the job, and therefore it is incorrect to regard the 5 kg as a direct cost to the job. If such losses are expected to occur from time to time, the cost of the lost materials should be charged to departmental overheads and included in the departmental overhead rate calculation. If such losses are abnormal (as indicated in the question), they should not be charged as product costs. Instead, they should be charged to an abnormal losses account (see Chapter 5) and written off to profit and loss account as a period cost.

(*W3*) 76 hours have been directly identified to the job at the hourly rate of £4.50. Six hours were overtime, resulting in excess payments. As these hours are likely to be due to the general high level of production, the overtime premium is included in the overhead rate and shared out amongst all jobs. An additional 3 hours rectification were spent on the job, but such work is a *normal* part of the work *generally* undertaken by the department. The cost of rectification is therefore charged to overheads and included in the overhead absorption rate.

(*W4*) 110 hours are charged to the job. Of these, 30 hours were overtime, but this was a direct result of a customer's requirement on another job. Therefore the overtime premium is not charged to the job.

(*W5*) All direct items can be ignored when calculating overhead rates, but direct materials include scrapped materials and direct labour includes rectification work. However, scrapped materials are to be regarded as abnormal costs, but 20 hours rectification should be charged to overheads. Department A overtime premium is part of the overhead cost, but the overtime premium for Department B is charged directly to another customer.

Calculation of overhead rates	Department A (£)	Department B (£)
Rectification (20 × £4.50)	90	—
Indirect labour	2420	2960
Overtime premium	450	—
Lubricants	520	680
Maintenance	720	510
Other	1200	2150
	5400	6300
Direct labour hours	$2000 \left(\dfrac{£9000^a}{£4.50}\right)$	$2800 \left(\dfrac{£11\,200}{£4}\right)$
Direct labour hour overhead rate	£2.70	£2.25

Note
^{a}£9000 − £90 rectification cost.

(b) Information on the cost of individual jobs can be used as follows:
   (i) for stock valuation of partly completed and completed jobs;
   (ii) to determine the selling price of a product where no established market price exists;
   (iii) as an assessment of the profitability of a job when the selling price is market determined.
   Note that the job cost calculation derived here may be inappropriate for decision-making purposes. The major objective is to use the cost for stock valuation purposes.

Accounting entries for a job costing system

Solutions to Chapter 4 questions

Question 4.27 (a)

Stores ledger control account

	(£)		(£)
Opening Balance	60 140	Finished Goods Control A/c (1)	95 200
Cost Ledger Control A/c	93 106	Closing Balance	58 046
	153 246		153 246

Production wages control account

	(£)		(£)
Cost Ledger Control A/c (2)	121 603	Finished Goods Control A/c	87 480
		Production Overhead	
		Control A/c (2)	34 123
		(indirect wages)	
	121 603		121 603

Production overhead control account

	(£)		(£)
Cost Ledger Control A/c	116 202	Finished Goods Control A/c (3)	61 236
Production Wages		Profit & Loss A/c – Fixed	
Control A/c (2)	34 123	Overhead (3)	90 195
Profit & Loss A/c – over			
absorbed variable			
production overhead (3)	1 106		
	151 431		151 431

Finished goods control account

	(£)		(£)
Opening Balance	147 890	Variable Production Cost of	
Stores Ledger Control A/c	95 200	Sales A/c (balance)	241 619
Production Wages Control A/c	87 480	Closing Balance	150 187
Production Overhead			
Control A/c	61 236		
	391 806		391 806

Workings

(1)

	(Kg)	(£)
Opening stock	540	7 663
Purchases	1 100	15 840
	1 640	23 503

Issue price £23 503/1 640 = £14.33 per kg
Cost of material issues: Material Y = £14.33 × 1 164kg = £16 680
Other materials = £78 520

£95 200

(2) *Analysis of wages*

	Direct labour (£)	Indirect labour (£)
Direct workers productive time (11 664 × £7.50)	87 480	
Direct workers unproductive time at £7.50 (12 215 hours – 11 664)		4 132.50
Overtime premium (1 075 hours × £2.50)		2 687.50
Indirect workers basic time (4 655 hours × £5.70)		26 533.50
Indirect workers overtime premium (405 hours × £1.90)		769.50
	87 480	34 123.00

Total wages for the period £121 603 (£87 480 + £34 123)

(3) *Analysis of overheads*
Production overheads = £150 325 (£116 202 + £34 123)
Fixed overheads = 90 195 (60% × £150 325)
Variable overheads = 60 130 (40% × £150 325)
Variable overheads
absorbed = 61 236 (70% of the direct labour cost of £87 480)
Over-absorbed overheads = 1 106 (£61 236 – £60 130)
Note that with a marginal costing system fixed overheads are charged directly to the profit and loss account and not included in the product costs. Therefore they are not included in the finished stocks.

(b) See working (2) in part (a) for the answer to this question.

(c)

	(£)	(£)
Sales		479 462
Less: Variable production cost of sales	241 619	
Variable selling and administration overheads	38 575	
Over-absorbed variable production overheads	(1 106)	279 088
Contribution		200 374
Less: Fixed production overheads	90 195	
Fixed selling and administration overheads	74 360	164 655
Net profit		35 819

(a)

Question 4.28

Stores ledger card

Date	Kilos	Total value (£)	Average price per kilo (£)	
Opening balance	21 600	28 944	1.34	
1 Issue	(7 270)	(9 742)	1.34	
7 Purchase	17 400	23 490		
	31 730	42 692	1.3455	(£42 692/31 730)
8 Issue	(8 120)	(10 925)	1.3455	
15 Issue	(8 080)	(10 872)	1.3455	
20 Purchase	19 800	26 730		
	35 330	47 625	1.348	(£47 625/35 330)

| 22 | Issue | (9 115) | (12 287) | 1.348 |
| | Closing balance | 26 215 | 35 338 | 1.348 |

Summary of transactions

	(£)
Opening balance	28 944
Purchases	50 220
Issues	(43 826)
Closing balance	35 338

Raw material stock control account

	(£)		(£)
Opening balance	28 944	WIP	43 826
Purchases	50 220	Closing balance	35 338
	79 164		79 164

Production costs for the period:	(£)
Raw materials	43 826
Labour and overhead	35 407
	79 233
Cost per unit (£79 233/17 150 units)	£4.62

Units sold = opening stock (16 960) + production (17 150)
   − closing stock (17 080) = 17 030 units

Finished goods stock control account

	(£)		(£)
Opening balance	77 168	Cost of sales	
Raw materials	43 826	(difference/balancing figure)	77 491
Labour and overhead	35 407	Closing balance	
		(17 080 × £4.62)	78 910
	156 401		156 401

(b) The financial ledger control account is sometimes described as a cost control account or a general ledger adjustment account. For an explanation of the purpose of this account see 'Interlocking accounting' in Chapter 4.

(c) Budgeted production (units):

Sales	206 000	
Add closing stock	18 128	(206 000 × 1.10 × 20/250)
Less opening stock	(17 080)	
	207 048	units

For month 12 the raw material usage is 1.90 kilos per unit of output:

(7270 + 8120 + 8080 + 9115 = 32 585 kg used)/17 150 units produced
∴ Budgeted material usage = 207 048 units × 1.9 kg per unit
                          = 393 391 kg

Budgeted material purchases

Budgeted usage	393 391 kg	
Add closing stock	22 230	(11 700 × 1.9)
Less opening stock	(26 215)	
	389 406 kg	

(a)

Raw material stock control account

	(£)		(£)
Opening balance	72 460	Finished goods (1)	608 400
Creditors	631 220	Closing balance	95 280
	703 680		703 680

Production overhead control account

	(£)		(£)
Bank/Creditors	549 630	Finished goods (3)	734 000
Wages (2)	192 970	P & L – under absorption (3)	8 600
	742 600		742 600

Finished goods stock control account

	(£)		(£)
Opening balance	183 560	Production cost of sales (6)	1 887 200
Raw materials	608 400	Closing balance	225 960
Wages (5)	587 200		
Production overhead	734 000		
	2 113 160		2 113 160

Workings

(1) Raw materials issues:

Product A: 41 000 units at £7.20 per unit   = £295 200
Product B: 27 000 units at £11.60 per unit = £313 200

                £608 400

(2) Indirect labour charged to production overhead:
3 250 overtime premium hours at £2 per hour = £6 500 + £186 470 = £192 970

(3) Production overhead absorbed charged to finished goods:

Product A: 41 000 × 1 hour × £10   = £410 000
Product B: 27 000 × 1.2 hours × £10 = £324 000

                £734 000

Production overhead under-absorbed = £549 630 + £192 970 – £734 000
= £8 600

(4) Direct labour charge to finished goods stock:

Product A: 41 000 × 1 hour × £8   = £328 000
Product B: 27 000 × 1.2 hours × £8 = £259 200

                £587 200

(5) Production cost of sales:

Cost of product A = £7.20 materials + £8 direct labour + £10 overhead =
£25.20
Cost of product B = £11.60 materials + £9.60 direct labour (1.2 hours × £8)
+ £12 overhead (1.2 hours × £10) = £33.20
Cost of sales: Product A = 38 000 units × £25.20 per unit = £957 600
Product B = 28 000 units × £33.20 per unit = £929 600

                £1 887 200

(6) Valuation of closing stocks of finished goods:

Product A: 6200 units at £25.20	=	£156 240	
Product B: 2100 units at £33.20	=	£69 720	
		£225 960	

The above figure can also be derived from the balance of the account.

(b)

	Product A (£000)	Product B (£000)	Total (£000)
Sales	1330	1092	2422
Production cost of sales	(957.6)	(929.6)	(1887.2)
Gross profit (before adjustment)	372.4	162.4	534.8
Under absorbed production overheads			(8.6)
Gross profit (after adjustment)			526.2
Non-production overheads			(394.7)
Net profit			131.5

(c) With a marginal costing system fixed production overheads are charged directly against profits whereas with an absorption costing system they are included in the product costs and therefore included in the stock valuations. This means that with absorption costing cost of sales and profits will be affected by the changes in stocks. An increase in stocks will result in some of the fixed overheads incurred during the period being deferred to future periods whereas with a decrease in stocks the opposite situation will apply. Thus, absorption costing profits will be higher than marginal costing profits when stocks increase and lower when stocks decrease. For a more detailed explanation of the difference in profits you should refer to 'Variable costing and absorption costing: a comparison of their impact on profit' in Chapter 8.

In this question there is a stock increase of 3000 units for product A resulting in absorption costing profits exceeding marginal costing profits by £20 400 (3000 units at £6.80 per unit fixed overhead). Conversely, for product B there is a 1000 units stock reduction resulting in marginal costing profits exceeding the absorption costing profits by £8160 (1000 units at £8.16 per unit fixed overhead). The overall impact is that absorption costing profits exceed marginal costing profits by £12 240.

Question 4.30

(a) A wages control account is a summary account which records total wages payable including employers' national insurance contributions. The account is cleared by a credit and corresponding debits in respect of total wages costs charged to WIP and the overhead control account. The detail which supports the control account is maintained in subsidiary payroll records.

(b) (i)

	Dr (£)	Cr (£)
Wages control	122 300	
Bank		122 300
Wages control	58 160	
Employees' National Insurance		14 120
Employees' pension fund contributions		7 200
Income tax		27 800

		1 840
Court order retentions		1 840
Trade union subscriptions		1 200
Private health plans		6 000
	180 460	180 460
Production overhead control Dr	18 770	
Employer's National Insurance		18 770
	18 770	18 770

(ii)

Work-in-progress control:		
Wages	77 460	
Overtime wages – direct	16 800	
Production overhead control:		
Overtime premium	9 000	
Shift premium	13 000	
Indirect wages	38 400	
Overtime wage – indirect	10 200	
Warehouse construction account	2 300	
Statutory sick pay	9 000	
Idle time	4 300	
Wages control		180 460
	180 460	180 460

Question 4.31

(a) *Calculation of gross wages:*

	Direct workers		Indirect workers		Total
		(£)		(£)	(£)
Attendance time	2640 × 5.00 =	13 200	940 × 4.00 =	3760	
Overtime premium	180 × 2 =	360	75 × 1.60 =	120	
Group bonuses		2 840		710	
Gross wages		16 400		4590	20 990

(b) *Analysis of gross wages:*

	Direct charge (to WIP)		Indirect charge to production overhead		Total
		(£)		(£)	(£)
Attendance time:					
Direct workers	2515 × 5.00 =	12 575	125 × 5.00 =	625	
Indirect workers			940 × 4.00 =	3760	
Overtime premium:					
Direct workers	72 × 2.00 =	144	108 × 2.00 =	216	
Indirect workers	30 × 1.60 =	48	45 × 1.60 =	72	
Group bonuses					
Direct workers				2840	
Indirect workers				710	
		12 767		8223	20 990

Wages control account

	(£)		(£)
Cost ledger control	20 990	Work in progress	12 767
(Gross wages)		Production overhead	8 223
	20 990		20 990

Production overhead control account:

	(£)
Wages control	8223
Cost ledger control	1865
(Employers' employment costs)	

Question 4.32

(a) (i) The overheads apportioned to Contract ABC are as follows:

Stores operations = £1.56 million × (£6.4 million × 6 months)/(76.2 million × 53 months) = £148 000

Contract general management = £1.22 million × (£1.017 million/9.762 million) = £127 000

Transport = £1.37 million × (23km × 6 months)/(16km × 53 months) = £223 000

General administration = £4.25 million × (6 months/53 months) = £481 000

Total overheads apportioned to Contract ABC = £979 000

(ii)

	(£ million)	(£ million)
Costs to 1.12.01		1.063
Additional costs from 1.12.01 to 31.5.02:		
Raw materials	1.456	
Direct labour	1.017	
Overheads	0.979	3.452
Costs to date		4.515
Costs to complete		0.937
Total costs		5.452
Contract value		6.400
Estimated contract profit		0.948

Amount of profit taken to be included in the profit statement for the period:

[Value of work certified (£5.18 million)/Contract value (£6.4 million)] × £0.948 million = £0.767 million

Note that with some questions on contract costing the profit to date is computed by deducting the cost of work certified from the value of work certified. However, the cost of work not yet certified or the cost of work certified is not given in the question so it is not possible to adopt this approach.

(b) Service costing represents a costing system where the cost objects are the cost of services rather than the cost of products. It is applied in the service sector but can be applied in other sectors where the objective is to calculate the cost of the service departments. The key factors to consider are as follows:

- determining which services are to be costed within the stores department (e.g. materials receiving, materials handling, etc.);
- establishing whether total costs or unit costs should be calculated. In the latter situation the output should be measurable to calculate the cost per unit of output;
- establishing how costs should be classified in determining the total costs of services (e.g. determining the different categories of direct and indirect costs to be reported);
- deciding the key financial and non-financial performance measures to be reported.

Contract accounts (for the previous year) **Question 4.33**

	MNO (£000)	PQR (£000)	STU (£000)		MNO (£000)	PQR (£000)	STU (£000)
Materials on site b/fwd			25	Wages accrued b/fwd		2	
Plant on site b/fwd		35	170	Plant control a/c		8	
Materials control a/c	40	99	180	Materials on site c/fwd	8		
Wages control a/c	20	47	110	Plant on site c/fwd	70		110
Subcontractors a/c			35	Prepayment c/fwd			15
Salaries	6	20	25	Cost of work not certified			
Plant control a/c	90	15		c/fwd			26
Wages accrued c/fwd		5		Cost of work certified			
Apportionment of				(balance)[c]	82	221	416
construction services[a]	4	10	22				
	160	231	567		160	231	567
Cost of work certified b/fwd	82	221	416	Attributable sales revenue	82	200	530
Profit taken this period[b]			114	Loss taken[b]		21	
	82	221	530		82	221	530
Cost of work not certified				Wages accrued b/fwd		5	
b/fwd			26				
Materials on site b/fwd	8						
Plant on site b/fwd	70		110				
Prepayment b/fwd			15				

Notes

[a]Costs incurred by construction services department:

	(£000)
Plant depreciation (12 – 5)	7
Salaries	21
Wages paid	8
	36

Wages incurred by each department are:

	(£000)
MNO	20
PQR	50 (47 + 5 − 2)
STU	110
	180

The costs apportioned to each contract are:

	(£000)
MNO	$4\left(\dfrac{[20]}{180} \times £36\right)$
PQR	$10\left(\dfrac{[50]}{180} \times £36\right)$
STU	$\dfrac{22}{36}\left(\dfrac{110}{180} \times £36\right)$

[b]See (b) (i) for calculation.
[c]Profit taken plus cost of sales for the current period or cost of sales less loss to date.

(b) (i) *Contract MNO*: Nil.
   Contract PQR:

	(£)
Cost of contract to date (see part (a))	411 000
Value of work certified	390 000
Recommended loss to be written off	21 000

Contract STU:

	(£)
Cost of work certified	786 000
Cost of work not yet certified	26 000
Estimated costs to complete	138 000
Estimated cost of contract	950 000
Contract price	1 100 000
Anticipated profit	150 000

The profit taken to date is calculated using the following formula:

$$\frac{\text{cash received to date } (£950\ 000)}{\text{contract price } (£1\ 100\ 000)} \times \text{estimated profit from the contract } (£150\ 000)$$

$$= £129\ 545 \text{ (say £129 000)}$$

The profit taken for the current period is £114 000, consisting of the profit to date of £129 000 less the profit previously transferred to the profit and loss account of £15 000.

(ii) *Contract MNO*: This contract is at a very early stage, and it is unlikely that the outcome can be reasonably foreseen. It is therefore prudent not to anticipate any profit at this stage.

Contract PQR: This contract has incurred a loss, and, applying the prudence concept, this loss should be written off as soon as it is incurred.

Contract STU: Applying the prudence concept, a proportion of the profit

$$\frac{\text{cash received to date}}{\text{contract price}}$$

is recognized in this period. The proportion of profit that is recognized is arbitrary and very much a matter of opinion. Alternative apportionments applying the concept of prudence could have been applied.

Process costing

Solutions to Chapter 5 questions

(a) (i)

Process A account

	(kg)	(£)		(kg)	(£)	(£)
Direct material	2000	10 000	Normal loss	400	0.50	200
Direct labour		7 200	Process B	1400	18.575	26 005
Process costs		8 400	Abnormal loss	200	18.575	3 715
Overhead		4 320				
	2000	29 920		2000		29 920

Unit cost = (£29 920 − £200)/1600 = £18.575

(ii)

Process B account

	(kg)	(£)		(kg)	(£)	(£)
Process A	1400	26 005	Finished goods	2620	21.75	56 989
Direct material	1400	16 800	Normal loss	280	1.825	511
Direct labour		4 200	(10% × 2800)			
Overhead		2 520				
Process costs		5 800				
		55 325				
Abnormal gain	100	2 175				
	2900	57 000		2900		57 500

Unit cost = (£55 325 − £511)/(2800 − 280) = £21.75

(iii)

Normal loss/gain account

	(kg)	(£)		(kg)	(£)
Process A	400	200	Bank (A)	400	200
Process B	280	511	Abnormal gain (B)	100	182.5
			Bank (B)	180	328.5
	680	711		680	711

(iv)

Abnormal loss/gain

	(£)		(£)
Process A	3715	Process B	2175
Normal loss/gain (B)	182.5	Bank	100
		Profit & Loss	1622.5
	3897.5		3897.5

(v)

Finished goods

	(£)		(£)
Process B	56 989		

(vi)

Profit and loss account (extract)

	(£)		(£)
Abnormal loss/gain	1622.5		

Question 5.29 (a) Units completed = 8250 − Closing WIP (1600) = 6650

Calculation of number of equivalent units produced

	Completed units	Closing WIP	Total equivalent units
Previous process	6650	1600	8250
Materials	6650	1600	8250
Labour and overhead	6650	960 (60%)	7610

(b)

	(£)	Total equivalent units	Cost per unit (£)
Previous process cost	453 750	8250	55
Materials	24 750	8250	3
Labour and overheads	350 060	7610	46
			104

(c)

Process account

	Units	(£)		Units	(£)
Input from previous process	8250	453 750	Finished goods[a]	6650	691 600
Materials		24 750	Closing WIP[b]	1600	136 960
Labour and overheads		350 060			
	8250	828 560		8250	828 560

Note
[a] Cost of completed production = 6650 units × £104 = £691 600
[b]

		(£)
Closing WIP: Previous process cost (1600 × £55) =		88 000
Materials (1600 × £3) =		4 800
Labour and overhead (960 × £46) =		44 160
		136 960

(d) See the introduction to Chapter 6 and 'Accounting for by-products' in Chapter 6 for the answer to this question.

Question 5.30 (a)

	Units
Input:	
Opening WIP	12 000
Transferred from process 1	95 000
	107 000
Output:	
Closing WIP	10 000
Normal loss	200
Completed units (balance)	96 800
	107 000

Statement of completed production and calculation of cost per unit (Process 2)

	Opening WIP (£)	Current cost (£)	Total cost (£)	Completed units	Closing WIP	Total equiv. units	Cost per unit (£)	WIP (£)
Previous process cost	13 440	107 790	121 230	96 800	10 000	106 800	1.135	11 350
Materials added	4 970	44 000	48 970	96 800	9 000	105 800	0.463	4 167
Conversion costs	3 120	51 480	54 600	96 800	7 000	103 800	0.526	3 682
	21 530	203 270	224 800				2.124	19 199

Completed units (96 800 × £2.124) 205 601

224 800

Note that the above answer is based on the short-cut approach described in Appendix 5.1

(b)

Process 2 Account

	Units	(£)		Units	(£)
Opening WIP	12 000	21 530	Finished goods	96 800	205 601
Transferred from process 1	95 000	107 790	Normal loss	200	—
Materials		44 000	Closing WIP	10 000	19 199
Conversion cost		51 840			
	107 000	224 800		107 000	224 800

(c) If losses are not expected to occur the loss would be abnormal. Because abnormal losses are not an inherent part of the production process and arise from inefficiencies they are not included in the process costs. Instead, they are charged with their full share of production costs and removed (credited) from the process account and reported separately as an abnormal loss. The abnormal loss is treated as a period cost and written off in the profit and loss account.

(d) Workings would be different because FIFO assumes that the opening WIP is the first group of units to be completed during the current period. The opening WIP is charged separately to completed production, and the cost per unit is based only on current period costs and production for the current period. This requires that opening WIP equivalent units are deducted from completed units to derive current period equivalent units. The cost per unit is derived from dividing current period costs by current period total equivalent units.

Question 5.31

(a) Fully complete production = Input (36 000) − Closing WIP (8000)
= 28 000 kg
Normal loss = 2 800 (10% × 28 000 kg)
Abnormal loss = 800 (Actual loss (3600) − 2800)
Good output = 24 400 (28 000 − 3600)

(b)

	(£)	Completed units (£)	Normal loss	Abnormal loss	Closing WIP	Total equiv. units	Cost per unit (£)
Previous process cost	166 000	24 400	2800	800	8000	36 000	4.61111
Conversion cost	73 000	24 400	2800	800	4000	32 000	2.28125
	239 000						6.89236

	(£)	(£)
Completed units (24 400 × £6.89236)	168 174	
Add normal loss (2800 × £6.89236)	19 298	
		187 472
Abnormal loss (800 × £6.89236)		5 514
WIP: Previous process cost (8000 × £4.61111)	36 889	
Conversion cost (4000 × £2.28125)	9 125	
		46 014
		239 000

The above computations assume that losses are detected at the end of the process when the units are fully complete. Therefore none of the normal loss is allocated to partly completed units (WIP). There is an argument for allocating the normal loss between completed units and the abnormal loss (see the section on equivalent units and abnormal losses in the appendix to Chapter 5) but it is unlikely to make a significant difference to the answer. Also examination questions are unlikely to require such sophisticated answers.

An alternative approach is to adopt the short-cut method described in Chapter 5. This method allocates the normal loss between completed units, WIP and the abnormal loss. Because the units actually lost are fully complete it is likely that losses are detected on completion. Therefore the short-cut method is not theoretically correct. Nevertheless the computations suggest that it was the examiner's intention that the question should be answered using the short-cut method. The revised answer is as follows:

		Completed units	Abnormal loss	WIP	Total equiv. units	Cost per unit	WIP
	(£)					(£)	(£)
Previous process cost	166 000	24 400	800	8000	33 200	5.00	40 000
Conversion cost	73 000	24 400	800	4000	29 200	2.50	10 000
	239 000					7.50	50 000

Completed units (24 400 × £7.50)		183 000
Abnormal loss (800 × £7.50)		6 000
		239 000

Distillation process account

	(kg)	(£)		(kg)	(£)
Input from mixing	36 000	166 000	Finished goods	24 400	183 000
Labour		43 800	Abnormal loss	800	6 000
Overheads		29 200	Normal loss	2 800	—
			Closing WIP	8 000	50 000
	36 000	239 000		36 000	239 000

(c) If the scrapped production had a resale value the resale value would be credited to the process account (thus reducing the cost of the process account). The accounting entries would be as follows:

Dr Cash
Cr Process Account (with sales value of normal loss)
Cr Abnormal Loss Account (with sales value of abnormal loss)

Question 5.32

a)

Expected output from an input of 39 300 sheets:	3 144 000 cans (39 300 × 80)	
Less 1% rejects	31 440 cans	
Expected output after rejects	3 112 560 cans	

The normal loss arising from the rejects (31 440 cans) is sold at £0.26 per kg. It is therefore necessary to express the rejects in terms of kilos of metal. Each sheet weighs 2 kilos but wastage in the form of offcuts is 2% of input. Therefore the total weight of 80 cans is 1.96 kg (0.98 × 2 kg) and the weight of each can is 0.0245 kilos (1.96 kg/80 cans). The weight of the normal loss arising from the rejects is 770.28 kg (31 440 × 0.0245 kg). The normal loss resulting from the offcuts is 1572 kg (39 300 × 2 kg × 0.02). Hence the total weight of the normal loss is 2342.28 kilos (1572 kg + 770.28 kg), with an expected sales value of £609 (2342.28 kg × £0.26).

Process account

	(£)		(£)
Direct materials		Finished goods	
(39 300 × £2.50)	98 250	(3 100 760 cans × £0.042[a])	130 232
		Normal loss	609
Direct labour and		Abnormal loss	
overheads	33 087	(11 800 kg[b] at £0.042[a])	496
	131 337		131 337

Abnormal loss account

	(£)		(£)
Process account	496	Sale proceeds[c]	75
		Profit and loss account	421
	496		496

Notes

[a]Cost per unit $= \dfrac{£98\ 250 + £33\ 087 - £609}{\text{expected output (3 112 560 cans)}} = £0.042$ per can

[b]Expected output (3 112 560) − actual output (3 100 760 cans) = 11 800 cans

[c]Abnormal loss = 11 800 cans (3 112 560 − 3 100 760)

This will yield 289.1 kilos (11 800 × 0.0245 kilos) of metal with a sales value of £75 (289.1 × £0.26).

(b) (i) See 'Opening and closing work in progress' in Chapter 5 for the answer to this question.

(ii) See 'Weighted average method' and 'First in, first out method' in Chapter 5 for the answer to this question.

Question 5.33

(a)

Production statement

	Units
Input:	
Opening WIP	20 000
Transfer from previous process	180 000
	200 000
Output:	
Closing WIP	18 000
Abnormal loss	60
Completed units (balance)	181 940
	200 000

Statement of equivalent production and calculation of cost of completed production and WIP

	Current costs (£)	Completed units less opening WIP equivalent units	Abnormal loss	Closing WIP equivalent units	Current total equivalent units	Cost per unit (£)
Previous process cost	394 200	161 940	60	18 000	180 000	2.19
Materials	110 520	167 940	60	16 200	184 200	0.60
Conversion cost	76 506	173 940	60	12 600	186 600	0.41
	581 226					3.20

		(£)	(£)
Cost of completed production:			
Opening WIP (given)		55 160	
Previous process cost (161 940 × £2.19)		354 649	
Materials (167 940 × £0.60)		100 764	
Conversion costs (173 940 × £0.41)		71 315	581 888
Cost of closing WIP:			
Previous process cost (18 000 × £2.19)		39 420	
Materials (16 200 × £0.60)		9 720	
Conversion costs (12 600 × £0.41)		5 166	54 306
Value of abnormal loss (60 × £3.20)			192
			636 386

Process 3 account

	(£)		(£)
Opening WIP	55 160	Transfer to finished goods	
Transfer from process 2	394 200	stock	581 888
Materials	110 520	Abnormal loss	192
Conversion costs	76 506	Closing WIP	54 306
	636 386		636 386

(b) Normal losses are unavoidable losses that are expected to occur under efficient operating conditions. They are an expected production cost and should be absorbed by the completed production whereas abnormal losses are not included in the process costs but are removed from the appropriate process account and reported separately as an abnormal loss. See 'Losses in process and partially completed units' in the appendix to Chapter 5 for a more detailed explanation of the treatment of normal losses.

(c) If the weighted average method is used, both the units and value of WIP are merged with current period costs and production to calculate the average cost per unit. The weighted average cost per unit is then applied to all completed units, any abnormal losses and closing WIP equivalent units. In contrast, with the FIFO method the opening WIP is assumed to be the first group of units completed during the current period. The opening WIP is charged separately to completed production, and the cost per unit is based only on current costs and production for the period. The closing WIP is assumed to come from the new units that have been started during the period.

Question 5.34   (a) It is assumed that the normal loss occurs at the start of the process and should be allocated to completed production and closing WIP. It is also assumed that process 2 conversion costs are not incurred when losses occur. Therefore losses should not be allocated to conversion costs.

Statement of input and output (units)

	Input		Output
Opening WIP	1 200	Completed output	105 400
Transferred from Process 1	112 000	WIP	1 600
		Normal loss (5% × 112,000)	5 600
		Abnormal loss (balance)	600
	113 200		113 200

Since the loss occurs at the start of the process it should be allocated over all units that have reached this point. Thus the normal loss should be allocated to all units of output. This can be achieved by adopting the short-cut method described in Chapter 5 whereby the normal loss is not included in the unit cost statement.

Calculation of cost per unit and cost of completed production (FIFO method)

	Current costs (£)	Completed units less opening WIP equiv. units	Abnormal loss	Closing WIP equiv. units	Current total equiv. units	Cost per unit (£)
Previous process cost	187 704					
Materials	47 972					
	235 676	104 200(105 400 − 1200)	600	1600	106 400	2.215
Conversion costs	63 176	104 800(105 400 − 600)	—	1200	106 000	0.596
	298 852					2.811

Cost of completed production:	(£)	(£)
Opening WIP (given)	3 009	
Previous process cost and materials (104 200 × £2.215)	230 803	
Conversion cost (104 800 × £0.596)	62 461	296 273
Abnormal Loss (600 × £2.215)		1 329
Closing WIP:		
Previous process cost and materials (1600 × £2.215)	3 544	
Conversion costs (1200 × £0.596)	715	4 259
		301 861

Process 2 account

	(£)		(£)
Opening WIP	3 009	Transfer to finished goods	296 273
Transfers from Process 1	187 704	Abnormal loss	1 329
Raw materials	47 972	Closing WIP	4 259
Conversion costs	63 176		
	301 861		301 861

(b) If the loss occurs at the end of the process then the normal loss should only be charged to those units that have reached the end of the process. In other words, the cost of normal losses should not be allocated to closing WIP. To meet this requirement a separate column for normal losses is incorporated into the unit cost statement and the normal loss equivalent units are included in the calculation of total equivalent units. The cost of the normal loss should be calculated and added to the cost of completed production. For an illustration of the approach see 'Losses in process and partially completed units' in the appendix to Chapter 5.

Question 5.35

The physical input and output to the process are as follows:

Input:	Rolls	Output:	Rolls
Opening WIP	1000	Spoiled	550
Started from new	5650	Closing WIP	800
Reworked	500	Completed (balance)	5800
	7150		7150

The 5800 rolls will include the reworked output of 500 rolls, which is assumed to be completed during the period. Therefore the un-reworked output is 5300 rolls. It is assumed that the normal loss is 10% of the un-reworked output of 5300 units. Hence the abnormal loss is 20 rolls (550 − 530 rolls).

(a) *Schedule of completed production and cost per roll*

	Current cost (£)	Un-reworked completed rolls less opening WIP equivalent rolls	Reworked equivalent rolls[a]	Normal loss	Abnormal loss	Closing WIP equivalent rolls	Total equivalent rolls	Cost per roll (£)
Materials	72 085	4300	300	530	20	640	5790	12.4499
Labour	11 718	4700	250	530	20	320	5820	2.0134
Overheads[b]	41 013	4700	250	530	20	320	5820	7.0469
	124 816							21.5102

Notes
[a] Reworked equivalent rolls refers to production for the current period only. Previous period costs are not included in the cost per unit calculation when the FIFO method is used.
[b] Note that overheads are charged to production at the rate of £3.50 per £1 of labour.

(b) *Allocation of costs*

Completed units:	
Un-reworked completed rolls	(£)
[(4300 × £12.4499) + (4700 × £2.0134) + (4700 × £7.0469)]	96 118
Reworked rolls	
[(300 × £12.4499) + (250 × £2.0134) + (250 × £7.0469)]	6 000
Cost of normal spoilage (530 × £21.5102)	11 400
Opening WIP (£12 000 + £4620 + £16 170[a])]	32 790
	146 308

Value of closing WIP	
[(640 × £12.4499) + (320 × £2.0134) + (320 × £7.0469)]	10 868
Cost of abnormal spoilage (20 × £21.5102)	430
	157 606

Note
[a] Overhead costs at the rate of £3.50 per £1 of labour should be added to the value of the opening WIP.

(c) The advantages of converting to a standard costing system are as follows:
   (i) Calculations of *actual* costs per unit for each period will not be required. Completed production and stocks can be valued at standard costs per unit for each element of cost.
   (ii) Targets can be established and a detailed analysis of the variances can be presented. This process should enable costs to be more effectively controlled.

(d) Actual costs computed in (a) and (b) imply that cost-plus pricing is used. Possible disadvantages of this approach include:
  (i) Prices based solely on costs ignore demand and the prices that competitors charge.
  (ii) Overheads will include fixed overheads, which are arbitrarily apportioned and may distort the pricing decision.
  (iii) Replacement costs are preferable to historic costs for pricing decisions. Standard costs represent future target costs and are therefore more suitable for decision-making than historic costs based on a FIFO system.

For additional comments see 'Limitations of cost-plus pricing' in Chapter 11.

(e) The implications are:
  (i) Replacement costs should be used for management accounting, but they will have to be adjusted for external reporting.
  (ii) Practical difficulties in using replacement costs. For example, it is necessary to constantly monitor the current market price for all stock items.
  (iii) The benefits from the use of replacement costs will depend upon the rate of inflation. The higher the rate of inflation, the greater the benefits.

Joint and by-product costing

Solutions to Chapter 6 questions

Question 6.19
(a) Normal loss (toxic waste) = 50 kg per 1000 kg of input (i.e. 5%)
Actual input = 10 000 kg
Abnormal loss = Actual toxic waste (600) less normal loss (500) = 100 kg

By-product R net revenues of £1750 are credited to the joint (main) process account and normal and abnormal losses are valued at the average cost per unit of output:

$$\frac{\text{Net cost of production } (£35\,750 - £1750)}{\text{Expected output of the joint products } (8500 \text{ kg})} = £4$$

The cost of the output of the joint products is £33 600 (8400 kg × £4) and this is to be allocated to the individual products on the basis of final sales value (i.e. 4800 kg × £5 = £24 000 for P and 3600 kg × £7 = £25 200 for Q):
P = £24 000/£49 200 × £33 600 = £16 390
Q = £25 200/£49 200 × £33 600 = £17 210

The main process account is as follows:

Main process account

	(kg)	(£)		(kg)	(£)
Materials	10 000	15 000	P Finished goods	4 800	16 390
Direct labour	—	10 000	Q Process 2	3 600	17 210
Variable overhead	—	4 000	By-product R	1 000	1 750
Fixed overhead	—	6 000	Normal toxic waste	500	—
Toxic waste disposal a/c	—	750	Abnormal toxic waste	100	400
	10 000	35 750		10 000	35 750

(b)
Toxic waste disposal (Creditors' account)

	(£)		(£)
Bank	900	Main process account	750
		Abnormal toxic waste	150
	900		900

Abnormal toxic waste account

		Profit and Loss Account	550
Main process account	400		
Toxic waste disposal account (100 × £1.50)	150		
	550		550

Process 2 account

	kg	(£)		kg	(£)
Main process Q	3600	17 210	Finished goods Q[b]	3 300	26 465
Fixed cost		6 000	Closing work-in-progress[b]	300	1 920
Variable cost		5 175[a]			
	3600	28 385		3600	28 385

Notes:

[a] $3300 + (50\% \times 300) \times £1.50 = £5175$

b

	(£)	Completed units	WIP equiv. units	Total equiv. units	Cost per unit
Previous process cost	17 210	3300	300	3600	£4.78
Conversion cost	11 175	3300	150	3450	£3.24
					£8.02

	(£)
Completed units (3 300 units × £8.02)	26 465
WIP (300 × £4.78) + (150 × £3.24)	1 920
	28 385

(c) See the section on methods of apportioning joint costs to joint products in Chapter 6 for the answer to this question.

(d)

	(£)
Incremental sales revenue per kg from further processing (£7 − £4.30)	2.70
Incremental (variable) cost per kg of further processing	1.50
Incremental contribution per kg from further processing	1.20

	(£)
At an output of 3600 kg the incremental contribution is	4320
Avoidable fixed costs	3600
Net benefit	720

$$\text{Break-even point} = \frac{\text{Avoidable fixed costs (£3600)}}{\text{Incremental unit contribution (£1.20)}} = 3000 \text{ kg}$$

Further processing should be undertaken if output is expected to exceed 3000 kg per week.

(a) See Figure Q6.20

Question 6.20

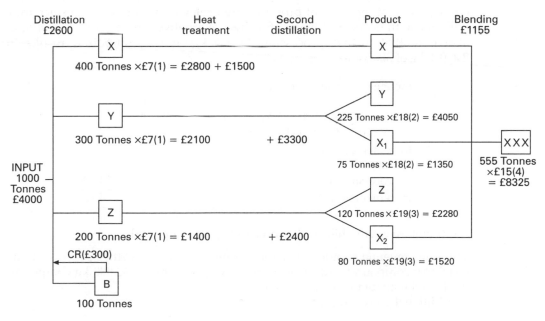

Figure Q6.20

Workings

(W1)	$(4000 + 2600 - 300)/900 = £7$
(W2)	$(2100 + 3300)/300 = £18$
(W3)	$(1400 + 2400)/200 = £19$
(W4)	$(2800 + 1500 + 1155 + 1350 + 1520)/555 = £15$

(b)

Product	Output (tonnes)	Total cost (£)	Cost per tonne (£)
XXX	555	8325	15
Y	225	4050	18
Z	120	2280	19

(c) An alternative treatment is to credit the income direct to the profit and loss account rather than crediting the proceeds to the process from which the by-product was derived.

Question 6.21

(a) You can see from the question that the input is 240 000 kg and the output is 190 000 kg. It is assumed that the difference of 50 000 kg is a normal loss in output which occurs at the start of processing. Therefore the loss should be charged to the completed production and WIP. By making no entry for normal losses in the cost per unit calculation the normal loss is automatically apportioned between completed units and WIP.

	Opening WIP (£)	Current cost (£)	Total cost (£)	Completed units	Closing WIP	Total equivalent units	Cost per unit (£)	WIP value (£)
Materials	20 000	75 000	95 000	160 000	30 000	190 000	0.50	15 000
Processing costs	12 000	96 000	108 000	160 000	20 000	180 000	0.60	12 000
			203 000				1.10	27 000
				Completed units (160 000 units × £1.10)				176 000
								203 000

(b) This question requires a comparison of incremental revenues and incremental costs. Note that the costs of process 1 are irrelevant to the decision since they will remain the same whichever of the two alternatives are selected. You should also note that further processing 120 000 kg of the compound results in 240 000 kg of Starcomp.

Incremental sales revenue:

	(£)	(£)
Starcomp (120 000 × 2 kg × £2)	480 000	
Compound (120 000 × £1.60)	192 000	288 000
Incremental costs:		
Materials	120 000	
Processing costs	120 000	240 000
Incremental profits		48 000

It is therefore worthwhile further processing the compound.

(c) The sales revenue should cover the additional costs of further processing the 40 000 kg compound and the lost sales revenue from the 40 000 kg compound if it is sold without further processing.
Additional processing costs:

$$
\begin{array}{lr}
 & (£) \\
\text{Materials } (£160\,000 - £120\,000) & 40\,000 \\
\text{Processing costs } (£140\,000 - £120\,000) & 20\,000 \\
\text{Lost compound sales revenue } (40\,000 \times £1.60) & \underline{64\,000} \\
 & \overline{124\,000}
\end{array}
$$

$$
\text{Minimum selling price per kg of Starcomp} = \frac{£124\,000}{40\,000\,\text{kg} \times 2}
$$

$$
= £1.55
$$

(a) *Profit and loss account*

	W	X	Z	Total
	(£)	(£)	(£)	(£)
Opening stock	—	—	8 640	8 640
Production cost	189 060	228 790	108 750	526 600
Less closing stock	(14 385)	(15 070)	(15 010)	(44 465)
Cost of sales	174 675	213 720	102 380	490 775
Selling and administration costs	24 098	27 768	10 011	61 877
Total costs	198 773	241 488	112 391	552 652
Sales	240 975	277 680	100 110	618 765
Profit/(loss)	42 202	36 192	(12 281)	66 113

Workings

Joint process cost per kilo of output = £0.685 per kg (£509 640/744 000 kg)
Production cost for products W, X and Y:

$$
\begin{array}{ll}
\text{Product W } (276\,000\,\text{kg} \times £0.685) = £189\,060 \\
\text{X } \ (334\,000\,\text{kg} \times £0.685) = £228\,790 \\
\text{Y } \ (134\,000\,\text{kg} \times £0.685) = \ £91\,790
\end{array}
$$

Closing stocks for products W and X:

$$
\begin{array}{ll}
\text{Product W } (21\,000\,\text{kg} \times £0.685) = £14\,385 \\
\text{X } \ (22\,000\,\text{kg} \times £0.685) = £15\,070
\end{array}
$$

Cost per kilo of product Z:

$$
\begin{array}{lr}
 & (£) \\
\text{Product Y } (128\,000\,\text{kg} \times £0.685) = & 87\,680 \\
\text{Further processing costs} & 17\,920 \\
\text{Less by-product sales } (8000 \times £0.12) = & \underline{(960)} \\
 & \overline{104\,640}
\end{array}
$$

Cost per kilo (£104 640/96 000 kg)   £1.09

$$
\begin{array}{lr}
\text{Closing stock of product Z } (10\,000\,\text{kg} \times £1.09) = & £10\,900 \\
\text{Add closing stock of input Y } (6000 \times £0.685) = & \underline{£4\,110} \\
\text{Closing stock relating to product Z} & £15\,010
\end{array}
$$

Production cost relating to final product Z:

$$
\begin{array}{lr}
 & (£) \\
\text{Product Y } (134\,000\,\text{kg} \times £0.685) = & 91\,790 \\
\text{Further processing costs} & 17\,920 \\
\text{Less by-product costs} & \underline{(960)} \\
 & \overline{108\,750}
\end{array}
$$

(b) The joint costs are common and unavoidable to both alternatives, and are therefore not relevant for the decision under consideration. Further processing from an input of 128 000 kg of Y has resulted in an output of 96 000 kg of Z. Thus it requires 1.33 kg of Y to produce 1 kg of Z (128/96).

	(£)
Revenue per kilo for product Z	1.065 (£100 110/94 000 kg)
Sale proceeds at split-off point (1.33 × £0.62)	0.823
Incremental revenue per kg from further processing	0.242
Incremental costs of further processing	0.177 [(£17 920 − £960)/96 000]
Incremental profit from further processing	0.065

It is assumed that selling and administration costs are fixed and will be unaffected by which alternative is selected. The company should therefore process Y further into product Z and not accept the offer from the other company to purchase the entire output of product Y.

(c) See 'Methods of allocating joint costs to joint products' in Chapter 6 for the answer to this question.

Question 6.23

(a) In a manufacturing organization product costs are required for stock valuation, the various types of decisions illustrated in Chapter 9 and pricing decisions (see 'Role of cost information in pricing decisions' in Chapter 11).

(b) The total net cost of the output for process 1 is calculated as follows:

	(£)
Materials (36 000 kg at £1.50)	54 000
Labour	28 000
Overheads (120%)	33 600
	115 600
Less: Sale of waste (14 400 kg at £0.30)	4 320
	111 280

Output for each category of fish is as follows:

Superior	3 600 kg
Special	7 200
Standard	10 800 (50% × (36 000 − 14 400))
	21 600

The allocation of costs based on weight and the resulting profits are as follows:

	Superior (£)	Special (£)	Standard (£)	Total (£)
Costs	18 547 [a]	37 093 [a]	55 640 [a]	111 280
Sales	27 000	48 960	43 200	119 160
Profit/(Loss)	8 453	11 867	(12 440)	7 880

Note
[a] Allocated pro-rata to output (e.g. Superior = £111 280 × 3600/21 600)

The allocation of costs based on market value and the resulting profits are as follows:

	Superior (£)	Special (£)	Standard (£)	Total (£)
Costs	25 215 [b]	45 722 [b]	40 343 [b]	111 280
Sales	27 000	48 960	43 200	119 160
Profit/(Loss)	1 785	3 238	2 857	7 880

Note

^b Allocated in proportion to sales revenues (e.g. Superior = £111 280 × £27 000/ 119 160)

(c) Since all of the costs are joint and unavoidable in relation to all products, dropping a product with a reported loss will not result in any reduction in costs but sales revenues from the product will be foregone. Therefore, an individual loss-making product should not be dropped provided that the process as a whole is profitable. In the circumstances given in the question, the emphasis should be on whether the joint process as a whole is making a profit. In the question none of the products incur further processing costs that can be specifically attributed to them. Where this situation occurs, a joint product should be produced as long as the sales revenues from the product exceed the costs that are specifically attributable to the product (assuming that the joint process as a whole makes a profit).

(d) Further process is worthwhile as long as the incremental revenues exceed the incremental costs. The calculations are as follows:

	Superior	£ per kilo Special	Standard
Incremental costs:			
Materials	0.10	0.10	0.10
Labour	0.60	0.60	0.60
Variable overhead	0.27	0.27	0.27
	0.97	0.97	0.97
Incremental revenue	1.20	0.70	1.20
Incremental contribution	0.23	(0.27)	0.23

The incremental revenues exceed the incremental costs for superior and standard. Special should not be further processed because the incremental revenues are insufficient to cover the incremental costs. Superior will generate a total contribution of £828 (3600 kg × £0.23) and the total contribution from standard is £2484 (10 800 kg × £0.23). Therefore, the total contribution from further processing is £3312. Further processing is profitable as long as the incremental contribution exceeds the fixed costs that are attributable to process 2 and that are avoidable. The fixed costs are not given but they would appear to exceed £3312. Assuming that the overhead rate has been derived from the output in (a) the total labour costs (included in the calculation in (d) are £12 960 (21 600 kg × £0.60). Fixed costs would appear to be £17 496 (0.75 × 180% × £12 960). The process would not appear to be worthwhile if all of the fixed costs can be avoided by not undertaking process 2.

Question 6.24

(a) Figure Q6.24 indicates that the relative sales value of each product is as follows:

	Boddie (£000)	Soull (£000)	Total (£000)
Total sales	8400	36 000	44 400
Plus NRV of Threekeys		2 170 *(W1)*	2 170
	8400	38 170	46 570

Workings

(W1)   (280 000 litres × £8) − £70 000 delivery costs

Allocation of joint costs:

$$\text{Boddie} = £840\,000 \left(\frac{8400}{46\,570} \times £4\,657\,000 \right)$$

$$\text{Soull} = \frac{£3\,817\,000}{4\,657\,000} \left(\frac{38\,170}{46\,570} \times £4\,657\,000 \right)$$

(b) *Profit and loss statement*

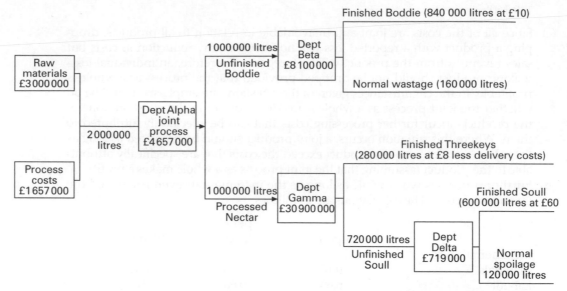

Figure Q6.24 *Diagram of joint cost system.*

	Boddie (£000)	Soull (£000)	Threekeys (£000)	Total (£000)
Sales	8400	36 000	2240	46 640
Less specifically attributable costs:				
Department Beta	8100			
Department Gamma		30 900		
Department Delta		719		
Delivery costs			70	
Contribution to joint costs	300	4 381	2170	6 851
Less apportioned joint costs	840	3 817	–	4 657
Profit/(loss)	(540)	564	2170	2 194

(c) The incremental revenues are in excess of the incremental costs for all three products. In other words, each product provides a contribution towards the joint costs. Consequently, all three products should be produced.

Question 6.25

(a) *Preliminary workings*

The joint production process results in the production of garden fertilizer and synthetic fuel consisting of 80% fertilizer and 20% synthetic fuel. The question indicates that 1 600 000 kg of fertilizer are produced. Therefore total output is 2 000 000 kg, and synthetic fuel accounts for 20% (400 000 kg) of this output. The question also states that a wholesaler bought 160 000 kg of the synthetic fuel, and the remaining fuel (400 000 kg − 160 000 kg = 240 000 kg) was used to heat the company greenhouses. The greenhouses produce 5 kg of fruit and vegetables per kg of fuel. Therefore 1 200 000 kg of fruit and vegetables were produced during the period.

Summary profit statements

	Garden fertilizer (£000)	Synthetic fuel (£000)	Fruit and vegetables (£000)
Sales revenue/internal transfers[a]	4800	560	600

Less costs:			
Internal transfers[a]			(336)
Joint costs[b]	(2880)	(720)	
Variable packing costs		(192)	
Direct fixed costs		(40)	
Variable costs			(420)
Fixed labour costs			(100)
Apportioned fixed costs	(720)	(18)	(90)
Net profit/(Loss)	1200	(410)	(346)

Notes

[a]Garden fertilizer: 1 600 000 kg at £3 per kg

Synthetic fuel: 160 000 kg external sales at £1.40 per kg

240 000 kg internal transfers at £1.40 per kg

Fruit and vegetables: 1 200 000 kg at £0.50 per kg

[b]The question states that the fertilizer has a contribution/sales ratio of 40% after the apportionment of joint costs. Therefore joint costs of £2 880 000 (60% × £4 800 000 sales) will be apportioned to fertilizers. Joint costs are apportioned on a weight basis, and synthetic fuel represents 20% of the total weight. Thus £2 880 000 joint costs apportioned to fertilizers represents 80% of the joint costs. The remaining 20% represents the joint costs apportioned to synthetic fuel. Joint costs of £720 000 [20% × (100/80) × £2 880 000] will therefore be apportioned to synthetic fuel.

(b) Apportioned joint and fixed costs are not relevant costs since they will still continue if the activity ceases. The relevant revenues and costs are as follows:

	(£)	
Relevant revenues	224 000	(160 000 kg at £1.40)
Less packing costs	(192 000)	
avoidable fixed costs	(40 000)	
Net benefit to company	(8 000)	

The percentage reduction in avoidable fixed costs before the relevant revenues would be sufficient to cover these costs is 20% (£8000/£40 000).

(c) The notional cost for internal transfers and the apportioned fixed costs would still continue if the fruit and vegetables activity were eliminated. These costs are therefore not relevant in determining the net benefit arising from fruit and vegetables. The calculation of the net benefit is as follows:

	(£)
Relevant revenues	600 000
Less variable costs	(420 000)
avoidable fixed labour costs	(100 000)
Net benefit	80 000

(d) Proposed output of synthetic fuel is 400 000 kg, but there is a contracted requirement to supply a minimum of 100 000 kg to the wholesaler. Consequently, the maximum output of fruit and vegetables is 1 500 000 kg (300 000 kg of synthetic fuel × 5 kg). In determining the optimum price/output level the fixed costs will remain unchanged whatever price/output combination is selected. Internal transfers are a notional cost and do not represent any change in company cash outflows arising from the price/output decision. The price/output decision should be based on a comparison of the relevant revenues less incremental costs (variable costs) for each potential output level. In addition, using synthetic fuel for fruit and vegetable production results in a loss of contribution of £0.20 per kg (£1.40 − £1.20 packing) of synthetic fuel used. This opportunity cost is a relevant cost which should be included in the analysis. The net contributions for the relevant output levels are as follows:

Sales (000kg)	Contribution per kg[a] (£)	Total contribution (£)	Contribution foregone on fuel sales (£)	Net contribution (£)
1200	0.15	180 000	0[b]	180 000
1300	0.145	188 500	4 000[c]	184 500
1400	0.135	189 000	8 000[d]	181 000
1500	0.125	187 500	12 000[e]	175 500

The optimum output level is to sell 1 300 000 kg of fruit and vegetables. This will require 260 000 kg of synthetic fuel. Sales of synthetic fuel to the wholesaler will be restricted to 140 000 kg.

Notes
[a]Average selling price less variable cost of fruit and vegetable production (£420 000/1 200 000 kg = £0.35 per kg).
[b]240 000 kg of synthetic fuel used, resulting in 160 000 kg being sold to the wholesaler. Therefore existing sales to the wholesaler of 160 000 kg will be maintained.
[c]260 000 kg of synthetic fuel used, resulting in 140 000 kg being sold to the wholesaler. Therefore sales will decline by 20 000 kg and the lost contribution will be £4000 (20 000 kg × £0.20 per kg).
[d]280 000 kg of synthetic fuel used, resulting in 120 000 kg being sold to the wholesaler. Therefore lost contribution is £8000 (40 000 kg × £0.20).
[e]300 000 kg used, resulting in 100 000 kg being sold to the wholesaler. Therefore the lost contribution is £12 000 (60 000 kg × £0.20).

Question 6.26

(a) Figure Q6.26 shows a flowchart for an input of 100 litres of raw material A and 100 litres of raw material B. The variable costs for an input of 100 litres of raw materials for each product are shown below:

Raw materials:	(£)	(£)	Fertilizer P (£)	Fertilizer Q (£)
100 litres of A at £25 per 100 litres	25.00			
100 litres of B at £12 per 100 litres	12.00	37.00		
Mixing:				
200 litres at £3.75 per 100 litres	7.50			
Residue × (10 litres at £0.03)	(0.30)	7.20		
Distilling:				
190 litres at £5 per 100 litres	9.50			
By-product Y (57 litres × £0.04)	(2.28)	7.22		
Total joint costs		51.42	25.71[a]	25.71[a]
Raw material C (114 litres at £20 per 100 litres)			22.80	
Raw material D (57 litres at £55 per 100 litres)				31.35
Blending:				
P (171 litres at £7 per 100 litres)			11.97	
Q (114 litres at £7 per 100 litres)				7.98
Cans:				
P (57 cans at £0.32 per can)			18.24	
Q (19 cans at £0.50 per can)				9.50

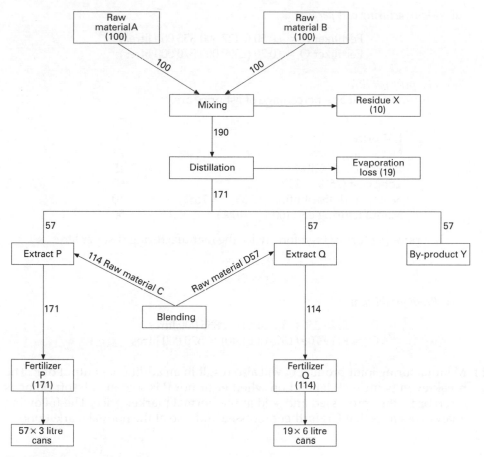

Figure Q6.26 *Flowchart for an input of 100 litres of raw materials A and B*

Labels:

P (57 cans at £3.33 per 1000 cans)	0.19	
Variable cost from 100 litres input of each raw material	78.91	74.54

Output is restricted to 570 000 litres of Q. An input of 100 litres of raw materials A and B yields an output of 114 litres of Q. Therefore an input of 500 000 litres [570 000/(114/110)] of each raw material will yield an output of 570 000 litres of Q. An input to the joint process of 500 000 litres of each raw material will yield an output of 855 000 litres (171 × 5000) of P. The total manufacturing cost based on an input of 500 000 litres of each raw material is shown below:

	Fertilizer P (£)	Fertilizer Q (£)
Total variable cost: 5000 × £78.91	394 550	
5000 × £74.54		372 700
Mixing and distilling fixed costs	13 000[a]	13 000[a]
Blending fixed costs	19 950[b]	13 300[b]
(i) *Total manufacturing cost*	427 500	399 000

Notes
[a]Joint costs are apportioned to the main products on the basis of the output from each process. The mixing and distilling processes yield identical outputs for each product. Therefore 50% of the costs are apportioned to each product.
[b]Apportioned on the basis of an output of 171 litres of P and 114 litres of Q.

(ii) *Manufacturing cost per litre*

$$\text{Fertilizer P} = £0.50 \ (£427\,500/855\,000 \text{ litres})$$
$$\text{Fertilizer Q} = £0.70 \ (£399\,000/570\,000 \text{ litres})$$

(iii) *List price per litre*
Costs and profit as a percentage of list price are:

	(%)
List price	100
Net selling price	75
Profit (20% × 75%)	15
Total cost (75% − 15%)	60
Selling and distribution (13.33% × 75%)	10
Manufacturing cost (60% − 10%)	50

List price per litre is, therefore, twice the manufacturing cost per litre:

$$P = £1.00$$
$$Q = £1.40$$

(iv) *Profit for the year*

$$P = £128\,250 \ (15\% \text{ of } £1) \times 855\,000 \text{ litres}$$
$$Q = £119\,700 \ (15\% \text{ of } £1.40) \times 570\,000 \text{ litres}$$

(b) Manufacturing joint product Q will also result in an additional output of P. The break-even point will depend on whether or not P is sold at split-off point as scrap or further processed and sold at the normal market price. The following analysis assumes that P is further processed and sold at the normal market price:

	(£)
Variable cost of producing 50 000 litres of Q	
[(50 000 × £372 700)/570 000]	32 693
Variable selling costs of Q	2 000
	34 693
Contribution from sale of 75 000 litres of P:	16 500
75 000 litres × £0.22[a]	
Net cost	18 193

The selling price should at least cover the net cost per litre of £0.364 (£18 193/ 50 000 litres). Therefore the break-even selling price is £0.364 per litre.

Note
[a]Output of P is 1.5 times the output of Q (see the Flowchart). Therefore output of P is 75 000 litres (50 000 × 1.5)
Variable manufacturing cost per litre of P = £0.46
$$(394\,500/855\,000 \text{ litres})$$
Variable selling cost per litre of P = £0.07
$$[0.7 \times (13.33\% \text{ of } £0.75)]$$
Selling price per litre = £0.75
Contribution per litre = £0.22

(c) There is no specific answer to this question. The recommendation should be based on price/demand relationships and the state of competition. The normal mark-up is 25% on cost (20% of selling price equals 25% mark-up on cost).

$$\text{Selling price based on normal mark-up} = [1.25 \ (£18\,193)]/50\,000 \text{ litres}$$
$$= £0.455$$

The above price assumes that the additional output of P can be sold at the normal market price. If P cannot be sold then the following costs will be incurred:

	(£)
Variable costs of Q	34 693
Pre-separation variable costs previously apportioned to P:	
5000 at £25.71 per 100 = £128 550 (for 570 000 output)	
Pre-separation variable costs for an output of 50 000 litres	
[(£128 550/570 000) × 50 000]	11 276
	45 969

Minimum selling price = £0.919 (£45 969/50 000)
Note that pre-separation variable costs previously allocated to P will still be incurred if P is not produced. The recommended price will depend on the circumstances, competition, demand and the company's pricing policy.

Income effects of alternative cost accumulation systems

Solutions to Chapter 7 questions

Question 7.22

(a) Manufacturing cost per unit of output = variable cost (£6.40) + fixed cost
(£92 000/20 000 = £4.60) = £11
Absorption costing profit statement

	(£000)
Sales (22 000 units at £14 per unit)	308.0
Manufacturing cost of sales (22 000 units × £11)	242.0
Manufacturing profit before adjustment	66.0
Overhead over-absorbed [a]	4.6
Manufacturing profit	70.6

Note:
[a] The normal activity that was used to establish the fixed overhead absorption rate was 20 000 units but actual production in period 2 was 21 000 units. Therefore a period cost adjustment is required because there is an over-absorption of fixed overheads of £4 600 [(22 000 units – 21 000 units) × £4.60].

(b)

	(£000)
Sales	308.0
Variable cost of sales (22 000 units × £6.40)	140.8
Contribution to fixed costs	167.2
Less fixed overheads	92.0
Profit	75.2

(c) (i) Compared with period 1 profits are £34 800 higher in period 2 (£70 600 – £35 800). The reasons for the change are as follows:

	(£000)
Additional sales (7000 units at a profit of £3 per unit)	21 000
Difference in fixed overhead absorption (3000 units extra production at £4.60 per unit) [a]	13 800
Additional profit	34 800

Note:
[a] Because fixed overheads are absorbed on the basis of normal activity (20 000 units) there would have been an under-recovery of £9200 (2000 units × £4.60) in period 1 when production was 18 000 units. In period 2 production exceeds normal activity by 1000 units resulting in an over-recovery of £4600. The difference between the under- and over-recovery of £13 800 (£9200 + £4600) represents a period cost adjustment that is reflected in an increase in profits of £13 800. In other words, the under-recovery of £9200 was not required in period 2 and in addition there was an over-recovery of £4600.

(c) (ii) Additional profits reported by the marginal costing system are £4600 (£75 200 – £70 600). Because sales exceed production by 1000 units in period 2 there is a stock reduction of 1000 units. With an absorption costing system the stock reduction will result in a release of £4600 (1000 units at £4.60) fixed overheads as an expense during the current period. With a marginal costing system changes in stock levels do not have an impact on the fixed overhead that is treated as an expense for the period. Thus, absorption costing profits will be £4600 lower than marginal costing profits.

Question 7.23

(a)

January	(£)	Marginal costing (£)	(£)	Absorption costing (£)
Sales revenue (7000 units)		315 000		315 000
Less: Cost of sales (7000 units)				
Direct materials	77 000		77 000	
Direct labour	56 000		56 000	
Variable production overhead	28 000		28 000	
Variable selling overhead	35 000	196 000		
Fixed overhead (7000 × £3)			21 000	182 000
Contribution		119 000		
Gross profit				133 000
Over absorption of fixed production overhead (1)				1 500
				134 500
Fixed production costs (2)	24 000			
Fixed selling costs (2)	16 000		16 000	
Variable selling costs			35 000	
Fixed admin costs (2)	24 000	64 000	24 000	75 000
Net profit		55 000		59 500

February	(£)	Marginal costing (£)	(£)	Absorption costing (£)
Sales revenue (8750 units)		393 750		393 750
Less: Cost of sales (8750 units)				
Direct materials	96 250		96 250	
Direct labour	70 000		70 000	
Variable production overhead	35 000		35 000	
Variable selling overhead	43 750	245 000		
Fixed overhead (8750 × £3)			26 250	227 500
Contribution		148 750		
Gross profit				166 250
Under absorption of fixed production overhead				750
				165 500
Fixed production costs (2)	24 000			
Fixed selling costs (2)	16 000		16 000	
Variable selling costs			43 750	
Fixed admin costs (2)	24 000	64 000	24 000	83 750
Net profit		84 750		81 750

Workings:

(1) Fixed production overhead has been unitized on the basis of a normal monthly activity of 8000 units (96 000 units per annum). Therefore monthly production fixed overhead incurred is £24 000 (8000 × £3). In January actual production exceeds normal activity by 500 units so there is an over-absorption of £1500 resulting in a period cost adjustment that has a positive impact on profits. In February production is 250 units below normal activity giving an under-absorption of production overheads of £750.

(2) With marginal costing fixed production overheads are treated as period costs and not assigned to products. Therefore the charge for fixed production overheads is £24 000 per month (see note 1). Both marginal and absorption costing systems treat non-manufacturing overheads as period costs. All of the non-manufacturing overheads have been unitized using a monthly activity level of 8000 units. Therefore the non-manufacturing fixed overheads incurred are as follows:

Selling   = £16 000 (8000 × £2)
Administration = £24 000 (8000 × £3)

(b) In January additional profits of £4500 are reported by the absorption costing system. Because production exceeds sales by 1500 units in January there is a stock increase of 1500 units. With an absorption costing system the stock increase will result in £4500 (1500 units × £3) being incorporated in closing stocks and deferred as an expense to future periods. With a marginal costing system changes in stock levels do not have an impact on the fixed overhead that is treated as an expense for the period. Thus, absorption costing profits will be £4500 higher than marginal costing profits. In February sales exceed production by 1000 units resulting in a stock reduction of 1000 units. With an absorption costing system the stock reduction will result in a release of £3000 (1000 units at £3) fixed overheads as an expense during the current period. Thus, absorption costing profits are £3000 lower than marginal costing profits.

(c) (i) Contribution per unit = Selling price (£45) – unit variable cost (£28) = £17
Break-even point (units) = Annual fixed costs (£64 000)/unit contribution (£17)
= 3765 units
Break-even point (£ sales) = 3765 units × £45 selling price = £169 424
The above calculations are on a monthly basis. The sales value of the annual break-even point is £2 033 100 (£169 425 × 12).

(ii) Required contribution for an annual profit of £122 800

= Fixed costs (£64 000 × 12) + £122 800
= £899 800

Required activity level   = $\dfrac{\text{Required contribution (£899 800)}}{\text{Unit contribution (£17)}}$

= 52 400 units

(d) See 'Cost–volume–profit analysis assumptions' in Chapter 8 for the answer to this question.

Question 7.24

(a) *Preliminary calculations*

	January–June (£)	July–December (£)
Production overheads	90 000	30 000
(Over)/underabsorbed	(12 000)	12 000
	78 000	42 000

Change in overheads		£36 000
Change in production volume (units)		12 000

Production variable overhead rate per unit		£3
Fixed production overheads (£78 000 – (18 000 × £3))		£24 000
Distribution costs	£45 000	£40 000
Decrease in costs		£5 000
Decrease in sales volume (units)		5 000
Distribution cost per unit sold		£1
Fixed distribution cost (£45 000 – (15 000 × £1))		£30 000

Unit costs are as follows:

	(£)	(£)
Selling price		36
Direct materials	6	
Direct labour	9	
Variable production overhead	3	
Variable distribution cost	1	19
Contribution		17

Note that the unit direct costs are derived by dividing the total cost by units produced

Marginal costing profit statement

	January–June		July–December	
	(£000)	(£000)	(£000)	(£000)
Sales		540		360
Variable costs at £19 per unit sold		285		190
Contribution		255		170
Fixed costs:				
Production overhead	24		24	
Selling costs	50		50	
Distribution cost	30		30	
Administration	80	184	80	184
Profit		71		(14)

(b) Marginal costing stock valuation per unit = £18 per unit production variable cost
    Absorption costing stock valuation per unit = £20 per unit total production cost

	January–June	July–December
	(£000)	(£000)
Absorption costing profit	77	(22)
Fixed overheads in stock increase of 3000 units	6	
Fixed overheads in stock decrease of 4000 units	—	(8)
Marginal costing profit	71	14

(c) Absorption gross profit per unit sold = Annual gross profit (£400 000)/Annual
                                    production (15 000 units)
                            = £16

	(£000)
Profit from January–June	77
Reduction in sales volume (5000 × £16)	(80)
Difference in overhead recovery (£12 000 over recovery and £12 000 under recovery)	(24)
Reduction in distribution cost	5
	(22)

Question 7.25

(d) Fixed cost £184 000 × 2 = £368 000
Contribution per unit   £17
Break-even point   21 647 units (Fixed costs/contribution per unit)

(e) See 'Some arguments in support of variable costing'in Chapter 7 for the answer to this question.

(a)
$$\text{Fixed overhead rate per unit} = \frac{\text{Budgeted fixed overheads (£300 000)}}{\text{Budgeted production (40 000 units)}} = £7.50$$

Absorption Costing (FIFO) Profit Statement:

		(£000)
Sales (42 000 × £72)		3024
Less cost of sales:		
Opening stock (2000 × £30)	60	
Add production (46 000 × £52.50[a])	2415	
	2475	
Less closing stock (6000 × £52.50)	315	2160
		864
Add over-absorption of overheads[b]		27
Profit		891

Notes:
[a] Variable cost per unit = £2070/46 000 = £45
Total cost per unit = £45 + £7.50 Fixed overhead = £52.50
[b] Overhead absorbed (46 000 × £7.50) = £345 000
Actual overhead incurred   = £318 000
Over-recovery   £27 000

Marginal Costing (FIFO) Profit Statement:

	(£000)	(£000)
Sales		3024
Less cost of sales:		
Opening stock (2000 × £25)	50	
Add production (46 000 × £45)	2070	
	2120	
Less closing stock (6000 × £45)	270	1850
Contribution		1174
Less fixed overheads incurred		318
Profit		856

Reconciliation:
Absorption profit exceeds marginal costing profit by £35 000 (£891 000 − £856 000). The difference is due to the fixed overheads carried forward in the stock valuations:

	(£)
Fixed overheads in closing stocks (6000 × £7.50)	45 000
Less fixed overheads in opening stocks (2000 × £5)	10 000
Fixed overheads included in stock movement	35 000

Absorption costing gives a higher profit because more of the fixed overheads are carried forward into the next accounting period than were brought forward from the last accounting period.

(b) *Absorption Costing (AVECO) Profit Statement:*

	(£000)	(£000)
Sales		3024
Opening stock plus production		
(48 000 × £51.56[a])	2475	
Less closing stock (6000 × £51.56)	309	2166
		858
Add over-absorption of overheads		27
Profit		885

Marginal Costing (AVECO) Profit Statement:

	(£000)	(£000)
Sales		3024
Less cost of sales		
Opening stock plus production		
(48 000 × £44.17[b])	2120	
Less closing stock (6000 × £44.17)	265	1855
Contribution		1169
Less fixed overheads		318
Profit		851

Notes:

[a] With the AVECO method the opening stock is merged with the production of the current period to ascertain the average unit cost:

Opening stock (2000 × £30) + Production cost (£2 415 000) = £2 475 000

Average cost per unit = £2 475 000/48 000 units

[b] Average cost = (Production cost (£2 070 000) + Opening stock (50 000))/48 000 units.

Reconciliation:

	(£000)
Difference in profits (£885 − £851)	34
Fixed overheads in closing stocks (309 − 265)	44
Less fixed overheads in opening stock (2000 × £5)	10
Fixed overheads included in stock movement	34

The variations in profits between (a) and (b) are £6000 for absorption costing and £5000 for marginal costing. With the FIFO method all of the lower cost brought forward from the previous period is charged as an expense against the current period. The closing stock is derived only from current period costs. With the AVECO method the opening stock is merged with the units produced in the current period and is thus allocated between cost of sales and closing stocks. Therefore some of the lower cost brought forward from the previous period is incorporated in the closing stock at the end of the period.

Question 7.26

(a) It is assumed that opening stock valuation in 2001 was determined on the basis of the old overhead rate of £2.10 per hour. The closing stock valuation for 2001 and the opening and closing valuations for 2002 are calculated on the basis of the new overhead rate of £3.60 per hour. In order to compare the 2001 and 2002 profits, it is necessary to restate the 2001 opening stock on the same basis as that which was used for 2002 stock valuations.

We are informed that the 2002 closing stock will be at the same physical level as the 2000 opening stock valuation. It should also be noted that the 2001 opening stock was twice as much as the 2000 equivalent. The 2000 valuation on the revised basis would have been £130 000, resulting in a 2001 revised valuation of £260 000. Consequently, the 2001 profits will be £60 000 (£260 000 − £200 000) lower when calculated on the revised basis.

From the 2001 estimate you can see that stocks increase and then decline in 2002. It appears that the company has over-produced in 2001 thus resulting in large opening stocks at the start of 2002. The effect of this is that more of the sales demand is met from opening stocks in 2002. Therefore production declines in 2002, thus resulting in an under recovery of £300 000 fixed overheads, which is charged as a period cost. On the other hand, the under recovery for 2001 is expected to be £150 000.

The reconciliation of 2001 and 2002 profits is as follows:

	(£)
2001 profits	128 750
Difference in opening stock valuation for 2001	(60 000)
Additional under recovery in 2002	(150 000)
Budgeted loss for 2002	(81 250)

(b) To prepare the profit and loss accounts on a marginal cost basis, it is necessary to analyse the production costs into the fixed and variable elements. The calculations are:

	2000 (£)	2001 (£)	2002 (£)
Total fixed overheads incurred	600 000	600 000	600 000
Less under recovery	300 000	150 000	300 000
Fixed overheads charged to production	300 000	450 000	300 000
Total production cost	1 000 000	975 000	650 000
Proportion fixed	3/10	6/13 (450/975)	6/13
Proportion variable (balance)	7/10	7/13	7/13

Profit and loss accounts (marginal cost basis)

	Actual 2000 (£)	(£)	Estimated 2001 (£)	(£)	Budget 2002 (£)	(£)
Sales		1 350 000		1 316 250		1 316 250
Opening finished goods stock at marginal cost	70 000[a]		140 000[a]		192 500[b]	
Variable factory cost	700 000[a]		525 000[b]		350 000[b]	
	770 000		665 000		542 500	
Closing finished goods stock at marginal cost	140 000[a]	630 000	192 500[b]	472 500	70 000[b]	472 500
		720 000		843 750		843 750
Fixed factory cost	600 000		600 000		600 000	
Administrative and financial costs	220 000		220 000		220 000	
		820 000		820 000		820 000
Profit/(loss)		(£100 000)		£23 750		£23 750

Notes
[a] 7/10 × absorption cost figures given in the question.
[b] 7/13 × absorption cost figures given in the question.

(c) The under absorption of overhead may be due to the fact that the firm is operating at a low level of activity. This may be due to a low demand for the firm's products. The increase in the overhead rate will cause the product costs to increase. When cost-plus pricing is used the selling price will also be increased. An increase in selling price may result in a further decline in demand. Cost-plus pricing ignores price/demand relationships. For a more detailed discussion of the answer required to this question see section on 'Limitations of cost-plus pricing' in Chapter 11.

(d) For an answer to this question see section on 'Reasons for using cost-based pricing formulae' in Chapter 11 and 'Some arguments in favour of absorption costing' in Chapter 7. Note that SSAP 9 requires that absorption costing (full costing) be used for external reporting.

Question 7.27

(a) Sales for the second six-monthly period have increased for department A, but profit has declined, whereas sales for department B have declined and profit has increased. This situation arises because stocks are valued on an absorption cost basis. With an absorption costing system, fixed overheads are included in the stock valuations, and this can result in the amount of fixed overhead charged as an expense being different from the amount of fixed overhead incurred during a period. The effect of including fixed overheads in the stock valuation is shown below:

	1 July–31 December		1 January–30 June	
	Department A	Department B	Department A	Department B
	(£000)	(£000)	(£000)	(£000)
Fixed overheads brought forward in opening stock of finished goods[a]	36	112	72	96
Fixed overheads carried forward in closing stock of goods[b]	72	96	12	160
Profit increased by	36			64
Profit reduced by		16	60	
Net profit as per absorption costing profit and loss account	94	50	53	83
Profit prior to stock adjustment	58	66	113	19

Notes
[a]Stocks are valued at factory cost with an absorption costing system. The opening stock valuation for department A for the first six months is £60 000 based on a product cost of £20 per unit. Therefore opening stock comprises 3000 units. Fixed manufacturing overheads are charged to the product made in department A at £12 per unit. Consequently, the stock valuation includes £36 000 for fixed overheads. The same approach is used to calculate the fixed overheads included in the opening stock valuation for the second period and department B.
[b]Closing stock for department B (first period) = 6000 units (£120 000/£20). Fixed overheads included in closing stock valuation = £72 000 (6000 units × £12).

The same approach is used to calculate fixed overheads included in the remaining stock valuations.

Comments
During the first six months for department A, stocks are increasing so that the stock adjustment results in a reduction of the fixed overhead charge for the period of £36 000. Fixed manufacturing overheads of £132 000 have been incurred during the period. Therefore the total fixed manufacturing overhead charge for the period is £96 000. In the first period for department B stocks are declining and the stock adjustment will result in an additional £16 000 fixed manufacturing overheads being included in the stock valuation. Consequently, the fixed manufacturing

overhead charge for the period is £320 000 (£304 000 + £16 000). When stocks are increasing, the stock adjustment will have a favourable impact on profits (department A, period 1), and when stocks are declining, the stock adjustment will have an adverse impact on profits (department B, period 1).

In the second period stocks decline in department A and the stock adjustment will have an adverse impact on profits, whereas in department B stocks increase and this has a favourable impact on profit. When the two periods are compared, the stock adjustment has an adverse impact on the profits of department A and a favourable impact on the profits of department B. With an absorption costing system, profit is a function of sales and stock movements, and these stock movements can have an adverse impact on profits even when sales are increasing.

(b) *Departmental profit and loss accounts (marginal costing basis)*

| | 1 July–31 December | | 1 January 30 June | |
| | Department A | Department B | Department A | Department B |
	(£000)	(£000)	(£000)	(£000)
Sales revenue	300	750	375	675
Variable manufacturing costs:				
Direct material	52	114	30	132
Direct labour	26	76	15	88
Variable overheads	26	76	15	88
Variable factory cost of production	104	266	60	308
Add opening stock of finished goods	24	98	48	84
	128	364	108	392
Less closing stock of finished goods	48	84	8	140
Variable factory cost of goods sold	80	280	100	252
Total contribution	£220	£470	£275	£423
Less:				
Fixed factory overheads	132	304	132	304
Fixed administrative and selling costs	30	100	30	100
Net profit	58	66	113	19

Cost–volume–profit analysis

Solutions to Chapter 8 questions

(a) See Figure Q8.29.

(b) See Chapter 8 for the answer to this question.

(c) The major limitations are:

   (i) Costs and revenue may only be linear within a certain output range.

  (ii) In practice, it is difficult to separate fixed and variable costs, and the calculations will represent an approximation.

 (iii) It is assumed that profits are calculated on a variable costing basis.

 (iv) Analysis assumes a single product is sold or a constant sales mix is maintained.

(d) The advantages are:

   (i) The information can be absorbed at a glance without the need for detailed figures.

  (ii) Essential features are emphasized.

 (iii) The graphical presentation can be easily understood by non-accountants.

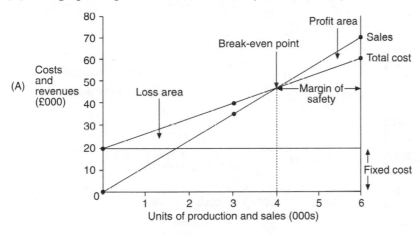

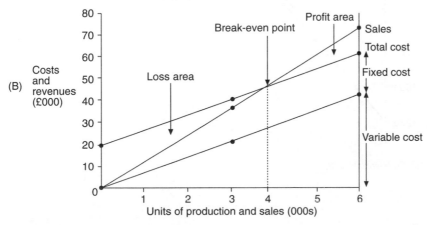

Figure Q8.29 *(A) Break-even chart. (B) Contribution graph*

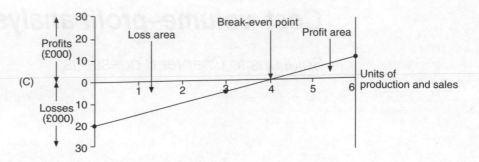

Figure Q8.29 *(C) Profit-volume graph*

Question 8.30

(a) Break-even point $= \dfrac{\text{fixed costs (£1 212 000)}}{\text{average contribution per £ of sales (£0.505)}} = £2\,400\,000$

Average contribution per £ of sales $= [0.7 \times (£1 - £0.45)] + [0.3 \times (£1 - £0.6)]$

(b) The graph (Figure Q8.30) is based on the following calculations:

Zero activity: loss $= £1\,212\,000$ (fixed costs)
£4 m existing sales: $(£4m \times £0.505) - £1\,212\,000 = £808\,000$ profit
£4 m revised sales: $(£4m \times £0.475) - £1\,212\,000 = £688\,000$ profit
Existing break-even point: £2 400 000
Revised break-even point: £2 551 579 ($£1\,212\,000/£0.475$)
Revised contribution per £ of sales: $(0.5 \times £0.55) + (0.5 \times £0.40) = £0.475$

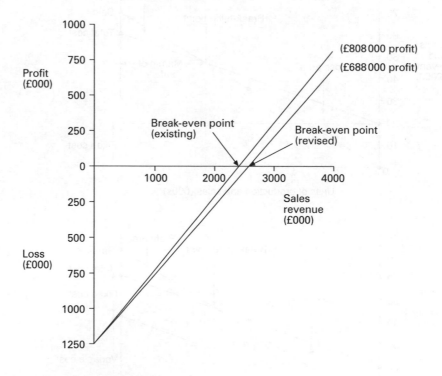

Figure Q8.30 *Profit-volume chart*

(c) $$\frac{\text{Required contribution}}{\text{Contribution per £ of sales}} = \frac{£455\,000 + £700\,000}{£0.55} = £2\,100\,000$$

(a) See Figures Q8.31(A) and Q8.31(B) for the break-even charts.

(b) Both charts indicate that each product has three break-even points. With the Standard quality, profits are earned on sales from 80 000 to 99 999 units and above 140 000 units; whereas with the De Luxe quality, profits are earned on sales from 71 429 − 99 999 units and above 114 286 units. The charts therefore provide guidance regarding the level of sales at which to aim.

(c) *Expected unit sales*

Standard: $(172\,000 \times 0.1) + (160\,000 \times 0.7) + (148\,000 \times 0.2) = 158\,800$
De Luxe: $(195\,500 \times 0.3) + (156\,500 \times 0.5) + (109\,500 \times 0.2) = 158\,800$

Expected profits

	Standard (£)	De Luxe (£)
Total contribution	397 000 (158 800 × £2.50)	555 800 (158 800 × £3.50)
Fixed costs	350 000	400 000
Profit	47 000	155 800

Margin of safety

Standard: expected sales volume (158 800) − break-even point (140 000)
   = 18 800 units
De Luxe: expected sales volume (158 800) − break-even point (114 286)
   = 44 514 units

(d) The profit probability distributions for the products are:

	Standard			De Luxe	
Demand	probability	Profits (£)	Demand	Probability	Profits/(loss) (£)
172 000	0.1	80 000	195 500	0.3	284 250
160 000	0.7	50 000	156 500	0.5	147 750
148 000	0.2	20 000	109 500	0.2	(16 750)

The De Luxe model has the higher expected profit, but is also more risky than the Standard product. There is a 0.2 probability that the De Luxe model will make a loss, whereas there is a zero probability that the Standard product will make a loss. The decision as to which product to produce will depend upon management's attitude towards risk and the future profitability from its other products. If the company is currently making a loss it may be inappropriate to choose the product that could make a loss. On the other hand, the rewards from the De Luxe model are much higher, and, if the company can survive if the worst outcome occurs, there is a strong argument for producing the De Luxe product.

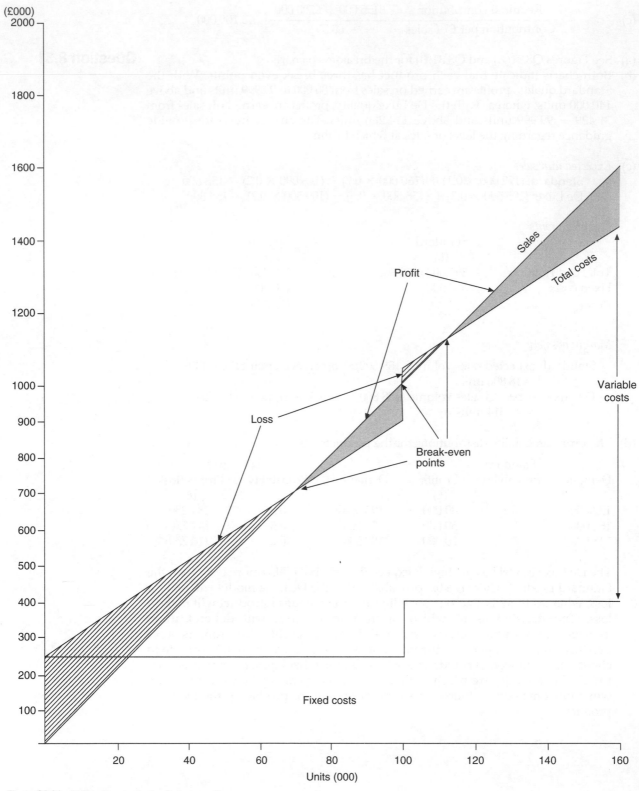

Figure Q8.31 *(A) Break-even chart – Deluxe quality*

COST–VOLUME–PROFIT ANALYSIS

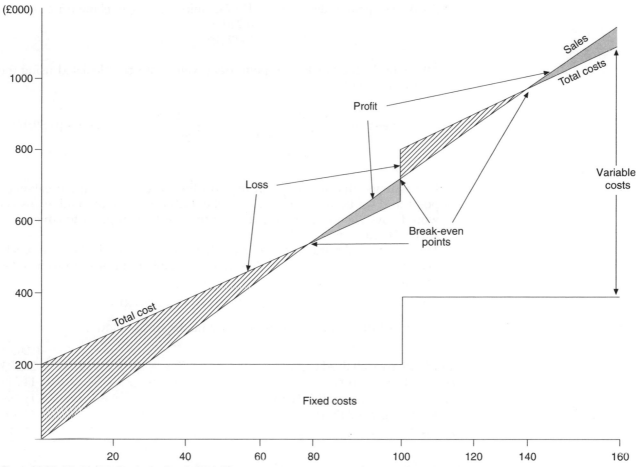

Figure Q8.31 *(B) Break-even chart – Standard quality*

(a) (i)

Products	1	2	3	Total
1. Unit contribution	£1.31	£0.63	£1.87	
2. Specific fixed costs per unit	£0.49	£0.35	£0.62	
3. General fixed costs per unit	£0.46	£0.46	£0.46	
4. Sales volume (000s units)	98.2	42.1	111.8	252.1
5. Total contribution (1 × 4)	£128.642	£26.523	£209.066	£364.231
6. Total specific fixed costs (2 × 4)	£48.118	£14.735	£69.316	£132.169
7. Total general fixed costs (3 × 4)	£45.172	£19.366	£51.428	£115.966
8. Unit selling price	£2.92	£1.35	£2.83	
9. Total sales revenue (8 × 4)	£286.744	£56.835	£316.394	£659.973

Average contribution per unit = Total contribution (£364.231)/sales volume (252.1)
= £1.4448

Average selling price per unit = Total sales revenue (£659.973)/sales volume (252.1)
= £2.6179

$$\text{Break-even point (units)} = \frac{\text{Total fixed costs}}{\text{Average contribution per unit}}$$

= (£132.169 + £115.966)/£1.4448
= 171.743 units

Break-even point (sales value) = 171.743 units × average selling price
(£2.6179)
= £449.606

Alternatively, the break-even point (sales value) can be calculated using the following formula:

$$\text{Break-even point} = \frac{\text{Fixed costs (£132.169 + £115.966)}}{\text{Total contribution (£364.231)}} \times \text{Total sales (£659.973)}$$

$$= £449.606$$

It is assumed that the question requires the calculation of the break-even point to cover both general and specific fixed costs. An alternative answer would have been to present details of the break-even point to cover only specific fixed costs.

(ii) The planned sales mix for Product 2 that was used to calculate the break-even point in (i) is 42.1/252.1. Therefore the number of units of Product 2 at the break-even point is:

$$42.1/252.1 \times 171\ 743 \text{ units} = 28\ 681$$

(b) At the forecast sales volume the profit/contributions are as follows:

	(£000s)
Contributions to all fixed costs	26.523
Less specific fixed costs	14.735
Contribution to general fixed costs	11.788
Less share of general fixed costs	19.366
Net loss	7.578

Product 2 provides a contribution of £11 788 towards general fixed costs and, unless savings in general fixed costs in excess of £11 788 can be made if Product 2 is abandoned, it is still viable to produce Product 2. If the company ceases production of Product 2 it will lose a contribution of £11 788 and total profits will decline by £11 788. The company should investigate whether a greater contribution than £11 788 can be generated from the resources. If this is not possible the company should continue production of Product 2.

Question 8.33

Task 1

	(£)	(£)
Sales		2 106 000
Less variable cost of sales:		
Cost of beds	1 620 000	
Commission	210 600	
Transport	216 000	2 046 600
Contribution		59 400

Average contribution per bed sold = £59 400/5400 = £11
Fixed costs (£8450 + £10 000 + £40 000 + £40 000) = £98 450

$$\text{Break-even point (units)} = \frac{\text{Fixed costs (£98 450)}}{\text{Contribution per unit (£11)}} = 8950 \text{ beds}$$

Average selling price per unit (£2 106 000/5400 beds) = £390
Break-even point (sales revenue) = 8950 beds at £390 = £3 490 500

Task 2
The letter should include the items listed in (a) to (e) below:

(a) Required contribution:

	(£)
Salary	36 550
Interest lost	15 000
Fixed costs shown in Task 1	98 450
	150 000
Less manager's salary saved	40 000
Total contribution	110 000

The minimum profit required to compensate for loss of salary and interest is £11 550 (£110 000 − £98 450 fixed costs).

(b) Required volume = Required contribution (£110 000)/Contribution per unit (£11)
= 10 000 beds

(c) Average life of a bed = (9 years × 0.10) + (10 years × 0.60) + (11 years × 0.3) = 10.2 years

Total bed population = 44 880 households × 2.1 beds per market = 94 248

$$\text{Estimated annual demand} = \frac{94\,248\text{ beds}}{\text{Average replacement period (10.2 years)}}$$
$$= 9\,240\text{ beds}$$

(d) The proposal will not achieve the desired profit. Estimated annual sales are 9240 beds but 10 000 beds must be sold to achieve the desired profit. The shortfall of 760 beds will result in profit being £8360 (760 × £11) less than the desired profit.

(e) The estimate of maximum annual sales volume may prove to be inaccurate because of the following reasons:
 (i) The population of Mytown may differ from the sample population. For example the population of Mytown might contain a greater proportion of elderly people or younger people with families. Either of these situations may result in the buying habits of the population of Mytown being different from the sample proportion.
 (ii) The data is historic and does not take into account future changes such as an increase in wealth of the population, change in composition or a change in buying habits arising from different types of beds being marketed.

Task 3
This question requires a knowledge of the material covered in Chapter 9. Therefore you should delay attempting this question until you have understood the content of Chapter 11.

	A (£)	B (£)	C (£)	Total
Selling price	240	448	672	
Unit purchase cost	130	310	550	
Carriage inwards	20	20	20	
Contribution	90	118	102	
Square metres per bed	3	4	5	
Contribution per square metre	£30	£29.50	£20.40	
Ranking	1	2	3	
Maximum demand	35	45	20	
Storage required (square metres)	105	180	100	385

Monthly sales schedule and statement of profitability:

	(£)	(£)
Contribution from sales of A (35 × £90)		3150
Contribution from sales of B (45 × £118)		5310
Contribution from sales of C (3[a] × £102)		306
		8766
Less specific avoidable fixed costs:		
Staff costs	3780	
Departmental fixed overheads	2000	5780
Contribution to general fixed overheads		2986
Less general fixed overheads		2520
Departmental profit		466

Note:
[a] The balance of storage space available for Model C is 300 square metres less the amount allocated to A and B (285 metres) = 15 metres. This will result in the sales of 3 beds (15 metres/5 metres per bed).

Question 8.34

(a) *Analysis of semi-variable costs[a]*

Method A: variable element $= \dfrac{\text{increase in costs}}{\text{increase in activity}} = \dfrac{£10\,000}{100\,000 \text{ copies}}$

$= £0.10$ per copy

fixed element $=$ total semi-variable cost (£55 000) − variable cost (£35 000) at an activity level of 350 000 copies

Therefore fixed element $= £20\,000$

Method B: variable element $= \dfrac{\text{increase in costs}}{\text{increase in activity}} = \dfrac{£5000}{100\,000 \text{ copies}}$

$= £0.05$ per copy

fixed element $=$ total semi-variable cost (£47 500) − variable costs (£17 500) at an activity level of 350 000 copies

Therefore fixed element $= £30\,000$

Note
[a]The analysis is based on a comparison of total costs and activity levels at 350 000 and 450 000 copies per year.

Contribution per copy of new magazine

	Method A (£)	Method B (£)
Selling price	1.00	1.00
Variable cost (given)	(0.55)	(0.50)
Variable element of semi-variable cost	(0.10)	(0.05)
Lost contribution from existing magazine	(0.05)	(0.05)
Contribution	0.30	0.40

Calculation of net increase in company profits

	Method A			Method B		
Copies sold	500 000	400 000	600 000	500 000	400 000	600 000
Contribution per copy	£0.30	£0.30	£0.30	£0.40	£0.40	£0.40
Total contribution	£150 000	£120 000	£180 000	£200 000	£160 000	£240 000
Fixed costs[a]	£100 000	£100 000	£100 000	£150 000	£150 000	£150 000
Net increase in profit	£50 000	£20 000	£80 000	£50 000	£10 000	£90 000

^{a}Method A = specific fixed costs (£80 000) + semi-variable element (£20 000)
= £100 000
Method B = specific fixed costs (£120 000) + semi-variable element (£30 000)
= £150 000

(b)
$$\text{Break-even point} = \frac{\text{fixed costs}}{\text{contribution per unit}}$$

Method A = £100 000/0.30 = 333 333 copies
Method B = £150 000/0.40 = 375 000 copies

The margin of safety is the difference between the anticipated sales and the break-even point sales:

Method A = 500 000 − 333 333 = 166 667 copies
Method B = 500 000 − 375 000 = 125 000 copies

(c) Method B has a higher break-even point and a higher contribution per copy sold. This implies that profits from Method B are more vulnerable to a decline in sales volume. However, higher profits are obtained with Method B when sales are high (see 600 000 copies in (B)).

The break-even point from the sale of the existing magazine is 160 000 copies (£80 000/£0.50) and the current level of monthly sales is 220 000 copies. Therefore sales can drop by 60 000 copies before break-even point is reached. For every 10 copies sold of the new publication, sales of the existing publication will be reduced by one copy. Consequently, if more than 600 000 copies of the new publication are sold, the existing magazine will make a loss. If sales of the new magazine are expected to consistently exceed 600 000 copies then the viability of the existing magazine must be questioned.

(a) (i) The opportunity costs of producing cassettes are the salary forgone of £1000 **Question 8.35** per month and the rental forgone of £400 per month.
(ii) The consultant's fees and development costs represent sunk costs.
(b) The following information can be obtained from the report.

	£10 selling price	£9 selling price
Sales quantity	7500–10 000 units	12 000–18 000 units
Fixed costs^a	£13 525	£17 525
Profit at maximum sales^b	£3 975	£4 975
Profit/(loss) at minimum sales^c	(£400)	(£2 525)
Break-even point^d	7 729 units	14 020 units
Margin of safety:		
Below maximum	2 271 units	3 980 units
Above minimum	229 units	2 020 units

Notes
^{a} Fixed production cost + £1400 opportunity cost
^{b} (10 000 units × £1.75 contribution) − £13 525 fixed costs = £3975 profit
(18 000 units × £1.25 contribution) − £17 525 fixed costs = £4975 profit
^{c} (7 500 units × £1.75 contribution) − £13 525 fixed costs = £400 loss
(12 000 units × £1.25 contribution) − £17 525 fixed costs = £2525 loss
^{d}Fixed costs/contribution per unit

Conclusions
(i) The £10 selling price is less risky than the £9 selling price. With the £10 selling price, the maximum loss is lower and the break-even point is only 3% above minimum sales (compared with 17% for a £9 selling price).

(ii) The £9 selling price will yield the higher profits if maximum sales quantity is achieved.

(iii) In order to earn £3975 profits at a £9 selling price, we must sell 17 200 units (required contribution of 17 525 fixed costs plus £3975 divided by a contribution per unit of £1.25).

Additional information required
  (i) Details of capital employed for each selling price.
 (ii) Details of additional finance required to finance the working capital and the relevant interest cost so as to determine the cost of financing the working capital.
(iii) Estimated probability of units sold at different selling prices.
(iv) How long will the project remain viable?
 (v) Details of range of possible costs. Are the cost figures given in the question certain?

Question 8.36

(a) *Impact of stitching elimination*

Loss of contribution from 10% sales reduction	
(£300 000 × 10% × £4.50)	£135 000
Production cost reduction (270 000 × £0.60)	£162 000
Net gain from the stitching elimination	£27 000

Note
Contribution per unit − Fixed cost per unit (£1.50) = Net profit per unit (£3). Therefore contribution per unit = £4.50.

Use of plastic eyes
The reduction in sales volume arising from the stitching elimination also applies to the evaluation of the proposals for the change in type of eye and change in filling.

Glass eyes required for production = £540 000 (270 000 × 2)	
Input required to allow for 5% input losses (540 000/0.95 × £0.20) =	£113 684
Plastic eyes required to allow for 10% input losses	
(540 000/0.90 × £0.15) =	£90 000
Net saving from plastic eyes	£23 684

Use of scrap fabric for filling

Cost of synthetic filling (270 000/2000 × £80)	£10 800
Additional production cost of scrap fabric (270 000 × £0.05)	£13 500
Net increase in cost from use of scrap fabric	£2 700

The overall net increase in annual net profit arising from the implementation of the three proposals is £47 984 − (£27 000 + £23 684 − £2700)

(b) Additional contribution from all three changes

(£162 000 + £23 684 − £2700)/270 000 =	£0.678
Existing contribution	£4.50
Revised contribution per unit	£5.178

Number of toys required to give the same contribution prior to the changes:
(£4.50 × 300 000)/£5.178 = 260 718 toys

Therefore the reduction in sales required to leave net profit unchanged
= (300 000 − 260 718)/300 000
= 13.1%

(c) The report should indicate that answers to the following questions should be obtained before a final decision is taken:
  (i) How accurate is the estimate of demand? Demand is predicted to fall by 10% but the answer to (b) indicates that if demand falls by more than 13%, profit will be lower if the changes are implemented.
  (ii) Have all alternative courses of action been considered? For example, would a price reduction, or advertising and a sales promotion, stimulate demand and profits?
  (iii) Will the change to using scrap fabric result in a loss of revenues from the sale of scrap?
  (iv) Will the elimination of stitching result in redundancy payments and possible industrial action?
  (v) Consideration should be given to eliminating stitching and using plastic eyes but not using scrap fabric for filling.

Question 8.37

(a) Actual patient days = 22 000 (£4.4 million/£200)

  Bed occupancy   = 75% (22 000/29 200)

Profit/(Loss)	(£)	(£)
Total revenue		4 400 000
Variable costs		1 100 000
Contribution to direct and general fixed costs		3 300 000
Staffing costs: Supervisors	4 × £22 000	
Nurses	13 × £16 000	
Assistants	24 × £12 000	584 000
Fixed charges		1 650 000
Profit		1 066 000

Break-even point = Fixed costs (£584 000 + £1 650 000)/ Contribution per patient day (£150) [a]
      = 14 893 patient days.

The above calculation is based on the actual outcomes for the period. Because of the stepped nature of the fixed costs other break-even points can be calculated based on actual patient days for the period being less than 20 500 or over 23 000.

Note
[a] £3 300 000/22 000 patient days

(b) It is assumed that estimated bed occupancy will be at the 2001 level plus an extra 20 beds for 100 days giving an occupancy of 24 000 patient days [22 000 + (100 × 20)]. This will result in an estimated bed occupancy of 66% (24 000/ (100 × 365)) = 66%.

Revised Profit/(Loss)

	(£)	(£)
Total revenue (24 000 × £200)		4 800 000
Variable costs (24 000 × £50)		1 200 000
Contribution to direct and general fixed costs		3 600 000
Staffing costs: Supervisors	4 × £24 200	
Nurses	15 × £17 600	
Assistants	28 × £13 200	730 400
Fixed charges (£1 650 000 × 100/80)		2 062 500
Profit		807 100

(c) Attempting to cover the 100 days demand by increasing capacity by 20 beds for 365 days has resulted in a decline in the occupancy percentage from 75% to 66%. To meet the increased demand of 2000 patient days (100 days × 20 beds) extra capacity of 7300 potential patient days were provided (365 days × 20 beds). This has had a detrimental impact on the occupancy percentage. The extra contribution from the increased demand was £300 000 but this was offset by a higher allocation of fixed charges of £412 500 arising from the increase in bed capacity. The additional personnel costs arising from increases in stepped fixed costs and increased salaries further contributed to the reduction in profit.

Assuming that fixed costs (administration, security and property costs) will remain unchanged the extra demand has generated an additional contribution to these common and unavoidable fixed costs and should therefore increase the profit for the hospital as a whole. However, the way in which the fixed costs are allocated reduces the profit for the paediatric unit. A possible solution to overcome this problem is to make the units accountable for the contribution to unavoidable fixed costs (assumed to be contribution less staffing costs). Adopting this approach would result in a contribution to general fixed costs of £2 716 000 being reported in 2001 and £2 869 000 in 2002. An alternative approach would be to allocate fixed costs on the basis of patient days rather than bed capacity. The danger with both approaches is that there is no incentive to encourage managers to restrict bed capacity.

(d) For organizations that have profit making objectives a reasonable financial return must be generated to satisfy the providers of the funds. However, for an organization to survive it must satisfy the objectives of other stakeholders (e.g. employees, customers and social objectives). Conflicts between financial and social objectives occur when a greater financial return can be achieved at the expense of poorer social provision or increased social provision can be obtained but this has a detrimental impact on meeting financial objectives. In a private healthcare organization higher profits might be obtained by charging higher fees and treating fewer patients compared with treating many patients at a lower fee. Thus financial objectives are being pursued at the expense of lower social provision. Determining the optimal balance between financial and social objectives represents a major problem for a private hospital. To ensure that an adequate level of social provision is provided, such as treating patients requiring expensive treatment, requires that the provision is provided within the public sector.

Question 8.38

(a)

	Estimated variable cost per unit Normal materials	Cheaper-grade materials
	(£)	(£)
Direct material	36.00	31.25
Direct labour	10.50	10.50
Variable overheads	10.50	10.50
	57.00	52.25
Wastage (5/95 × £52.25)		2.75
	57.00	55.00

Contribution from using normal grade of materials

Selling price (£)	80	84	88	90	92	96	100
Variable cost (£)	57	57	57	57	57	57	57
Unit contribution (£)	23	27	31	33	35	39	43
Demand (000)	25	23	21	20	19	17	15
Contribution to general fixed costs (£000)	575	621	651	660	665	663	645

Contribution from using cheaper grade of materials

	80	84	88	90	92	96	100
Selling price (£)	80	84	88	90	92	96	100
Variable cost	55	55	55	55	55	55	55
Unit contribution	25	29	33	35	37	41	45
Demand (000)	25	23	21	20	19	17	15
Contribution to specific fixed costs (£000)	625	667	693	700	703	697	675
Specific fixed costs (£000)	30	30	30	30	30	30	30
Contribution to general fixed costs (£000)	595	637	663	670	673	667	645

The selling price that maximizes profit is £92 and the optimum output is 19 000 units. For all levels of demand (other than 15 000 units), profits are higher for the cheaper-grade material. At 15 000 units, profits are identical for both grades of materials.

If the reject rate for the cheaper grade of materials increased from 5% to 6% then at the optimum output level higher profits would be earned from using the normal grade of materials. Fixed inspection costs can increase by 10%, and profits will still be higher with the cheaper-grade materials for all output levels other than 15 000 units. As long as demand is in excess of 15 000 units (£30 000 inspection costs/£2 variable cost saving), it is preferable to use the cheaper-grade materials. Profits are not very sensitive to selling prices within the range £90–£96.

(b) Total revenues and total costs are required to construct a cost–volume–profit graph (Figure Q8.38).

Demand (000)	25	23	21	20	19	17	15
Total revenue (£000)	2000	1932	1848	1800	1748	1632	1500
Total variable cost (£000) (normal grade)	1425	1311	1197	1140	1083	969	855
Total variable cost plus £30 000 inspection cost (cheaper grade)	1405	1295	1185	1130	1075	965	855

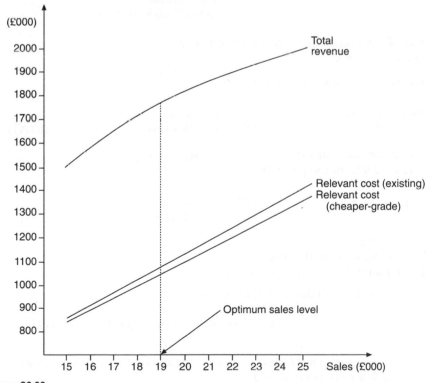

Figure Q8.38

The above costs and revenues are plotted on the CVP diagram, and optimum output is determined at the point where the difference between the total cost and revenue line is the greatest. This occurs at an output level of 19 000 units. The selling price with a demand of 19 000 units is £92.

Question 8.39

(a)

	Manual production		Computer-aided	
	Thingone	Thingtwo	Thingone	Thingtwo
	(£)	(£)	(£)	(£)
Selling price	20	50	20.00	50.00
Variable production costs	(15)	(31)	(12.75)	(26.35)
Bad debts^a	—	(2)	—	(2.00)
Finance cost^b	—	(3)	—	(3.00)
Contribution	5	14	7.25	18.65
Fixed costs per month	£31 500		£43 500	

Notes
^{a} 4% of selling price
^{b} 2% × £50 × 3 months

(i) *Thingone only is sold*
Manual process break-even point = 6300 units (£31 500/£5)
= £126 000 sales revenue
Computer-aided break-even point = 6000 units (£43 500/£7.25)
= £120 000 sales revenue

Point of indifference:
Let x = point of indifference
Then indifference point is where:

$$5x - 31\,500 = 7.25x - 43\,500$$
$$= 5333.33 \text{ units}$$
$$= £106\,667 \text{ sales revenue}$$

(ii) *Sales of Thingone and Thingtwo in the ratio 4 : 1*
Manual process:

$$\text{average contribution per unit} = \frac{(4 \times £5) + (1 \times £14)}{5} = £6.80$$

break-even point = 4632.35 units (£31 500/£6.80)
= £120 441 sales revenue (4632.35 × £26 (W1))

Computer-aided process:
$$\text{average contribution per unit} = \frac{(4 \times £7.25) + (1 \times £18.65)}{5} = £9.53$$

break-even point = 4564.53 units (£43 500/£9.53)
= £118 678 sales revenue (4564.53 × £26 (W1))

Indifference point:
Let x = point of indifference
Then indifference point is where:

$$6.80x - 31\,500 = 9.53x - 43\,500$$
$$= 4395.60 \text{ units}$$
$$= £114\,286 \text{ sales revenue} (4395.60 \times £26 (W1))$$

Workings
(W1) Break-even point (sales revenue) = break-even point in units × average selling price per unit sold

$$\text{Therefore, average sales revenue per unit} = \frac{(4 \times £20) + (1 \times £50)}{5} = £26$$

(b) If Thingone alone is sold, budgeted sales are 4000 units, and break-even sales are 6000 units (computer-aided process) and 6300 units (manual process). Hence there is little point producing Thingone on its own. Even if the two products are substitutes, total budgeted sales are 6000 units, and Thingone is still not worth selling on its own. Only if sales are limited to £180 000 (budgeted sales revenue) is Thingone worth selling on its own. However, the assumption that the products are perfect substitutes and £180 000 sales can be generated is likely to be over-optimistic. In other words, the single-product policy is very risky.

Assuming that Thingone and Thingtwo are sold in the ratio of 4:1, the break-even point is 4565 units using the computer-aided process. This consists of a sales mix of 3652 units of Thingone and 913 units of Thingtwo, representing individual margins of safety of 348 units and 1087 units when compared with the original budget. Launching both products is clearly the most profitable alternative.

It should be noted that the budgeted sales mix is in the ratio of 2:1, and this gives an average contribution per unit of £8 (manual process) and £11.05 (computer-aided process). The break-even point based on this sales mix is 3937 units for both the manual and computer-aided process, consisting of 2625 units of Thingone and 1312 units of Thingtwo. This represents a margin of safety of 1375 units of Thingone (34%) and 688 units of Thingtwo (34%). It is obviously better to sell Thingtwo in preference to Thingone. It is recommended that both products be sold and the computer-aided process be adopted.

(c) For the answer to this question see 'Pricing policies' in Chapter 11. In particular, the answer should stress the need to obtain demand estimates for different selling prices and cost estimates for various demand levels. The optimal *short-run* price is where profits are maximized. However, the final price selected should aim to maximize *long-run* profits and the answer should include a discussion of relevant pricing policies such as price skimming and pricing penetration policies. Competitors' reactions to different selling prices should also be considered.

Before demand estimates are made, market research should be undertaken to find customers' reaction to the new product. In addition, research should be undertaken to see whether a similar product is being developed or sold by other firms. This information might be obtained from trade magazines, market research or the company's sales staff. If a similar product is currently being sold, a decision must be made whether to compete on price or quality. The degree of interdependence of new and existing products must also be considered, and any lost sales from existing products should be included in the analysis. It may be necessary to differentiate the new product from existing products.

Measuring relevant costs and revenues for decision-making

Solutions to Chapter 9 questions

Question 9.35

a)

	(£)
Purchase price of component from supplier	50
Additional cost of manufacturing (variable cost only)	34
Saving if component manufactured	16

The component should be manufactured provided the following assumptions are correct:

(i) Direct labour represents the *additional* labour cost of producing the component.

(ii) The company will not incur any additional fixed overheads if the component is manufactured.

(iii) There are no scarce resources. Therefore the manufacture of the component will not restrict the production of other more profitable products.

(b) (i) Additional fixed costs of £56 000 will be incurred, but there will be a saving in purchasing costs of £16 per unit produced. The break-even point is 3500 units (fixed costs of £56 000/£16 per unit saving). If the quantity of components manufactured per year is less than 3500 units then it will be cheaper to purchase from the outside supplier.

(ii) The contribution per unit sold from the existing product is £40 and each unit produced uses 8 scarce labour hours. The contribution per labour hour is £5. Therefore if the component is manufactured, 4 scarce labour hours will be used, resulting in a lost contribution of £20. Hence the relevant cost of manufacturing the components is £54, consisting of £34 incremental cost plus a lost contribution of £20. The component should be purchased from the supplier.

(c) The book value of the equipment is a sunk cost and is not relevant to the decision whether the company should purchase or continue to manufacture the components. If we cease production now, the written-down value will be written off in a lump sum, whereas if we continue production, the written-down value will be written off over a period of years. Future cash outflows on the equipment will not be affected by the decision to purchase or continue to manufacture the components. For an illustration of the irrelevance of the written down value of assets for decision-making purposes see 'Replacement of equipment' in Chapter 9.

Question 9.36

(a) *Calculation of minimum selling price:*

	(£)
Direct materials: Steel[a]	55.00
Brass Fittings[b]	20.00
Direct Labour: Skilled[c]	300.00
Semi-skilled[d]	—

Overhead[e]	7.50
Estimating time[f]	—
Administration[g]	—
Relevant cost of the order	382.50

Notes:

[a] Using the materials for the order will result in them having to be replaced. Therefore future cash outflows will increase by £55.

[b] Future cash outflows of £20 will be incurred.

[c] The required labour hours can be obtained by reducing production of another product involving a lost contribution before deducting the labour cost of £21 (£13 + £8) per hour (note that the labour cost will be incurred for all alternatives and therefore is not an incremental cash flow). Alternatively, the company can pay additional wages involving overtime of £300 (25 hours × £12). Therefore the latter course of action is the most economical and the incremental cash flows from undertaking the order will be £300.

[d] No incremental cost is involved since the alternative is paid idle time.

[e] The only incremental cost is power consisting of 10 hours at £0.75 per hour.

[f] Estimating time is a sunk cost.

[g] Administration does not involve any incremental cash flows.

(b) Factors to be considered include:
   (i) time period for repeat orders, the number of repeat orders and the likely demand;
   (ii) the cash flows generated from the alternative use of the capacity;
   (iii) competition to obtain future orders from Exe plc;
   (iv) estimated price quotations from competitors.

(c) *Limiting factor presentation:*

	Product X	Product Y
Product contribution	£10	£20
Kg of material used per product	1	4
Contribution per kg	£10	£5

Thus scarce materials should be allocated to Product X since it yields a contribution of £5 per kg in excess of the contribution derived from Product Y.

Opportunity cost approach:

	Product X	Product Y
Product contribution at acquisition cost	£10	£20
Lost contribution from alternative use:		
1 kg allocated to Y at £5 per kg	(£5)	
4 kg allocated to X at £10 per kg		£40
Cash flow impact per product	+£5	−£20
Cash flow impact per kg	+£5 (£5/1 kg)	−£5 (£20/4 kg)

The above analysis shows that X yields a contribution of £5 per kg when taking alternative uses of the materials into consideration. Producing Product Y results in the contribution being reduced by £5 per kg taking into account the alternative use of the materials. This is consistent with the limiting factor approach which indicates that the company is £5 per kg better off using the materials for X or £5 per kg worse off from using the materials for Y.

Question 9.37   (a)   (i)

	Product I (£000)	Product II (£000)	Product III (£000)	Total (£000)
Sales	2475	3948	1520	7943
Contribution	1170	1692	532	3394
Attributable fixed costs	(275)	(337)	(296)	(908)
General fixed costs[a]	(520)	(829)	(319)	(1668)
	(795)	(1166)	(615)	(2576)
Profit	375	526	(83)	818
	= £1.6/unit	= £1.40/unit	= (£0.04/unit)	

Note
[a]General fixed costs are allocated to products at 21% of total sales revenue (£1668/£7943)

(ii) If Product III is discontinued it is assumed that variable costs and attributable (i.e. specific) fixed costs are avoidable. It is assumed that general fixed costs are common and unavoidable to all products and will remain unchanged if Product III is discontinued. However, it is possible that some general fixed costs may be avoidable in the longer term. The revised profits if Product III is discontinued will be:

	(£000s)
Contribution of Products I and II (£1170 + £1692)	2862
Attributable fixed costs (£275 + £337)	(612)
General fixed costs	(1668)
Profit	582

Profits will decline by £236 000 (£818 − £582) if Product III is discontinued because A Ltd will no longer obtain a contribution of £236 000 (£532 − £296) towards general fixed costs.

(iii) Extra sales of 15 385 units (£80 000 additional fixed costs/£5.20 unit contribution) will be required to cover the additional advertising expenditure. It is assumed that existing fixed costs will remain unchanged.

(iv) The revised unit contribution will be £3.45 (£9.45 − £6).

$$\text{Required sales} = \frac{\text{£1 692 000 (existing total contribution)}}{\text{£3.45 revised unit contribution}}$$

= 490 435 units (an increase of 30.4% over the budgeted sales of 376 000 units)

(b) The following factors will influence cost behaviour in response to changes in activity:

  (i) The magnitude of the change in activity (more costs are likely to be affected when there is a large change in activity).

 (ii) Type of expense (some expenses are directly variable with volume such as direct materials, whereas others are fixed or semi-fixed).

(iii) Management policy (some expenses are varied at the discretion of management, e.g. advertising).

(iv) The time period (in the long term, all costs can be changed in response to changes in activity whereas in the short term, some costs, e.g. salaries of supervisors, will remain unchanged).

Task 1

(a) and (b)

	£60	£70	£80	£90
Selling price				
Sales volume (units)	25 000	20 000	16 000	11 000

	(£ per unit)	(£ per unit)	(£ per unit)	(£ per unit)
Direct material	14.00	14.00	14.00	16.10 (£14 × 115/100)
Direct labour	13.00	13.00	11.70 (90%)	11.70
Variable production overhead	4.00	4.00	4.00	4.00
Sales commission (10% of selling price)	6.00	7.00	8.00	9.00
Total variable cost per unit	37.00	38.00	37.70	40.80
Contribution per unit	23.00	32.00	42.30	49.20
	£000	£000	£000	£000
Total contribution	575	640	676.8	541.2

Fixed costs:

	£000	£000	£000	£000
production overhead (25 000 × £8)	200	200	190	190
selling and distribution (25 000 × £3)	75	70	70	70
administration (25 000 × £2)	50	50	50	50
Total fixed costs	325	320	310	310
Total annual profit	250	320	366.8	231.2

Task 2

(a) A selling price of £80 maximizes company profits at £366 800 per annum.

(b) Factors to be considered include:

(i) The effect on morale arising from a large reduction in direct labour and the resulting redundancies.

(ii) If competitors do not increase their prices customers may migrate to competitors in the long term and long-term annual profits may be considerably less than the profits predicted in the above schedule. The migration of customers may also enable competitors to reap the benefits of economies of scale thus resulting in their having lower unit costs than Rane Ltd.

Task 3

(a) The products should first be ranked according to their contribution per component used.

	Product A	Product B	Product C	Product D
	£ per unit	£ per unit	£ per unit	£ per unit
Selling price	14	12	16	17
Variable costs	11	11	12	12
Contribution	3	1	4	5
Number of components used per unit	2 (£4/£2)	1 (£2/£2)	3 (£6/£2)	4 (£8/£2)
Contribution per component	£1.50	£1.00	£1.33	£1.25
Ranking	1	4	2	3

The scarce components should be allocated as follows:

Product	Units	Components used	Balance unused
A	4000	8 000	14 400
C	3600	10 800	3 600
D	900	3 600	—
		22 400	

(b) Profit to be earned next period:

Product	Units	Contribution per unit (£)	Total (£)
A	4000	3	12 000
C	3600	4	14 400
D	900		4 500
Total contribution			30 900
Fixed costs			8 000
Profit			22 900

Question 9.39

(a)

	Product X	Product Y	Total
(1) Estimated demand (000 units)	315	135	
(2) Machine hours required (per 000 units)	160	280	
(3) Machine hours required to meet demand (1 × 2)	50 400	37 800	88 200

The machine hours required to meet demand are in excess of the machine hours that are available. Therefore machine hours are the limiting factor and the company should allocate capacity according to contribution per machine hour.

	Product X (£)	Product Y (£)
Selling price	11.20	15.70
Variable cost	6.30	8.70
Contribution	4.90	7.00
Machine hours required per unit[a]	0.16	0.28
Contribution per machine hour	£30.625	£25

Note:
[a] Product X = 160/1000   Product Y = 280/1000

The company should concentrate on maximizing output of Product X. Meeting the maximum demand of Product X will require 50 400 machine hours and this will leave 34 600 hours (85 000 hrs − 50 400 hrs) to be allocated to Product Y. Therefore 123 571 units (34 600 hrs/0.28 hrs) of Y and 315 000 units of X should be produced.

(b)

	Product X (£)	Product Y (£)	Total (£)
Contribution per unit	4.90	7.00	
Sales volume	315 000	123.571	
Contribution (£000s)	1543.5	864.997	2 408.497
Less fixed costs[a]			2 124.997
Profit			283.500

Note:
[a] Fixed costs: Product X = 315 000 units × £4 per unit   = £1 260 000
                Product Y = 123 571 units × £7 per unit   =   £864 997
                                                                 2 124 997

(c) There are now two limiting factors and linear programming techniques must be used.

Let X = Number of units of X produced (in 000s of units)
Y = Number of units of Y produced (in 000s of units)

$160X + 280Y = 85\,000$ Machine hours (1)
$120X + 140Y = 55\,000$ Labour hours (2)

Multiply equation (2) by 2 and equation (1) by 1

$160X + 280Y = 85\,000$ (1)
$240X + 280Y = 110\,000$ (2)

Subtract equation (2) from equation (1)

$-80X = -25\,000$
$X = 312.5$ (i.e. 312 500 units)

Substitute for X in equation (1)

$160\,(312.5) + 280Y = 85\,000$
$50\,000 + 280Y = 85\,000$
$280Y = 35\,000$
$Y = 125$ (i.e. 125 000)

Therefore the optimal output to fully utilize both labour and machine capacity is 312 500 units of Product X and 125 000 units of Product Y.

(a) The statement includes the following errors:

1 It focuses only on next year's figures but this is not a typical year. Some of the costs are one-off costs and will not be repeated each year. The decision is also likely to be influenced by the level of demand and this varies over the years. Therefore, the analysis should be over a longer time period.

2 The additional cost of purchasing SCB's ignores relevant costs. It should be based on the purchase price less incremental cost and not the full cost of £112 per unit.

3 Half of the purchasing officer's salary is unlikely to be saved since there is no evidence to suggest that he/she will be placed on a fractional contract.

4 The cost of placing orders are not an incremental cost since they are already reflected in the salary, which is likely to remain unchanged.

5 The new liaison officer's salary and redundancy costs are omitted.

6 The cost of transportation of materials is unlikely to be an incremental cost. The cost will be included within the cost of direct materials.

(b) (i) There are a number of different approaches that can be adopted to answer this question. Where you are faced with more than two alternatives, you will probably find it easier to list the costs and revenues associated with each of the alternatives. For the irrelevant costs you can either ensure that the same amount is included in all alternatives, thus ensuring that they become irrelevant, or omit them from the analysis.

Question 9.40

Evaluation of the three alternatives

	2002/03	2003/04	2004/05	Total
Produce internally (Alternative 1)				
Sales volume (units)	58 000	60 500	60 500	
	(£000's)	(£000's)	(£000's)	(£000's)
Sales at normal contribution of £312				
(£400 – £88) per unit	18 096	18 876	18 876	
Less: Overtime at £75 per unit in excess				
of 55 000 units	(225)	(412.5)	(412.5)	

Avoidable fixed costs – SCB's	(250)	(380)	(380)	
Fixed costs – sensors [a]	(2 600)	(2 900)	(2 900)	
Contribution to profits	15 021	15 183.5	15 183.5	45 388

Purchase SCB's externally (Alternative 2)

Sales volume (units)	58 000	62 000	65 000	
	(£000's)	(£000's)	(£000's)	(£000's)
Sales at a contribution of £284 (£400 – £116) per unit	16 472	17 608	18 460	
Less: Extra stockholding costs	(10)	(10)	(10)	
Redundancy costs (72 × £4 000)	(288)			
Liaison officer	(30)	(30)	(30)	
Fixed costs – sensors [a]	(2 600)	(2 900)	(3 100)	
Contribution to profits	13 544	14 668	15 320	43 532

Purchase SCB's externally and rental of extra space (Alternative 3)

Sales volume (units)	58 000	60 500	60 500	
	(£000's)	(£000's)	(£000's)	(£000's)
Sales at a contribution of £284 (£400 – £116) per unit	16 472	17 182	17 182	
Additional rental income (240 × 120 × £45)		1 296	1 296	
Less: Extra stockholding costs	(10)	(10)	(10)	
Redundancy costs (72 × £4 000)	(288)			
Liaison officer	(30)	(30)	(30)	
Fixed costs – sensors [a]	(2 600)	(2 900)	(2 900)	
Contribution to profits	13 544	15 538	15 538	44 620

Note
[a] Note that the same amount is entered for 2002/03 and 2003/04 for the fixed costs relating to sensors, thus making them irrelevant. In 2004/05 the figures reflect incremental fixed costs of £200 000 associated with the higher output level for the second alternative in 2004/05.

Based on the time horizon specified in the question it is preferable to continue producing SCB's and work overtime.

(b) (ii) It is assumed that, in the long term, annual output for the first and third alternatives would still be restricted to 60 500 units but with the second alternative output can be increased to 70 000 units. Over the three year time horizon shown in (b) (i) the first alternative generates £1 856 000 (£45 388 – £43 532) greater contribution than the second alternative and £768 000 (£45 388 – £44 620) more than the third alternative. Assuming that demand remains at 65 000 units the second alternative will generate an extra contribution of £136 500 each year compared with the first alternative (difference between year 3 figures for the two alternatives) thus taking approximately another 13 years (£1 856 000/£136 500) to make up the shortfall in contribution. However, if demand increases to 68 000 units (based on the same 3000 units increase in 2004/05) an additional contribution of £852 000 (3000 units × £284) will be obtained for the second alternative from 2005/06 onwards thus exceeding alternative 1 by £988 500 (£852 000 + £136 500) per annum. Therefore, after two years alternative 2 would be preferred to the first alternative.

A similar analysis could be undertaken based on a comparison of alternatives 1 and 3 to show that in 2004/05 alternative 3 generates £354 500 (£15 538 – £15 183.5) greater contribution. Thus after approximately two years the shortfall in profits would be achieved and beyond a five-year time horizon alternative 3 would be preferred to alternative 1.

MEASURING RELEVANT COSTS AND REVENUES FOR DECISION-MAKING

The choice of alternatives therefore depends on future demand levels. If demand can be maintained at 68 000 units, alternative 2 is the most attractive option. If demand is expected to remain at 65 000 units the third alternative is preferable. It should be noted that qualitative factors, such as the impact of redundancies on the morale of the workforce, should be incorporated into the final decision.

Question 9.41

(a) The relevant cost of producing the new product is the variable cost plus the lost contribution from selling the processing time to another manufacturer. It is assumed that it is more profitable to spend three days per week producing the established main products. The calculations of the variable overhead rates are:

	Department 4	Department 5
Normal hours (0.9 × 40 hrs × 50 weeks)	1800	1800
Fixed overhead rate per hour (£)	20 (36 000/1800)	28 (50 400/1800)
Total overhead rate per hour (£)	40	40
Variable overhead rate per hour (£)	20	12

The variable costs per hour are:

> Department 4: £60 (£40 power cost + £20 variable overhead)
> Department 5: £72 (£60 power cost + £12 variable overhead)

Note that labour costs are fixed.

If the new product is not developed, Department 4 should sell unused processing time at £70 per hour, but it is not profitable for Department 5 to sell processing time because hourly variable cost is in excess of the selling price. Therefore the relevant costs per processing hour are:

> Department 4: £70 (£60 variable cost + £10 lost contribution)
> Department 5: £72

We can now calculate the relevant cost of producing the new product:

	(£)
Direct material	10.00
Department 4 variable operating cost (0.75 hrs × £70)	52.50
Department 5 variable operating cost (0.33 hrs × £72)	24.00
	86.50

The total *additional* contributions for various selling prices and demand levels are:

	(£)	(£)	(£)
Selling price	100	110	120
Unit contribution	13.50	23.50	33.50
Demand	1067[a]	1000	500
Total contribution	14 404	23 500	16 750

Note
[a]Maximum output in Department 4 is 1067 units [(16 weeks × 50 hrs)/0.75 hrs] and 2400 units in Department 5. Output is therefore restricted to 1067 units. Optimum output of the new product is 1000 units at a selling price of £110. An output of 1000 units will require 15 hours per week (20 units per week × 0.75 hrs) in Department 4 and 6.67 hours in Department 5. Department 4 should therefore sell 1 hour per week at £70 per hour, but it is not profitable for Department 5 to sell its spare capacity of 9.33 hours per week.

The weekly *additional* gain from this programme is £470 (20 units × £23.50 contribution). The overall weekly gain is calculated without including the lost contribution of £10 per hour for Department 4. Variable cost is £79 (£86.50 relevant cost less opportunity cost of 0.75 hrs at £10) and contribution is £31 per unit. The total week gain is £630 (20 units at £31 per week plus £10 from the sale of one hour). Without the new product, weekly contribution will be £160 (16 hrs × £10). Therefore there is an additional gain of £470 from introducing the new product.

(b) The shadow prices indicate that if an hour is lost from the existing optimum plan, contribution will decline by £76 for Department 4 and £27 for Department 5. The relevant hourly cost for a scarce resource is:

Variable cost per hour plus lost contribution per hour

Therefore the relevant cost of producing the new product is:

	(£)
Direct material	10
Department 4: 0.75 hrs × (£60 + £76)	102
Department 5: 0.33 hrs × (£72 + £27)	33
	145

The new product will not increase total contribution if the selling price is less than £145.

(c) The shadow price of a scarce resource represents the increase in total contribution that will be obtained if a scarce resource can be increased by 1 unit. Alternatively, the shadow price can be expressed as the loss in total contribution that will occur if the availability of a scarce resource is reduced by 1 unit. The opportunity cost of using a resource is the lost benefit that occurs from using it in the most profitable manner. Shadow prices represent the contribution that would be lost if one unit of a resource were removed from the optimal production programme. In other words, it represents the lost benefit from using it in the most profitable manner. Therefore shadow prices are equivalent to opportunity costs.

Question 9.42

(a) *Alternative uses of spare electric motor*

Use with exhaust gas extraction equipment

Production/sales enhancement resulting in the reduction of the loss in production enhancement from 30% to 10% of 30 000 units thus increasing sales volume by

2000 units at a contribution of £5 (£8–£3)	£10 000
Less fitting and dismantling costs	(2 500)
Add sales value after one year	2 000
Net cash flow	9 500

Use in cooling process	
Hiring cost avoided	£3000
Less modification cost	(1000)
Less disposal cost	(250)
Net cash flow	1750

Hold in store and sell in one year	
Net cash flow (sale proceeds in one year)	£3500

The company should use the motor in conjunction with the exhaust gases for the space heating proposal during the coming year.

(b) The answer in part (a) indicates that if conversion is implemented now, the spare electric motor should be used in the coming year to enhance production and then sold after one year for £2000. The consequences of adopting this alternative are incorporated into the financial evaluation of converting now or in one year's time. Note that the production enhancement will therefore be 9000 units (10 000 units less 10%) for one year only and 10 000 units after the running in period.

Evaluation of decision to convert now or in one year's time

	Convert now	Convert in one year's time	Net benefit/ (cost) of delay for one year
	(£)	(£)	(£)
Cash inflows:			
Production/sales enhancement (at £8)	72 000	80 000	8 000
Sales of space heating equipment (ducted air)	20 000	18 000	(2 000)
Gas extraction machine sale	40 000	30 000	(10 000)
Electric motor sale	2 000	3 500	1 500
	134 000	131 500	
Cash outflows:			
Production/sales enhancement – (VC at £3)	27 000	30 000	(3 000)
Exhaust gas extraction machine			
Incremental fixed costs		16 000	(16 000)
dismantling cost	5 000	5 500	(500)
Space heating (ducted air)			
running costs		10 000	(10 000)
dismantling cost	3 000	3 500	(500)
Alternative exhaust gas extraction machinery			
running cost	12 000		12 000
leasing cost	4 000		4 000
Electric motor conversion cost	2 500		2 500
	53 500	65 000	
Net cash flow	80 500	66 500	
Net cost of delay for one year (£14 000)			(£14 000)

(a) In order to evaluate the three alternatives, it is necessary to estimate the annual income receivable from customers if the company undertakes to service the appliances itself. The calculation of income receivable from customers is:

	(£)
Labour: maintenance contract (100/10 × £30 000)	300 000
Labour: ad hoc work (100/15 × £12 000)	80 000
Materials: maintenance contract (137.5[a]/10 × £18 000)	247 500
Materials: ad hoc work (137.5[a]/10 × £6000)	82 500
	710 000

Note
[a]The material price calculation per £100 cost is:

	(£)
Company cost	100
Contractors' price (£100 + 10%)	110
Customers' price (£110 + 25%)	137.5

In other words, it is assumed that for every £137.50 charged to customers the subcontractor obtains £27.50 profit and the remaining £10 represents income received by the company from the sub-contractor.

Option 1

	(£)	(£)
Sales from small items (40% × £710 000)		284 000
Costs: Incremental fixed costs	148 000	
Materials [40% × 100/137.5 × (247 500 + 82 500)]	96 000	244 000
Income from own operations		40 000
Income from subcontractors of large items (60% × £66 000)		39 600
Total net income		79 600

Option 2

	(£)	(£)
Sales from large items (60% × £710 000)		426 000
Costs: Incremental fixed costs	285 000	
Materials [60% × 100/137.5 × (247 500 + 82 500)]	144 000	429 000
Deficit from own operations		(3 000)
Income from subcontracting small items (40% × £66 000)		26 400
Total net income		23 400

Option 3

	(£)	(£)
Sales from large and small items		710 000
Costs: Incremental fixed costs	385 000	
Materials [100/137.5 × (247 500 + 82 500)]	240 000	625 000
Income from own operations		85 000

It is assumed that all of the fixed costs relating to own operations represent incremental costs.

Option 3 is recommended since it yields the highest profit and is £19 000 in excess of existing operations. Insufficient information is given to incorporate in the answer the effect of repair work undertaken in the first 6 months of operation for which the subcontractor receives 3.5% of the selling price. It is assumed that this payment is common and unavoidable for all alternatives.

(b) Favourable non-financial features:
 (i) The company will have better control over repairs and maintenance of its products and can ensure that a good customer service is provided.
 (ii) The company's mechanics will specialize only in maintaining the company's own appliances, whereas the subcontractors may service many different manufacturers' appliances. Consequently, the company mechanics may become more experienced in maintaining the appliances.
 Adverse non-financial features:
 (i) The new system requires the customers to bring the small appliances to the repair centre. Customers may find this inconvenient compared with the present system.
 (ii) The subcontractors may compete and seek to offer present customers a better service.

Activity-based costing

Solutions to Chapter 10 questions

(a) (i) *Conventional Absorption Costing Profit Statement:*

		XYI	YZT	ABW
(1)	Sales volume (000 units)	50	40	30
		£	£	£
(2)	Selling price per unit	45	95	73
(3)	Prime cost per unit	32	84	65
(4)	Contribution per unit	13	11	8
(5)	Total contribution in £000s (1 × 4)	650	440	240
(6)	Machine department overheads[a]	120	240	144
(7)	Assembly department overheads[b]	288.75	99	49.5
	Profit (£000s)	241.25	101	46.5

Total profit = £388 750

Notes:
[a] XYI = 50 000 × 2 hrs × £1.20, YZT = 40 000 × 5 hrs × £1.20
[b] XYI = 50 000 × 7 hrs × £0.825, YZT = 40 000 × 3 hrs × £0.825

(ii) *Cost pools:*

	Machining services	Assembly services	Set-ups	Order processing	Purchasing
£000	357	318	26	156	84
Cost drivers	420 000 machine hours	530 000 direct labour hours	520 set-ups	32 000 customer orders	11 200 suppliers' orders
Cost driver rates	£0.85 per machine hour	£0.60 direct labour hour	£50 per set-up	£4.875 per customer order	£7.50 per suppliers' order

ABC Profit Statement:

	XYI (£000)	YZT (£000)	ABW (£000)
Total contribution	650	440	240
Less overheads:			
Machine department at £0.85 per hour	85	170	102
Assembly at £0.60 per hour	210	72	36
Set-up costs at £50 per set-up	6	10	10
Order processing at £4.875 per order	39	39	78
Purchasing at £7.50 per order	22.5	30	31.5
Profit (Loss)	287.5	119	(17.5)

Total profit = £389 000

(b) See the sections on 'Comparison of traditional and ABC costing systems' and 'Volume-based and non-volume-based cost drivers' in Chapter 10 for the answer to this question.

Question 10.30 (a) (i) The package material requirements are as follows:

John Ltd	30 000 units	(30 000 × 1)
George Ltd	90 000 units	(45 000 × 2)
Paul Ltd	75 000 units	(25 000 × 3)
	195 000 units	

Cost per unit of packaging = £1 950 000/195 000 = £10

Product costs per cubic metre

	John Ltd	George Ltd	Paul Ltd
	(£)	(£)	(£)
Packaging material	10 (1 × £10)	20 (2 × £10)	30 (3 × £10)
Labour and overhead[a]	9.40	9.40	9.40
	19.40	29.40	39.40

Note
[a]Labour and overhead average cost per metre = £940 000/100 000 metres
= £9.40.

(ii) The costs are assigned to the following activities:

	Receipt and inspection	Storage	Packing
	(£)	(£)	(£)
Labour: Basic	52 500 (15%)	35 000 (10%)	262 500 (75%)
Overtime	15 000 (50%)	4 500 (15%)	10 500 (35%)
Occupancy	100 000 (20%)	300 000 (60%)	100 000 (20%)
Administration and management	24 000 (40%)	6 000 (10%)	30 000 (50%)
	191 500	345 500	403 000

The resource usage for each of the cost drivers is:

	Receipt and inspection hours	Storage (m²)	Packing hours
John Ltd.	2 500 (30 000 × 5 mins.)	9 000 (30 000 × 0.3)	18 000 (30 000 × 36 min)
George Ltd.	6 750 (45 000 × 9 mins.)	13 500 (45 000 × 0.3)	33 750 (45 000 × 45 min)
Paul Ltd.	6 250 (25 000 × 15 mins.)	5 000 (25 000 × 0.2)	25 000 (25 000 × 1 hr)
	15 500	27 500	76 750

The cost driver rates are:

£12.355 per receipt and inspection hour (£191 500/15 500 hours)
£12.564 per m² of material stored (£345 500/27 500 m²)
£5.251 per packing hour (£403 000/76 750 hrs)

Product cost per cubic metre

	John Ltd	George Ltd	Paul Ltd
	(£)	(£)	(£)
Packing material	10.00	20.00	30.00
Receipt and inspection[a]	1.03	1.85	3.09

Storage cost[b]	3.77	3.77	2.51
Packing cost[c]	3.15	3.94	5.25
	17.95	29.56	40.85

Notes
[a] $£12.355 \times 5/60$ hrs $= £1.03$;
$£12.355 \times 9/60$ hrs $= £1.85$; $£12.355 \times 15/60$ hrs $= £3.09$.
[b] $£12.564 \times 0.3$ m $= £3.77$; $£12.564 \times 0.2$ m $= £2.51$.
[c] $£5.25 \times 36/60$ hrs $= £3.15$; $£5.25 \times 45/60$ hrs $= £3.94$, $£5.25 \times 1$ hr.

(b) The company has established cost pools for three major activities (receipt and inspection, storage and packing). The cost driver that causes the receipt and inspection costs to be incurred is the fragility of the different goods (measured by receipt and inspection time). The storage cost is influenced by the average size (measured in square metres) of the incoming product and packing costs are caused by the complexity of packaging and this is measured by the time required to pack the products.

ABC results in the computation of more accurate costs by seeking to measure resources consumed by products. ABC systems assume that activities cause costs and that products create the demand for activities. Costs are assigned to products based on individual products' consumption or demand for each activity. ABC systems simply recognize that businesses must understand the factors that cause each major activity, the cost of activities and how activities relate to products.

ABC has attracted a considerable amount of interest because it provides not only a basis for calculating more accurate product costs but also a mechanism for managing and controlling overhead costs. By collecting and reporting on the significant activities in which a business engages, it is possible to understand and manage costs more effectively. The aim is to manage the forces that cause activities (i.e. the cost drivers), and by reducing cost driver volume, costs can be managed and controlled in the long run.

Question 10.31

(a) For the answer to this question see Chapter 10.

(b) *Machine-related costs*
Machine hours for the period:

$$A = 500 \times \tfrac{1}{4} = 125$$
$$B = 5000 \times \tfrac{1}{4} = 1\,250$$
$$C = 600 \times 1 = 600$$
$$D = 7000 \times 1\tfrac{1}{2} = 10\,500$$
$$12\,475$$

Machine hour rate $= £3$ per hour ($£37\,424/12\,475$ hrs)

Set-up related costs
Cost per set-up $= £256.18$ ($£4355/17$)
Set-up cost per unit of output:

$$\text{Product A } (1 \times £256.18)/500 = £0.51$$
$$B \ (6 \times £256.18)/5000 = £0.31$$
$$C \ (2 \times £256.18)/600 = £0.85$$
$$D \ (8 \times £256.18)/7000 = £0.29$$

Material ordering related costs
Cost per order $= £1920/10$ orders $= £192$ per order

Material ordering cost per unit of output:

$$\begin{array}{lll} \text{Product A} & (1 \times £192)/500 & = £0.38 \\ \text{B} & (4 \times £192)/5000 & = £0.15 \\ \text{C} & (1 \times £192)/600 & = £0.32 \\ \text{D} & (4 \times £192)/7000 & = £0.11 \end{array}$$

Material handling related costs
Cost per material handing = £7580/27 = £280.74
Material handling cost per unit of output:

$$\begin{array}{lll} \text{Product A} & (2 \times £280.74)/500 & = £1.12 \\ \text{B} & (10 \times £280.74)/5000 & = £0.56 \\ \text{C} & (3 \times £280.74)/600 & = £1.40 \\ \text{D} & (12 \times £280.74)/7000 & = £0.48 \end{array}$$

Spare parts
Cost per part = £8600/12 = £716.67
Administration of spare parts cost per unit of output:

$$\begin{array}{lll} \text{Product A} & (2 \times £716.67)/500 & = £2.87 \\ \text{B} & (5 \times £716.67)/5000 & = £0.72 \\ \text{C} & (1 \times £716.67)/600 & = £1.19 \\ \text{D} & (4 \times £716.67)/7000 & = £0.41 \end{array}$$

Overhead cost per unit of output

Product	A	B	C	D
	(£)	(£)	(£)	(£)
ABC overhead cost:				
Machine overheads	0.75	0.75	3.00	4.50
Set-ups	0.51	0.31	0.85	0.29
Material ordering	0.38	0.15	0.32	0.11
Material handling	1.12	0.56	1.40	0.48
Spare parts	2.87	0.72	1.19	0.41
	5.63	2.49	6.76	5.79
Present system	1.20	1.20	4.80	7.20
Difference	+4.43	+1.29	+1.96	−1.41

The present system is based on the assumption that all overhead expenditure is volume-related, measured in terms of machine hours. However, the overheads for the five support activities listed in the question are unlikely to be related to machine hours. Instead, they are related to the factors that influence the spending on support activities (i.e. the cost drivers). The ABC system traces costs to products based on the quantity (cost drivers) of activities consumed. Product D is the high volume product, and thus the present volume-based system traces a large share of overheads to this product. In contrast, the ABC system recognizes that product D consumes overheads according to activity consumption and traces a lower amount of overhead to this product. The overall effect is that, with the present system, product D is overcosted and the remaining products are undercosted. For a more detailed explanation of the difference in resource consumption between products for an ABC and traditional cost system see 'A comparison of traditional and ABC systems' and 'Volume-based and non-volume-based cost drivers' in Chapter 10 for the answer to this question.

Question 10.32 (a) For short-term decision-making, contribution to fixed costs is often advocated. Contribution is defined as sales less variable costs. It therefore attempts to include only those costs and revenues that will change as a result of a decision. Fixed costs are assumed to be unavoidable and remain unchanged and irrelevant for decision-making. Ignoring fixed costs can only be justified in certain circumstances. For example, the contribution approach can be applied to one-time only special orders where the company has a temporary excess supply of spare capacity. In this situation a short-term approach can be adopted by focusing only on the sales revenues and variable costs. The contribution approach is also advocated for pricing off-peak business and ranking products where limiting factors apply (see 'Product-mix decisions when capacity constraints apply' in Chapter 9). In the latter situation a company may be faced with short-term capacity constraint and profit is maximized by ranking products by their contributions per limiting factor.

The contribution approach can only be applied when decisions have no long-term implications. However, most decisions do have long-term implications and in these circumstances fixed costs cannot be ignored. With the contribution approach there is a danger that only those direct costs that are uniquely attributable to individual products will be regarded as relevant for decision-making. Those fixed costs relating to the joint resources that fluctuate according to the demand for them will also be relevant for decision-making. An ideal answer should emphasize, why in the longer-term, fixed costs are likely to change and be relevant for decision-making. For a more detailed discussion of this issue you should refer to 'The need for a cost accumulation system in generating relevant cost information for decision-making' in Chapter 10. Points 1 (many indirect costs are relevant for decision-making) and 3 (product decisions are not independent) are of particular importance.

(b) See section 'Designing ABC systems' in Chapter 10 for the answer to this question.

(c) See sections on 'A comparison of traditional and ABC systems' and 'Volume-based and non-volume-based cost drivers' in Chapter 10 for the answer to this question.

(d) See 'Activity hierarchies' in Chapter 10 for the answer to this question.

Pricing decisions and profitability analysis

Solutions to Chapter 11 questions

Question 11.24   (a)   *Computation of full costs and budgeted cost-plus selling price*

	EXE (£m)	WYE (£m)	Stores (£m)	Maintenance (£m)	Admin (£m)
Material	1.800	0.700	0.100		
Other variable	0.800	0.500	0.100	0.200	0.200
Gen factory	1.440	1.080	0.540	0.180	0.360
					0.560
Admin reallocation	0.224	0.168	0.112	0.056	(0.560)
				0.536	
Maintenance reallocation	0.268	0.134	0.134	(0.536)	
			0.986		
Stores	0.592	0.394	(0.986)		
	5.124	2.976			
Volume	150 000	70 000			
	(£)	(£)			
Full cost	34.16	42.51			
Mark up (25%)	8.54	10.63			
Price	42.70	53.14			

(b)   (i) The incremental costs for the order consist of the variable costs. The calculation of the unit variable cost is as follows:

	EXE (£m)	WYE (£m)	Stores (£m)	Maintenance (£m)	Admin (£m)
Material	1.800	0.700	0.100	0.100	
Other variable	0.800	0.500	0.100	0.200	0.200
Admin	0.080	0.060	0.040	0.020	(0.200)
				0.320	
Maintenance	0.160	0.080	0.080	(0.320)	
			0.320		
Stores	0.192	0.128	(0.320)		
	3.032	1.468			
Volume	150 000	70 000			
	(£)	(£)			
Variable cost	20.21	20.97			

The proposed selling price exceeds the incremental cost and provides a contribution towards fixed costs and profits of £14.03 (£35 – £20.97) per unit thus giving a total contribution of £42 090. Given that the company has spare capacity no lost business will be involved and it appears that the order is a one-off short-term special order. Therefore the order is acceptable provided it does not have an impact on the selling price in the existing market or utilize capacity that has alternative uses. Given that the markets are segregated the former would appear to be an unlikely event. However, if the order were to generate further regular business the longer-term cost considerations described in Chapter 11 should be taken into account in determining an acceptable long-run price.

(b) (ii) The proposed selling price is £46.76 (full cost of £42.51 plus 10%). This will generate a contribution of £25.79 (£46.76 – £20.97) per unit. Un-utilized capacity is 30 000 units but the order is for 50 000 units. Therefore the order can only be met by reducing existing business by 20 000 units. The financial evaluation is as follows:

Increase in contribution from existing business	
(50 000 units at a contribution of £25.79)	£1 289 500
Lost contribution from existing business	
(20 000 units at a contribution of (£53.14 – £20.97))	643 400
Net increase in contribution	646 100

Before accepting the order the longer term implications should be considered. The inability to meet the full demand from existing customers may result in a significant reduction in customer goodwill and the lost contribution from future sales to these customers may exceed the short-term gain of £646 100. Also the above analysis has not considered the alternative use of the un-utilized capacity of 30 000 units. If the cost savings from reducing the capacity exceed £646 100 for the period under consideration the order will not be worthwhile. The order will also result in the company operating at full capacity and it is possible that the cost structure may change if the company is operating outside its normal production range.

If the company does not rely on customer repeat orders and customer goodwill it is unlikely to be affected and the order would appear to be profitable. It is important, however, that long-term considerations are taken into account when evaluating the order. In particular, consideration should be given to the negotiation of a longer-term contract on both price and volume.

(c) See 'Alternative denominator level measures' in Chapter 7 and 'Selecting the cost driver denominator level' in Chapter 10 for the answer to this question.

Question 11.25

(a) For the answer to this question you should refer to Chapter 11. In particular the answer should discuss the role of cost information in the following situations:
1   a price setting firm facing short-run pricing decisions;
2   a price setting firm facing long-run decisions;
3   a price taker firm facing short-run product-mix decisions;
4   a price taker firm facing long-run decisions.

(b) *Calculation of variable overhead absorption rates*

	Moulding (£000)	Finishing (£000)	General Factory (£000)
Allocated overheads	1600	500	1050
Reallocation of General Factory			
based on machine hours	600	450	(1050)
	2200	950	
Machine hours	800	600	
Variable overhead rate per hour	£2.75	£1.583	

Calculation of fixed overhead absorption rates

	Moulding (£000)	Finishing (£000)	General Factory (£000)
Allocated overheads	2500	850	1750
Reallocation of General Factory based on machine hours	1050	700	(1750)
	3550	1550	
Machine hours	800	600	
Variable overhead rate per hour	£4.4375	£2.583	

Calculation of full manufacturing cost

		(£)
Direct material		9.00
Direct labour	10.00 (2 × £5)	
	16.50 (3 × £5.50)	26.50
Variable overheads	11.00 (4 × £2.75)	
	4.75 (3 × £1.583)	15.75
Variable manufacturing cost		51.25
Fixed overheads	17.75 (4 × £4.4375)	
	7.75 (3 × £2.583)	25.50
Full manufacturing cost		76.75

Prices based on full manufacturing cost
25% mark up = £95.94
30% mark up = £99.78
35% mark up = £103.61

Minimum prices based on short-term variable cost and incremental cost are as follows:

Variable cost = £51.25
Incremental cost = £59.60 (£51.25 plus specific fixed costs of £8.35)

The specific fixed cost per unit is calculated by dividing the fixed costs of £167 000 by the estimated sales volume (10% × 200 000).

(c) The cost information is more likely to provide a general guide to the pricing decision but the final pricing decision will be influenced by the prices of competitors' products (£90 – £100). The full cost prices indicate prices within a range of £96 – £104. The variable/incremental price indicates a minimum short-run price that may be appropriate if the company wishes to pursue a price skimming policy. Given that the product is an improvement on competitors, a price in the region of £100 would seem to be appropriate but the final decision should be based on marketing considerations drawing off the knowledge of the marketing staff. The role of the cost information has been to indicate that a price within this range should provide a reasonable margin and contribution to general fixed costs.

Question 11.26

(a) Presumably the question is intended to indicate that if competitors increase their prices by 6% and the company maintains its current price then this is equivalent to a price reduction by the company of 6%. An estimated price reduction of 6% and a price elasticity of demand of 1.5 would be expected to increase demand by 9%.

To predict costs for the next period it is necessary to analyse the costs into their fixed and variable elements. The high–low method can be used by comparing the changes in costs between the periods with the changes in activity. However, the current period costs must be deflated by the inflation factor so that they are expressed in the current prices for the previous period.

Current period's costs adjusted to previous period's prices = £1036 (£1077.4/ 1.04. Applying the high–low method:

	Units (000)	Costs (£000)
Current period	106	1036
Previous period	100	1000
	6	36

Variable cost per unit = Increase in costs (£36 000)/Increase in activity (6000 units)
= £6 per unit
Fixed costs = £1 000 000 − (100 000 units × £6) = £400 000

Costs have increased by 4% from the previous to the current period and by a further 6% from the current to the next period:

Variable cost per unit next period = £6 (1.04) (1.06) = £6.6144
Fixed costs next period = £400 000 (1.04) (1.06) = £440 960

Budgeted profit at a selling price of £13

	(£)
Sales (106 000 × 1.09[a] × £13)	1 502 020
Variable costs (106 000 × 1.09[a] × £6.6144)	764 228
Contribution	737 792
Less fixed costs	440 960
Profit	296 832

Note
[a]It is assumed that sales volume and production increase by 9% as a result of the price increase by competitors.

(b) *Budgeted profit assuming that the selling price is increased by 6%*

	(£)
Sales (106 000 × £13 (1.06))	1 460 680
Variable costs (106 000 × £6.6144)	(701 126)
Contribution	759 554
Fixed costs	440 960
	318 594

If the selling price is increased to match that of the competitors it is assumed that demand will remain unchanged.

(c) The report should indicate that on the basis of the information specified in parts (a) and (b) the price should be increased by 6%.

(d) It is assumed that:
  (i) Total market volume will remain unchanged and that the sales of the company will not decline as a result of both the firm and its competitors increasing prices by 6%;
  (ii) The estimate of the elasticity of demand is correct;
  (iii) All costs are affected by the same rate of inflation;
  (iv) All other factors remain constant so that sales will not be influenced by changes in advertising, customer preferences and general economic conditions.

Question 11.27 (a) The following represents the quantity of sales that would be required to break even for a range of selling prices within each of the three selling price categories:

	Selling price (£)	Variable costs[a] (£)	Unit contribution (£)	Break-even point[b] (units)	Break-even % share of market
Category 1					
Low selling price	600	850	0	Not applicable	—
Medium selling price	825	917.50	0	Not applicable	—
High selling price	1050	985	65	8462	38
Category 2					
Low selling price	1450	1105	345	1594	27
Medium selling price	1675	1172.5	502.5	1095	18
High selling price	1900	1240	660	833	14
Category 3					
Low selling price	2500	1420	1080	509	68
Medium selling price	2750	1495	1255	438	58
High selling price	3000	1570	1430	385	51

Notes
[a] (30% × selling price) + £670 variable cost.
[b] (£550 000 fixed costs)/unit contribution.

The average market share per manufacturer in category 1 is 5500 units. AB Ltd would have to sell 8462 units (that is, capture a 38% share of the market) at the maximum price within the range in order to break even. It is likely that there will be a significant demand in the category 1 market for a lower-quality and lower-priced product. It may therefore be unwise to enter the category 1 market.

The average market share per manufacturer in the category 2 market is 1200 units. Given that AB will be able to enter the market with a product of advanced technology and distinctive design, it is likely that it will be able to sell the break-even sales volume of 1594 units (that is, obtain a market share of 27%) at the lowest selling price within the range. At the medium and high selling prices the break-even sales volume is below the average sales volume per manufacturer.

For the category 3 market the average market share per manufacturer is 375 units. This is in excess of the break-even point for the three prices considered in the above analysis. The company would also have to obtain a market share in excess of 50% in order to break even. The technology in this market is also advanced, and consequently competition will be more intensive.

It is therefore suggested that the company market the product within a selling price range of £1450–£1900.

(b) The question does not provide any details of demand information within each price range, and it is therefore questionable whether or not it is possible to recommend a price from the data given. AB's product incorporates some of the most advanced techniques available, together with a very distinctive design, and it is therefore likely that a large market share will be obtained at selling prices at the lower end of the price range. Assuming that a 50% market share could be obtained at a £1500 selling price, 40% at £1700, 30% at £1800 and 20% at £1900, the profits would be as follows:

Selling price	£1500	£1700	£1800	£1900
3000 units (50%)	£590 000			
2400 units (40%)		£698 000		
1800 units (30%)			£512 000	
1200 units (20%)				£242 000

Note that the above figures have been calculated as follows:

demand × (70% of selling price − £670 variable cost) − £550 000 fixed costs

Assuming that the above estimates of demand were correct, a selling price of £1700 would be recommended.

(a) The answer should include a discussion of the following points:
- the benefits and limitations of cost-plus pricing;
- price skimming and price penetration policies;
- pricing based on demand estimates approximating economic theory.

A detailed description of each of the above approaches is provided in Chapter 11. You will find an explanation of the approach involving demand estimates in the sections relating to economic theory and pricing non-customized products in Chapter 11.

(b) (i) To increase demand by one unit, price must be reduced by £0.01 (£10/1000) so that:
Selling price = £750 − £0.10x
Marginal revenue = £750 − £0.02x
Marginal cost = £320
At the optimum output level where MR = MC:
£320 = £750 − £0.02x
x = 21 500
Selling price = £750 − 21 500 (0.01) = £535
Therefore the maximum annual profit is:

Total contribution (21 500 × unit contribution (£535 − £320)	=	£4 622 500
Less fixed costs (15 000 × £80)	=	1 200 000
	=	3 422 500

(b) (ii) Current contribution = £4 622 500

Contribution from exporting to L = [(930 × 0.60) − £300] × 25 000 = £6 450 000

Based on the above information R Ltd. should sell all of the output to L. However, if the exchange rate falls below €1 = £0.521 R Ltd. will be worse off. This rate is calculated as follows:

Required unit contribution = £4 622 500/25 000 = £184.90

Required selling price in UK currency = £484.90 (£300 variable cost + £184.90)

The exchange rate can fall to €1 = £0.521 (£484.90/[€]930) before R Ltd. will be worse off.

Also note that if the exchange rate falls to €1 = £0.25 the following negative contribution will be generated:

((€930 × 0.25) − £300) × 25 000 = − £1 687 500

The above items can now be plotted on the graph (see Figure 11.28).

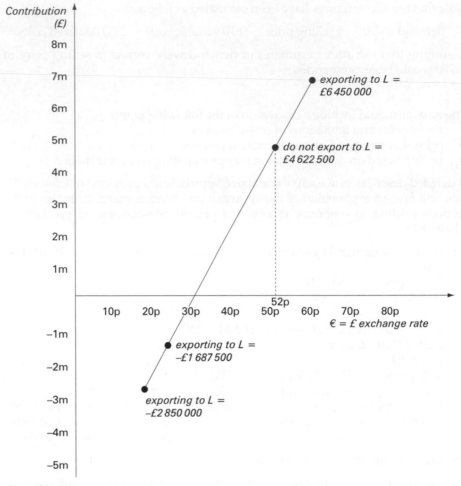

Figure Q11.28

(c)

Purchase Year	Outlay	Capital allowances	Tax savings on capital allowances[a]	Net cash flow	Discount factor	Present value
	(£)	(£)	(£)	(£)	(£)	(£)
0	(1 000 000)			(1 000 000)	1.000	(1 000 000)
1		(250 000)	37 500	37 500	0.893	33 488
2		(187 500)	65 625	65 625	0.893	52 303
3		(140 625)	49 219	49 219	0.712	35 044
4		(421 875)	84 375	84 375	0.636	53 663
5			63 281	63 281	0.567	35 880
		(1 000 000)				(789 622)

Lease Year	Payments	Tax cash flow	Net cash flow	Discount factor	Present value
	(£)	(£)	(£)	(£)	(£)
0	(300 000)	45 000	(255 000)	1.000	(255 000)
1	(300 000)	90 000	(210 000)	0.893	(187 530)
2	(300 000)	90 000	(210 000)	0.797	(167 370)
3	(300 000)	90 000	(210 000)	0.712	(149 520)
4		45 000	45 000	0.636	28 620
					(730 800)

therefore, leasing is the least cost option with savings of £58 822.

Note

[a]Capital allowances cannot be claimed if the machine is hired. The tax saving for year 2 is $(0.30 \times £250\,000 \times 0.5) + (0.30 \times £187\,500 \times 0.5)$

(a) (i) If the selling price is £200, demand will be zero. To increase demand by one unit, selling price must be reduced by £1/1000 units or £0.001. Hence the maximum selling price attainable for an output of x units is:

$$P = £200 - 0.001x$$

At an output level of 100 000 units,

$$P = £200 - £0.001 \times 10\,000$$
$$= £100 \text{ per unit}$$

Total contribution at an output level of 100 000 units

$100\,000 \times (£100 - £50)$	5 000 000
Less fixed costs $(100\,000 \times £25)$	2 500 000
Profit	2 500 000

(ii) Profit is maximized where MC = MR

$$MC = £50 \text{ per unit variable cost (given)}$$

$$MR = \frac{dTR}{dx}$$

$$TR = x(200 - 0.001x)$$
$$= 200x - 0.001x^2$$

$$\frac{dTR}{dx} = 200 - 0.002x$$

Therefore optimum output is where $50 = 200 - 0.002x$ (i.e. where MC = MR). And so

$$150 = 0.002x$$

That is,

$$x = 75\,000 \text{ units}$$

At an output level of 75 000 units, the selling price is $£200 - (£0.001 \times 75\,000) = £125$. Therefore profit at 75 000 units:

	(£)
Contribution $(75\,000 \times £75)$	5 625 000
Less fixed costs	2 500 000
	3 125 000

(b) (i) Revised fixed costs = £3 000 000.
The optimal output level will not be affected by a change in fixed costs. Therefore the selling price should not be changed. Profit will decline by £500 000.

(ii) Revised marginal cost = £60.
The new optimum is where $60 = 200 - 0.002x$
$$0.002x = 140$$
Therefore $x = 70\,000$ units
At this output level, $P = £200 - £0.001 \times 70\,000$
$$= £130$$

(c) Profit before advertising expenditure:

	(£)
Total contribution [70 000 × (£130 − £60)]	4 900 000
Less fixed costs	3 000 000
Profit	1 900 000

After the introduction of the advertising expenditure:

$$P = 210 - 0.001x$$
$$TR = x (210 - 0.001x)$$
$$= 210x - 0.001x^2$$
$$\text{Therefore MR} = 210 - 0.002x$$

The revised optimum output is where $60 = 210 - 0.002x$
$$0.002x = 150$$
$$x = 75\,000$$

The optimum price at this output level is where $P = £210 - £0.001 \times 75\,000$
$$= £135$$

	(£)
Total contribution [75 000 × (£135 − £60)]	5 625 000
Revised fixed costs	4 000 000
Profit	1 625 000

Therefore profits will decline by £275 000 if the advertising campaign is undertaken.

(d) The original budgeted output of 100 000 units was higher than the optimum output level. The solution to (a) (ii) indicates that the optimum output level is achieved by reducing production to 75 000 units and increasing the selling price to £125. Beyond an output level of 75 000 units, marginal cost per unit is in excess of marginal revenue. This is because selling price is reduced in order to expand output. Consequently, marginal revenue declines and is less than marginal cost. This means that profits decline when output is in excess of 75 000 units. This analysis is based on the following assumptions:

  (i) The demand schedule can be predicted accurately.
 (ii) Marginal cost per unit is constant at all output levels.
(iii) Fixed costs are constant throughout the entire output range.

The analysis also showed that the change in fixed costs had no effect on the MR and MC function, so that the optimum output level and price did not change. When MC increases, the effect is to decrease output level and increase price.

The effect of the advertising campaign is to shift the demand curve to the right, thus causing sales demand to be higher at each selling price or the selling price to be higher at each demand level. However, the increased advertising costs are in excess of the additional revenue, thus resulting in a reduction in profits.

Decision-making under conditions of risk and uncertainty

Solutions to Chapter 12 questions

(a) *Profit and Loss Statement for Period Ending 31 May 2000*

Question 12.17

	(£)
Revenue (14 400 000 journeys):	
0–3 miles (7 200 000 × £0.20)	1 440 000
4–5 miles (4 320 000 × £0.30)	1 296 000
Over 5 miles (2 880 000 × £0.50)	1 440 000
Juvenile fares (4 800 000 × £0.15)	720 000
Senior citizen fares (4 800 000 × £0.10)	480 000
	5 376 000
Advertising revenue	250 000
	5 626 000
Less: Variable costs (20 routes × 4 buses × 150 miles × 330 days × £0.75)	(2 970 000)
Fixed costs	(1 750 000)
Net profit	906 000

(b) Assuming the same passenger mix as 2000 the weighted average fare per passenger for year ending 31 May 2001 is (£5 376 000 × 1.05)/24 000 000 = £0.2352. The break-even point is where:

Total revenue from fares + Advertising revenue = Total cost

Let x = number of passenger journeys

$$\text{Break-even point: } 0.2352x + £250\,000 = (2\,970\,000 + £1\,750\,000)\,1.1$$
$$0.2352x = £4\,942\,000$$
$$x = 21\,011\,905$$

Maximum capacity utilization = 40 000 000 passenger journeys (24 000 000/0.6)
Break-even capacity utilization = 21 011 905/40 000 000 = 52.5%

(c) (i)

Expected value and probability estimates for 2001

Capacity Utilization		Revenue		Inflation		Costs	Combined probability	Net profit	Expected value
%	(Probability)	Fares (£000)	Adverts (£000)	(%)	(Probability)	(£000)		(£000)	(£000)
70	0.1	6585.6[a]	250	8	0.3	5097.6[b]	0.03	1738.0	52.14
		6585.6	250	10	0.6	5192.0[b]	0.06	1643.6	98.62
		6585.6	250	12	0.1	5286.4[b]	0.01	1549.2	15.49
60	0.5	5644.8[a]	250	8	0.3	5097.6	0.15	797.2	119.58
		5644.8	250	10	0.6	5192.0	0.30	702.8	210.84
		5644.8	250	12	0.1	5286.4	0.05	608.4	30.42
50	0.4	4704.0[a]	250	8	0.3	5097.6	0.12	−143.6	−17.23
		4704.0	250	10	0.6	5192.0	0.24	−238.0	−57.12
		4704.0	250	12	0.1	5286.4	0.04	−332.4	−13.30
							1.00		439.44

[a]Fare revenues at 60% capacity for 2000 were £5 376 000. Assuming 5% inflation fare revenues for 2001 at 60% capacity will be £5 644 800 (£5 376 000 × 1.05). At 70% and 50% capacity utilization fare revenues will be as follows:

$$70\% = 70/60 \times £5\,644\,800 = £6\,585\,600$$
$$50\% = 50/60 \times £5\,644\,800 = £4\,704\,000$$

[b]Variable costs vary with bus miles which are assumed to remain unchanged. Predicted costs at the different inflation levels are as follows:

$$8\% = (£2\,970\,000 + £1\,750\,000)1.08 = £5\,097\,600$$
$$10\% = (£2\,970\,000 + £1\,750\,000)1.10 = £5\,192\,000$$
$$12\% = (£2\,970\,000 + £1\,750\,000)1.12 = £5\,286\,400$$

(c) (ii) The answer to this question requires the preparation of a cumulative probability distribution that measures the cumulative probability of profits/ (losses) being greater than specified levels.

Cumulative probability distribution

Losses greater than £300 000	= 0.04 probability
Probability of a loss occurring	= 0.40
Profits greater than £600 000	= 0.60
Profits greater than £700 000	= 0.55
Profits greater than £800 000	= 0.10
Profits greater than £1 500 000	= 0.10

(d) The following factors have not been incorporated into the analysis:
   (i) Change in the passenger mix.
   (ii) Changes in the number of routes and the number of days operation per year.
   (iii) Changes in fare structure such as off-peak travel or further concessions for juveniles and senior citizens.
   (iv) Changes in cost levels due to factors other than inflation (e.g. more efficient operating methods).

Question 12.18

(a) For each selling price there are three possible outcomes for sales demand, unit variable cost and fixed costs. Consequently, there are 27 possible outcomes. In order to present probability distributions for the two possible selling prices, it would be necessary to compute profits for 54 outcomes. Clearly, there would be insufficient time to perform these calculations within the examination time that can be allocated to this question. It is therefore assumed that the examiner requires the calculations to be based on an expected value approach.
The expected value calculations are as follows:

(i) *Variable cost*		(£)	(ii) *Fixed costs*		(£)
(£10 + 10%) × 10/20	=	5.50	£82 000 × 0.3	=	24 600
£10 × 6/20	=	3.00	£85 000 × 0.5	=	42 500
(£10 − 5%) × 4/20	=	1.90	£90 000 × 0.2	=	18 000
		10.40			85 100

(iii) *£17 selling price*			(iv) *£18 selling price*		
		(units)			(units)
21 000 units × 0.2	=	4 200	19 000 units × 0.2	=	3 800
19 000 units × 0.5	=	9 500	17 500 units × 0.5	=	8 750
16 500 units × 0.3	=	4 950	15 500 units × 0.3	=	4 650
		18 650			17 200

Expected contribution

$$£17 \text{ selling price} = (£17 - £10.40) \times 18\,650 = £123\,090$$
$$£18 \text{ selling price} = (£18 - £10.40) \times 17\,200 = £130\,720$$

The existing selling price is £16, and if demand continues at 20 000 units per annum then the total contribution will be £112 000 [(£16 − £10.40) × 20 000 units]. Using the expected value approach, a selling price of £18 is recommended.

(b) Expected profit = £130 720 − £85 100 fixed costs = £45 620

Break-even point = fixed costs (£85 100)/contribution per unit (£7.60)

$$= 11\,197 \text{ units}$$

Margin of safety = expected demand (17 200 units) − 11 197 units = 6003 units

% margin of safety = 6003/17 200 = 34.9% of sales

Note that the most pessimistic estimate is above the break-even point.

(c) An expected value approach has been used. The answer should draw attention to the limitations of basing the decision solely on expected values. In particular, it should be stressed that risk is ignored and the range of possible outcomes is not considered. The decision ought to be based on a comparison of the probability distributions for the proposed selling prices. For a more detailed answer see 'Probability distributions and expected value' and 'Measuring the amount of uncertainty' in Chapter 12.

(d) Computer assistance would enable a more complex analysis to be undertaken. In particular, different scenarios could be considered, based on different combinations of assumptions regarding variable cost, fixed cost, selling prices and demand. Using computers would also enable Monte Carlo simulation (see Chapter 14) to be used for more complex decisions.

Question 12.19

(a)

Alternative types of machine hire	Possible outcomes (level of orders)	Probability of outcomes	Payoff (£000)
High	High	0.25	2200 [(0.3 × £15 000) − £2300]
	Medium	0.45	250 [(0.3 × £8500) − £2300]
	Low	0.30	−1100 [(0.3 × £4000) − £2300]
Medium	High	0.25	1700 (0.3 × £15 000) − £1500 − £1300
	Medium	0.45	1050 [(0.3 × £8500) − £1500]
	Low	0.30	−300 [(0.3 × £4000) − £1500]
Low	High	0.25	1350 (0.3 × £15 000) − £1000 − £2150
	Medium	0.45	700 (0.3 × £8500) − £1000 − £850
	Low	0.30	200 [(0.3 × £4000) − £1000]

(b) Expected values:

$$\text{High hire level} = (0.25 \times £2200) + (0.45 \times £250) - (0.3 \times £1100)$$
$$= £332\,500$$
$$\text{Medium hire level} = (0.25 \times £1700) + (0.45 \times £1050) - (0.3 \times £300)$$
$$= £807\,500$$
$$\text{Low hire level} = (0.25 \times £1350) + (0.45 \times £700) + (0.3 \times £200)$$
$$= £712\,500$$

Using the expected value decision rule, the medium hire contract should be entered into.

(c) Managers may be risk-averse, risk-neutral or risk-seeking. A risk-averse manager might adopt a maximin approach and focus on the worst possible outcome for each alternative and then select the alternative with the largest payoff. This approach would lead to the selection of the low initial hire level. A risk-seeking manager might adopt a maximax approach and focus on the best possible outcomes. This approach would lead to choosing the high initial hire contract, since this has the largest payoff when only the most optimistic outcomes are considered.

(d) With perfect information, the company would select the advance plant and machinery hire alternative that would maximize the payoff. The probabilities of the consultants predicting high, medium and low demand are respectively 0.25, 0.45 and 0.30. The expected value calculation with the consultant's information would be:

	Advance hire level	Payoff (£000)	Probability	Expected value (£000)
High market	high	2200	0.25	550
Medium market	medium	1050	0.45	472.5
Low market	low	200	0.30	60
				1082.5

	(£)
Expected value with consultant's information	1 082 500
Expected value without consultant's information	807 500
Maximum amount payable to consultant	275 000

Question 12.20

(a)

Selling price (£)	70	80	90
Maximum demand (£)	75 000	60 000	40 000
Maximum revenue (£)	5 250 000	4 800 000	3 600 000
Total variable cost (£)	3 750 000	3 000 000	2 000 000
Fixed costs (£)	800 000	800 000	800 000
R & D cost (£)	250 000	250 000	250 000
	4 800 000	4 050 000	3 050 000
Estimated profit (£)	450 000	750 000	550 000

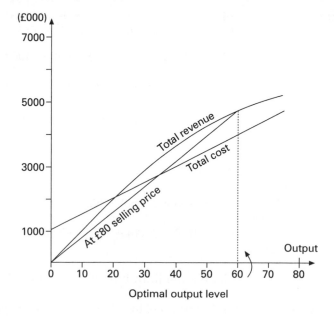

Figure Q12.20

The above analysis is based on the maximum sales demand. On this basis, the analysis indicates that profits are maximized at an output level of 60 000 units when the selling price is £80. It is preferable to use the 'most likely' demand level and to incorporate uncertainty around the 'most likely' demand into the analysis.

(b) For a selling price of £90 there are three different demand levels, and for each demand level there are three different outcomes for actual unit variable cost. Therefore there are nine possible outcomes. The contribution and probability of each outcome is presented in the following schedule:

(1) Demand (000)	(2) Probability	(3) Unit variable cost (£)	(4) Probability	(5) Unit contribution (£)	(6) Total contribution (£000)	(7) Joint probability (2 × 4)	(8) Weighted outcome (6 × 7) (£000)
20	0.2	60	0.2	30	600	0.04	24.00
20	0.2	55	0.7	35	700	0.14	98.00
20	0.2	50	0.1	40	800	0.02	16.00
35	0.7	60	0.2	30	1050	0.14	147.00
35	0.7	55	0.7	35	1225	0.49	600.25
35	0.7	50	0.1	40	1400	0.07	98.00
40	0.1	60	0.2	30	1200	0.02	24.00
40	0.1	55	0.7	35	1400	0.07	98.00
40	0.1	50	0.1	40	1600	0.01	16.00
						1.00	1121.25

	(£)
Expected total contribution	1 121 250
Fixed costs	1 050 000
Expected profit	71 250

(c) To compare the three selling prices, it is necessary to summarize the information in part (b) for a £90 selling price in the same way as part (c) of the question. Note that fixed costs are deducted from the total contribution column in the schedule presented in (b) to produce the following statement:

		Prices under review		
		£70	£80	£90
Probability of a loss				
Greater than or equal to	£500 000	0.02	0	0
	£300 000	0.07	0.05	0.18
	£100 000	0.61	0.08	0.20
	0	0.61	0.10	0.34
Probability of a profit				
Greater than or equal to	0	0.39	0.91	0.80
	£100 000	0.33	0.52	0.66
	£300 000	0.03	0.04	0.15
	£500 000	0	0.01	0.01
Expected profit		Loss (£55 750)	£68 500	£71 250

The following items should be included in the memorandum:
   (i) The £90 selling price has the largest expected profit, but there is also a 0.34 probability of not making a profit.
  (ii) Selling price of £80 may be preferable, because there is only a 0.10 probability of not making a profit. A selling price of £80 is least risky, and the expected value is only slightly lower than the £90 selling price.

(iii) Subjective probability distributions provide details of the uncertainty surrounding the estimates and enable the decision-maker to select the course of action that is related to his personal risk/profit trade-off (see Chapter 12 for an explanation of this).

(iv) Subjective probabilities are subject to all the disadvantages of any subjective estimate (e.g. bias).

(v) Calculations are based on discrete probabilities. For example, this implies that there is a 0.7 probability that demand will be exactly 35 000. A more realistic interpretation is that 35 000 represents the mid-point of demand falling within a certain range.

(d) If the increase in fixed costs represents an additional cost resulting from an increase in volume then this incremental cost is relevant to the pricing decision. If the fixed costs represent an apportionment then it is not relevant. Nevertheless, we noted in Chapter 11 that selling prices should be sufficient to cover the common and unavoidable long-run fixed costs.

The research and development expenditure is a sunk cost, and is not a relevant cost as far as the pricing decision is concerned. However, the pricing policy of the company may be to recover the research and development expenditure in the selling price. The amount recovered per unit sold should be a policy decision. Note that the decision to write off research and development in one year instead of three will affect the reported profits.

Question 12.21

(a) The calculations of the product variable costs per unit are:

	Newone (£)	Newtwo (£)
Labour and materials	82	44
Variable overheads	6 (6 hrs × £1)	2 (2 hrs × £1)
Unit variable cost	88	46

Low-price alternative: The contributions per unit are £32 for Newone (£120 − £88) and £14 (£60 − £46) for Newtwo. The probability distributions are as follows:

	Newone			Newtwo	
Demand	Probability	Contribution (£)	Demand	Probability	Contribution (£)
1000	0.2	32 000	3000	0.2	42 000
2000	0.5	32 000[a]	3000	0.5	42 000
3000	0.3	32 000[a]	3000	0.3	42 000

Note

[a]Machine capacity restricts outputs to 1000 units of Newone and 3000 units of Newtwo.

Note that estimates indicate with 100% certainty that Newone will yield a contribution of £32 000 and Newtwo will yield a contribution of £42 000.

Higher price alternative: The contributions per unit are £42 for Newone (£130 − £88) and £24 (£70 − £46) for Newtwo. The probability distributions are as follows:

	Newone			Newtwo	
Demand	Probability	Contribution (£)	Demand	Probability	Contribution (£)
500	0.2	21 000	1500	0.2	36 000
1000	0.5	42 000	2500	0.5	60 000
1500	0.3	42 000[a]	3500	0.3	72 000[a]
	Expected value	37 800		Expected value	58 800

Note
[a]Output is restricted to 1000 units of Newone and 3000 units of Newtwo.

Recommendations
The above probability distributions indicate that Newtwo is preferable to Newone, irrespective of which price is set. At the higher selling price Newtwo yields a higher expected value. There is only a 0.2 probability that a lower contribution will be earned if the higher price is selected in preference to the lower price. The advantage of the lower price is that the outcome is certain, but, given the high probability (0.8) of earning higher profits with the higher-price alternative, a selling price of £70 is recommended. With the higher-price alternative, there is a 0.70 probability that machine hours will not be utilized. Any unused capacity should be used to sell Newone at £130 selling price.

(b) Decision problems require estimates of changes in costs and revenues for choosing alternative courses of action. It is therefore necessary to distinguish between fixed and variable costs. Regression analysis can be used to estimate a cost equation, and tests of reliability can be applied to ascertain how reliable the cost equation is in predicting costs. For a description of regression analysis and tests of reliability you should refer to Chapter 24. A common test of reliability is the coefficient of determination, which can be calculated by squaring the correlation coefficient. The coefficient of determination for the cost equation used in the question is 0.64 (0.8^2). Consequently, 36% of the variation in cost is not explained by the cost equation used in the question. It is possible that activity bases other than machine hours might provide a better explanation of the relationship between costs and activities. Alternatively, changes in costs might be a function of more than one variable. In such circumstances, cost equations based on multiple regression techniques should provide more reliable cost estimates.

The following is a decision tree relating to the question:

Question 12.22

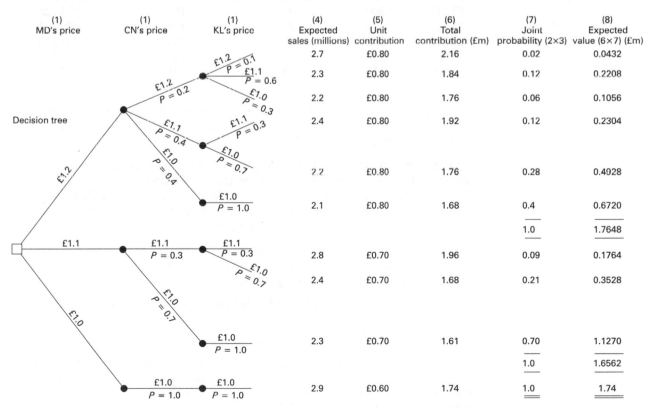

(1) MD's price	(1) CN's price	(1) KL's price	(4) Expected sales (millions)	(5) Unit contribution	(6) Total contribution (£m)	(7) Joint probability (2×3)	(8) Expected value (6×7) (£m)
			2.7	£0.80	2.16	0.02	0.0432
			2.3	£0.80	1.84	0.12	0.2208
			2.2	£0.80	1.76	0.06	0.1056
			2.4	£0.80	1.92	0.12	0.2304
			2.2	£0.80	1.76	0.28	0.4928
			2.1	£0.80	1.68	0.4	0.6720
						1.0	1.7648
			2.8	£0.70	1.96	0.09	0.1764
			2.4	£0.70	1.68	0.21	0.3528
			2.3	£0.70	1.61	0.70	1.1270
						1.0	1.6562
			2.9	£0.60	1.74	1.0	1.74

Figure Q12.22

The variable cost per litre is as follows:

	(£)
Direct materials	0.12
Direct wages	0.24
Indirect wages etc. $(16\frac{2}{3}\% \times £0.24)$	0.04
	0.40

and the range of contributions are:

£0.80 for a selling price of £1.20
£0.70 for a selling price of £1.10
£0.60 for a selling price of £1.00

The decision tree indicating the possible outcomes presented in Figure Q12.22 shows that the expected value of the contribution is maximized at a selling price of £1.20. Fixed costs are common and unavoidable to all alternatives, and are therefore not included in the analysis. However, management might prefer the certain contribution of £1.74 million at a selling price of £1.00. From columns 6 and 7 of the decision tree it can be seen that there is a 0.60 probability that contribution will be in excess of £1.74 million when a selling price of £1.20 is implemented. The final decision depends on management's attitude towards risk.

Question 12.23

(a) Budgeted net Profit/Loss outcomes for year ending 30 June

Client Days	Fee per Client day (£)	Variable cost per client day (£)	Contribution per client day (£)	Total contrib. per year (£)
15 750	180	95	85	1 338 750
15 750	180	85	95	1 496 250
15 750	180	70	110	1 732 500
13 125	200	95	105	1 378 125
13 125	200	85	115	1 509 375
13 125	200	70	130	1 706 250
10 500	220	95	125	1 312 500
10 500	220	85	135	1 417 500
10 500	220	70	150	1 575 000

(b) The *maximax* rule looks for the largest contribution from all outcomes. In this case the decision maker will choose a client fee of £180 per day where there is a possibility of a contribution of £1 732 500.

The *maximin* rule looks for the strategy which will maximize the minimum possible contribution. In this case the decision maker will choose client fee of £200 per day where the lowest contribution is £1 378 125. This is better than the worst possible outcome from client fees per day of £180 or £220 which will provide contribution of £1 338 750 and £1 312 500 respectively.

The *minimax regret* rule requires the choice of the strategy which will minimize the maximum regret from making the wrong decision. Regret represents the opportunity lost from making the wrong decision.

The calculations in part (a) are used to list the opportunity losses in the following regret matrix:

State of nature

	Low variable cost of £70	Most likely variable cost of £85	High variable cost of £95
Choose a fee of £180	0	£13 125	£39 375
Choose a fee of £200	£26 250	0	0
Choose a fee of £220	£157 500	£91 875	£65 625

At a variable cost of £70 the maximum contribution is £1 732 500 derived from a fee of £180. Therefore there will be no opportunity loss. At a fee of £200 the opportunity loss is £26 250 (£1 732 500 – £1 706 250) and at the £220 fee the opportunity loss is £157 500 (£1 732 500 – £1 575 000). The same approach is used to calculate the opportunity losses at variable costs of £85 and £95.

The maximum regrets for each fee are as follows:

	(£)
£180	39 375
£200	26 250
£220	157 500

The minimum regret is £26 250 and adopting a minimum regret strategy will result in choosing the £200 fee per day alternative.

(c) The expected value of variable cost

$$= £95 \times 0.1 + £85 \times 0.6 + £70 \times 0.3 = £81.50$$

For each client fee strategy the expected value of budget contribution for the year is calculated as follows:

* fee of £180 : 15 750 (180 – 81.50) = £1 551 375
* fee of £200 : 13 125 (200 – 81.50) = £1 555 312.50
* fee of £220 : 10 500 (220 – 81.50) = £1 454 250

A client fee of £200 per day is required to give the maximum expected value contribution of £1 555 312.50. Note that there is virtually no difference between this and the contribution where a fee of £180 per day is used.

(d) Profit can be increased by making cost savings provided that such actions do not result in a fall in demand and a reduction in revenues. Alternatively, investments may be made that will increase the level of service and thus demand. Profits will increase if the extra revenues exceed the increase in costs. The balanced scorecard approach to performance measurement and the determinants of performance measurement relating to service organizations described in Chapter 23 can be used to identify appropriate performance areas for the health centre. The performance areas identified in Exhibit 23.5 in Chapter 23 include quality of service, flexibility, resource utilization and innovation. Each of these areas is discussed below.

(i) Quality of service may be improved by upgrading facilities such as a cafeteria, free daily newspapers and better waiting room facilities. This may increase demand and generate additional revenues which exceed the cost increases.

(ii) Flexibility of service may be improved by providing additional sports/exercise facilities that are not currently available. In addition, additional exercise and dietary consultants who can provide services that are not currently available.

(iii) Resource utilization may be improved by better scheduling relating to the use of the exercise equipment and staff time and extending the opening hours. The aim should be to provide at least the same level of service with fewer resources.

(iv) Innovation may take the form of *new* services such as an extension of the range of health advice that can be provided and introducing on-line booking systems which can be directly accessed by the clients.

Capital investment decisions: 1

Solutions to Chapter 13 questions

Question 13.24

(i) Net present values:

Year	0% NPV (£)	10% Discount Factor	10% NPV (£)	20% Discount Factor	20% NPV (£)
0	(142 700)	1 000	(142 700)	1.000	(142 700)
1	51 000	0.909	46 359	0.833	42 483
2	62 000	0.826	51 212	0.694	43 028
3	73 000	0.751	54 823	0.579	42 267
NPV	43 300		9 694		(14 922)

(ii) **Project NPV Profile**

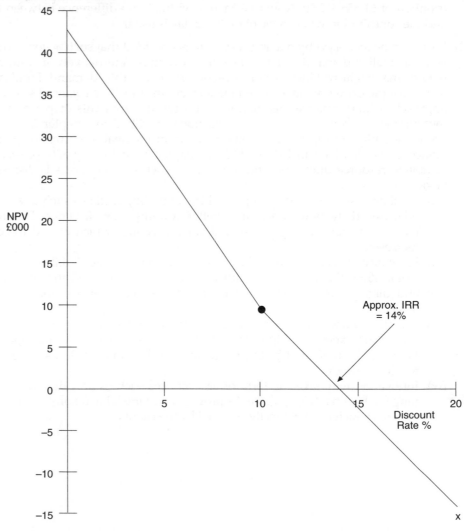

Figure Q13.24

(a) The answer should include the following points:

   1   Computations of the payback period and accounting rate of return (see below for the calculations), a description of the methods and their benefits and limitations (see text for a discussion of the payback and accounting rate of return methods).

   2   A computation of the net present value (see below) and an explanation as to why this method is preferred to the other methods (see text for an explanation).

   3   A recommendation that since the project has a positive net present value it should be accepted.

   4   A discussion of the difficulties associated with NPV. These include the greater potential for a lack of understanding by non-accountants, difficulties in estimating cash flows over the whole life of the asset and the difficulty in deriving the discount rate.

Computation of the payback period

The cumulative cash flows for years 4 and 5 are £1 700 000 and £2 200 000. Therefore, the payback period occurs between years 4 and 5. Assuming that cash flows accrue evenly throughout the year, a cash flow of £300 000 is required in year 5 to reach the payback period. This represents 7 months (£300 000/£500 000 × 12 months). Therefore, the payback period is 4 years and 7 months. This is above the target payback period of 4 years, so the project would be rejected using this method.

Computation of accounting rate of return

Total cash flows = (£400 × 3) + (£500 × 2) + (£450 × 3) + (£400 × 2)	= £4 350 000
Less depreciation/initial outlay	= £2 000 000
Total profits over the period	= £2 350 000
Average annual profit	= £235 000
Average investment (Initial cost/2)	= £1 000 000
Accounting rate of return	= 23.5%

This is below the target return so the project would be rejected.

Computation of NPV

Year	Cash flows (£000's)	Discount factor (15%)[a]	Present value (£000's)
1 – 3	400	2.283	913.20
4 – 5	500	1.069	534.50
6 – 8	450	1.135	510.75
9 – 10	400	0.531	212.40
			2170.85
Less initial outlay			2000.00
NPV			170.85

Note
[a] The discount factors are derived by summing the factors for years 1–3, 4–5, 6–8 and 9–10 in the discount tables.

The project has a positive NPV and should be accepted.

(b)   1 For the answer to this question see 'Controlling the capital expenditure during the installation stage' and 'Post-completion audits' in Chapter 13.

Estimated incremental net cash flows and NPV from project VZ

Inflows:	20X1 (£000)	20X2 (£000)	20X3 (£000)	20X4 (£000)	20X5 (£000)
Sales[a]	916	1269	1475	1780	160
Savings in salaries of employees made redundant[b]		42	44.1	46.3	
Residual value of new machine					242
Material XNT, savings on cost of disposal	2				
	918	1311	1519.1	1826.3	402

Outflows:					
Purchases[c]	320	480	570	610	120
Loss of sale proceeds from old machine		12			
Employee promoted[d]	10	10.5	11.03	11.58	
Redundancy pay		62			
Material XPZ, lost residual value	3				
Sub-contractors	60	90	80	80	
Lost contribution from existing product	30	40	40	36	
Overheads and advertising[e]	130	100	90	100	
Taxation		96	142	174	275
	553	890.5	933.03	1011.58	395

	20X1	20X2	20X3	20X4	20X5	Total
Incremental net cash flow	365	420.5	586.01	814.72	7	
Discount factors at 10%	0.9091	0.8264	0.7513	0.683	0.6209	
Present value (£000)	331.8	347.5	440.3	556.4	4.3	1680.3
Less net investment outlay (1640–16)						1624.0
NPV (£000s)						56.3

Notes
[a]The cash inflows from sales are calculated as follows:

	20X1 (£000)	20X2 (£000)	20X3 (£000)	20X4 (£000)	20X5 (£000)
Opening debtors	—	84	115	140	160
Add sales	1000	1300	1500	1800	—
	1000	1384	1615	1940	160
Less closing debtors	84	115	140	160	—
Cash from sales	916	1269	1475	1780	160

[b]Four employees at £10 000 per year inflated at 5% per annum
[c]The cash outflows for purchases is calculated as follows:

Opening creditors	—	80	100	110	120
Add purchases	400	500	580	620	—
	400	580	680	730	120
Less closing creditors	80	100	110	120	—
Cash paid for purchases	320	480	570	610	120

[d]£10 000 incremental costs inflated at 5% per annum
[e]Difference in costs between new and old product line

(b) (i) The report should explain that the figures incorporate only the incremental cash flows arising from undertaking the project. In addition the following information should be included in the report:
 (i) The feasibility study is a sunk cost.
 (ii) Depreciation is a non-cash item and the net investment cost is incorporated as a deduction from the total present value of the net cash flows. Including depreciation will result in double counting.
 (iii) The £12 000 paid to the three employees is not a relevant cash flow because it will be paid whether or not the project goes ahead.
 (iv) The original purchase price for both types of materials is a sunk cost and is not relevant to the decision.
 (v) The relevant figures for a NPV calculations are cash flows and therefore no adjustment is required for prepayments.

(b) (ii) The report should indicate that on the basis of the financial appraisal the project should be undertaken because it has a positive NPV. However, it should be pointed out that the cash flows have been discounted at the company's average cost of capital of 10%. If the risk of the project is higher than the average for the firm as a whole then a higher cost of capital should be used. Other factors that should be incorporated in the report include the effect on staff morale of the redundancies, the reliability of the estimates, the likely response from the competitors and the alternative use of the capacity.

(a) *Alternative 1*
NPV:

Year	Cash flow (£000)	Discount factor	PV (£000)
0	−100	1.00	−100
1	+255	0.83	+211.65
2	−157.5	0.69	−108.675
		NPV =	2.975

IRR: The cash flow sign changes after year 1, which implies that the project will have two IRRs. Using the interpolation method, the NPV will be zero at a cost of capital of 5% and 50%. Therefore the IRRs are 5% and 50%.

Alternative 2
NPV:

Year	Cash flow (£000)	Discount factor	PV (£000)
0	−50	1.00	−50
1	0	0.83	0
2	+42	0.69	+28.98
3	+42	0.58	+24.36
		NPV =	+3.34

IRR: At a 25% discount rate the project has an NPV of -1.616. Using the interpolation formula:

$$\text{IRR} = 20 + \frac{3340}{3340 - (-1616)} \times (25 - 20)$$

$$= 23.4\%$$

Summary

	NPV	IRR
Alternative 1	£2975	5% or 50%
Alternative 2	£3340	23.4%

(b) The projects are mutually exclusive and capital rationing does not apply. In these circumstances the NPV decision rule should be applied and alternative 2 should be selected. Because of the reasons described in Chapter 13, the IRR method should not be used for evaluating mutually exclusive projects. Also, note that alternative 1 has two IRRs. Therefore, the IRR method cannot be used to rank the alternatives.

Before a final decision is made, the risk attached to each alternative should be examined. For example, novelty products are generally high-risk investments with short lives. Therefore alternative 1 with a shorter life might be less risky. Other considerations include the possibility of whether the promotion of this novelty product will adversely affect the sales of the other products sold by the company. Also, will the large expenditure on advertising for alternative 1 have a beneficial effect on the sales of the company's other products?

(c) The answer should include a discussion of the payback method, particularly the limitations discussed in Chapter 13. It should be stressed that payback can be a useful method of investment appraisal when liquidity is a problem and the speed of a project's return is particularly important. It is also claimed that payback allows for uncertainty in that it leads to the acceptance of projects with fast paybacks. This approach can be appropriate for companies whose products are subject to uncertain short lives. Therefore there might be an argument for using payback in Khan Ltd.

The second comment by Mr Court concerns the relationship between reported profits and the NPV calculations. Projects ranked by the NPV method can give different rankings to projects that are ranked by their impact on the reported profits of the company. The NPV method results in the maximization of the present value of future cash flows and is the correct decision rule. If investors give priority to reported profits in valuing shares (even if reported profits do not give an indication of the true economic performance of the company) then Mr Court's comments on the importance of a project's impact on reported profits might lead to the acceptance of alternative 1. However, if investors are aware of the deficiencies of published reported profits and are aware of the company's future plans and cash flows then share values will be based on PV of future cash flows. This is consistent with the NPV rule.

Question 13.28

(a) *Attending 6 training courses per year*

Year	Travel and accommodation etc. (£000's)[a]	Course costs (£000's)[a]	Total cash flows (£000's)	Discount factor	Present value (£000's)
1	522.00	70.50	592.50	0.877	519.62
2	548.10	72.26	620.36	0.769	477.06
3	575.51	74.07	649.58	0.675	438.47
4	604.29	75.92	680.21	0.592	402.68
5	634.50	77.82	712.32	0.519	369.69
					2207.52

Note:
[a] Travel etc. = £870 × 100 delegates × 6 courses = £522 000
  Courses = £11 750 × 6 courses = £70 500
  Travel etc. Year 2 = £522 (1.05), Year 3 = £522 (1.05)^2 and so on.
  Course costs Year 2 = £70.5 (1.025), Year 3 = £70.5 (1.025)^2 and so on.

Proposed e-learning solution

Year	0	1	2	3	4	5
	(£000's)	(£000's)	(£000's)	(£000's)	(£000's)	(£000's)
Hardware[a]	1500					(50)
Software	35	35	35	35	35	
Technical manager and trainers (30 + 12)[b]		42	44.52	47.19	50.02	53.02
Camera and sound		24	24	25.44	26.97	28.59
Broadband connection		30	28.50	27.08	25.73	24.44
		131	132.02	134.71	137.72	56.05
Discount factor	1.000	0.877	0.769	0.675	0.592	0.519
Present value	1 535	114.89	101.52	90.93	81.53	29.09

Total present value = £1 953 257
The e-learning solution should be recommended since this has the lowest present value.

Notes:
[a] Depreciation is not a relevant cost and should not be included in the analysis.
[b] The technical manager will have to be replaced resulting in an incremental cash flow of £20 000 per annum.

(b) (i) Note that equivalent annual costs/cash flows are explained in Chapter 14. To answer this question it is necessary to separate those costs that are variable with the number of delegates and those that are fixed and thus do not change with the number of candidates. It is assumed that 6 courses will be provided per year. For the course attendance alternative, the course costs are fixed and travel, etc. is variable with the number of delegates. Separate present values must be calculated for course costs and travel, etc. If you discount the second and third columns for the course attendance alternative you will find that the present values are £1 954 800 (variable cost) and £252 720 (fixed cost). Dividing both of these items by an annuity factor for 5 years at 14% (3.433) gives annual equivalent costs of £569 415 (variable costs) and £73 615 (fixed cost).

For the e-learning costs alternative, the broadband connection is variable with the number of delegates and the remaining costs are fixed. The respective present values are £94 421 (variable) and £1 858 836 (fixed) giving equivalent annual costs of £27 504 (variable) and £541 461 (fixed). Therefore, the additional annual equivalent fixed costs for the e-learning alternative are £467 846. The savings in annual equivalent variable costs from this alternative are £541 911 (£569 415 – £27 504) per 100 delegates or £5419 per delegate. Therefore the minimum number of delegates required to achieve the fixed cost savings is 86.33 (£467 846/£5419).

(b) (ii) The required number of delegates to break even is 87%. This is a very high required take-up rate and so the company must ensure that virtually all of the delegates will favour this method of delivery.

Question 13.29

(a) Three alternatives can be identified from the question:
1 Produce product A and replace it with AA at the UK factory.
2 Produce product A, then sell the UK factory in year 2 and make AA in Eastern Europe for 8 years.
3 Produce product A for a limited period, replace with product X and sell the UK factory in year 4 and make Product AA in Eastern Europe for 8 years.

Alternative 1

Years		Cash flows (£m)	Discount factor	NPV (£m)
1	Normal sales of product A	3.0	0.952	2.856
2	Normal sales of product A	2.3	0.907	2.086
2	Equipment and training costs for product AA	−6.0	0.907	−5.442
3–10	Net cash inflows from AA	5.0	5.863 (7.722 − 1.859)	29.315
10	Sale of factory ª	3.85	0.614	2.364
				31.179

Note:
ª £5.5m + £0.35m − redundancy costs (2m) = 3.85m

Alternative 2

Years		Cash flows (£m)	Discount factor	NPV (£m)
1	Normal sales of product A	3.0	0.952	2.856
2	Normal sales of product A	2.3	0.907	2.086
2	Sale of factory	3.85	0.907	3.492
2	Equipment and training costs for product AA	−6.0	0.907	−5.442
3–10	Net cash flows from AA with additional transport costs	3.0	5.863 (7.722 − 1.859)	17.589
				20.581

Alternative 3

Years		Cash flows (£m)	Discount factor	NPV (£m)
1	Purchase of equipment for X	−4.0	0.952	−3.808
1	Normal sales of product A	3.0	0.952	2.856
2	Sales of stock of A (0.125 × £3m)	0.375	0.907	0.340
2	Inflows from product X (50 000 × £70)	3.5	0.907	3.175
3	Inflows from product X (75 000 × £70)	5.25	0.864	4.536
4	Inflows from product X (75 000 × £70)	5.25	0.823	4.321
4	Sale of factory	3.85	0.823	3.169
2	Equipment and training costs for product AA	−6.0	0.907	−5.442
3–10	Sales of AA with additional transport costs	3.0	5.863 (7.722 − 1.859)	17.589
				26.736

The first alternative yields the highest NPV.

(b) (i) Both alternatives 2 and 3 involve the same transport cost but alternative 3 yields a significantly higher NPV. Therefore it is appropriate to test the sensitivity of transport costs by comparing alternative 3 against alternative 1, which does not involve transport costs. The NPV of alternative 1 exceeds the NPV of alternative 3 by £4.443m (£31.179m − £26.736). The present value of the transport costs is £11.726m (200 000 × £10 × a discount factor of 5.863 for years 3–10). Therefore, the present value of transport costs would have to fall below £7.283m (£11.726m – £4.443m) for alternative 3 to be preferred to alternative 1. This represents annual cash flows of £1 242 000 (£7.283m/5.863 discount factor). Estimated annual cash flows for transport costs are £2m so cash flows would have to decline by £758 000 which represents a 37.9% decline.

(b) (ii) Based on the discussion in (b) (i), it is again appropriate to compare alternatives 1 and 3 where the NPV for alternative 1 exceeds that of alternative 3 by £4 443 000.

Let SV = net difference in sales value for NPV to be the same for both alternatives so that:
SV × year 4 discount factor (0.823) – SV × year 10 discount factor (0.614)
$$= £4\,443\,000$$
0.209SV $\quad = £4\,443\,000$
SV $\qquad = £21\,258\,373$

Given that the existing sales value is £5.5m, the sales value can increase to £26.758m (£21.258m + £5.5m), representing an increase of approximately 400%.

(c) The answer should include a discussion of the following points:
1   the availability of skilled labour;
2   closeness to the market in terms of being able to respond quickly to demand;
3   taxation implications;
4   management problems arising from differences in national cultures;
5   the difficulties that may be encountered in operating a business that is located a considerable distance from central headquarters.

(a) The expected number of passengers is derived from the demand at each **Question 13.30** exchange rate:
Expected demand at 1.52 €/£ = 0.33 (500 + 460 + 420) = 460
Expected demand at 1.54 €/£ = 0.33 (550 + 520 + 450) = 506.67
Expected demand at 1.65 €/£ = 0.33 (600 + 580 + 500) = 560
Expected demand = 0.2(460) + 0.5(506.67) + 0.3(560) = 513.335 per train (or 1026.7 per day).

(b) *Cash flows: in-house option*

Year	1	2	3	4	5
Sales[a]	748 440	748 440	748 440	748 440	748 440
Variable costs[b]	(501 455)	(501 455)	(501 455)	(501 455)	(501 455)
Contribution	246 985	246 985	246 985	246 985	246 985
Labour costs[c]	(74 844)	(78 586)	(82 516)	(86 641)	(90 973)
Purchase and insurance[d]	(37 422)	(37 422)	(37 422)	(37 422)	(37 422)
Asset sale/purchase		(500 000)			280 000
Net cash flow	134 719	(369 023)	127 047	122 922	398 590
Discount factor at 12%	0.893	0.797	0.712	0.636	0.567
Present value	120 304	(294 111)	90 457	78 178	226 000

Net present value = £220 828

Cash flows: contract out option

Year	0	1	2	3	4	5
Contract fee[f]		(90 000)	(90 000)	(90 000)	(90 000)	(90 000)
Asset purchase/sale	650 000					
Purchase and insurance[e]		(16 422)	(16 422)	(16 422)	(16 422)	(16 422)

Net cash flow	650 000	(106 422)	(106 422)	(106 422)	(106 422)	(106 422)
Discount factor	1.0	0.893	0.797	0.712	0.636	0.567
Present value	650 000	(95 035)	(84 818)	(75 772)	(67 684)	(60 341)

Net present value = £266 350

The contract out option is preferred because it has the higher NPV of £45 522.

Notes:
[a] Sales revenues = 0.45 × 513.335 × £9 ×360 = £748 440
[b] Direct materials = 0.55 × £748 440 = £411 642
  Variable overhead = 0.12 × £748 440 = £89 813
  Variable costs = £501 455
[c] Labour costs = 0.10 × £748 440 = £74 844 for year 1, Year 2 = £74 844 (1.05), Year 3 = £74 844 $(1.05)^2$
[d] Purchase and insurance = 0.05 × £748 440 = £37 422 (for in-house provision)
[e] Purchase and insurance = £37 422 – £21 000 = £16 422 (for contracting out)
[f] Provision of catering service by outside supplier = £250 × 360 days = £90 000
[g] Gross catering receipts are £2079 per day (£748 440/360) do not exceed £2200 so the 5% commission does not apply.
[h] Depreciation is not a cash flow and is therefore not a relevant cost.

(c) A 10% increase in sales would increase the annual contribution by £24 699 giving an increase in present value of £89 040 (£24 699 × 3.605 discount factor at 12%). The present value of the additional costs is £36 050 (£10 000 × 3.605) resulting in an increase in NPV of £52 990. This exceeds the NPV of £45 522 from changing to the contracting out alternative. However, the revised annual sales per day would be £2287 (£2079 × 1.10), thus enabling the company to receive 5% of gross sales receipts once sales exceed £2200 per day. The company would therefore receive £41 164 per annum (5% × £748 440 sales × 1.10). This would result in the contracting out alternative having the higher NPV. The choice is highly dependent on future sales being in excess of £2200 per day.

(d) The answer should draw attention to the difficulties in deriving probabilities and using past data to estimate probabilities based on the view that the past is indicative of the future. The outcome using probabilities represents an average outcome, which may be unlikely to occur. Also expected values ignore risk. For a more detailed discussion of these points you should refer to the sections on probabilities, probability distributions and expected value and measuring the amount of uncertainty in Chapter 12.

(e) The following non-financial factors need to be taken into account:
1 The loss of ability to control the quality and reliability of the service if the service is contracted out. These factors may influence the number of passengers choosing to travel with Amber plc.
2 Impact on staff morale as a result of the reduction in labour costs. Existing staff may be concerned that their jobs are under threat and may leave the company.
3 The difficulty and high costs of changing back to in-service provision once the company has contracted out the service.
4 Willingness of the supplier to respond to changes in market demand.

Capital investment decisions: 2

Solutions to Chapter 14 questions

(a) See 'Payback method' and 'Accounting rate of return' in Chapter 13 for the **Question 14.23**
answer to this question.

(b) (i) For the answer to this question you should refer to the sections on the concept of NPV, calculating NPV's, the internal rate of return (IRR) and comparison of NPV and IRR in Chapter 13.

(b) (ii) NPV of one year replacement = £1200/1.14 – 2400 = – £1347

Equivalent annual cost of one year replacement = £1347/0.877ᵃ = £1535.91

NPV of two year replacement = 800/1.14² – 75/1.14 – 2400 = – £1850.21

Equivalent annual cost of two year replacement = 1850.21/1.647ᵃ = 1123.38

NPV of three year replacement = 300/1.14³ – 150/1.14² – 75/1.14 – 2400 = – £2378.72

Equivalent annual cost of three year replacement = £2378.72/2.322ᵃ = 1024.43

Note:

ᵃ Annuity factors for 1, 2 or 3 years at 14%.

The three year replacement has the lowest equivalent annual cost. Therefore the three year replacement is the preferred alternative. However, the following factors should also be taken into account:

1 Likely changes in technology. If there are rapid changes in technology, the three year replacement will result in a failure to obtain the benefits of any improvement in technology.

2 Compatibility with the company's other computer systems. If the company's other computer systems are frequently updated the laptop computers may not be compatible with them.

(a) Expected value of the annual sales = (4m × 0.2) + (£5m × 0.4) + (£7m × 0.3) + **Question 14.24**
(£10m × 0.1) = £5.9m

The market research survey (note vii) is a sunk cost.

Cash flows £'000s	Year						
	0	1	2	3	4	5	6
Purchase of Company	(400)						
Legal/professional		(20)	(20)	(20)	(20)	(20)	
Lease rentals		(12)	(12)	(12)	(12)	(12)	
Studio hire		(540)	(540)	(702)	(702)	(702)	
Camera hire		(120)	(120)	(120)	(120)	(120)	
Technical staff		(1560)	(1716)	(1888)	(2077)	(2285)	
Screenplay		(150)	(173)	(199)	(229)	(263)	
Actors salaries		(2100)	(2310)	(2541)	(2795)	(3074)	
Costumes/wardrobe		(180)	(180)	(180)	(180)	(180)	
Non production staff wages		(60)	(66)	(73)	(80)	(88)	
Set design		(450)	(450)	(450)	(450)	(450)	
Lost income from office accommodation		(20)	(20)	(20)	(20)	(20)	
Sales		5900	6195	6505	6830	7172	

Cash flow before tax	(400)	688	588	300	145	(42)	
Tax		–	(227)	(194)	(99)	(48)	14
Net Cash Flow	(400)	688	361	106	46	(90)	14
Disc. Factor	1	0.877	0.769	0.675	0.592	0.519	0.456
P.V. Cash Flow	(400)	603	278	72	27	(47)	6

NPV = £539 000

(b) Limitations of expected values include:
1 Expected values represent average outcomes based on the assumption that decisions will be repeated but a specific investment decision is likely to occur once so the average outcome is unlikely to occur.
2 Deriving probabilities is highly subjective.
3 Expected values do not take into account the range of outcomes. A probability distribution is likely to provide more meaningful information.

For a more detailed discussion of the above points you should refer to the sections on probability distributions and expected values and measuring the amount of uncertainty in Chapter 12.

(c) (i) See 'Profitability index' in Chapter 14 for the answer to this question.
(c) (ii) Profitability index = Present value/investment outlay

Profitability index for the filmmaking acquisition $= \dfrac{\text{NPV (£539 000)} + \text{Investment outlay (£400 000)}}{\text{Investment outlay (£400 000)}}$
$= 2.347$

Investment X present value:
$(200 \times 0.877) + (200 \times 0.769) + (150 \times 0.675) + (100 \times 0.592) + (100 \times 0.519) + (100 \times 0.456) = £587$
Profitability index = £587/200 = 2.935

Investment Y present value:
$(80 \times 0.877) + (80 \times 0.769) + (40 \times 0.675) + (40 \times 0.592) + (40 \times 0.519) + (40 \times 0.456) = £221$
Profitability index = £221/100 = 2.21

Given that projects are indivisible the choice is between:
1 Investing in X and Y, yielding an NPV of £508 000 (587 + 221 – 300 investment outlay). The un-utilized funds of £100 000 can only be reinvested to obtain a zero NPV.
2 Investing all of the £400 000 in the filmmaking company yielding an NPV of £539 000.

The company should choose to invest in the filmmaking company.

(c) (iii) For a discussion of the limitations of the profitability index you should refer to the final paragraph in the section on capital rationing in Chapter 14. In addition, the answer should point out that the profitability index does not take into account:
1 How projects interact to reduce risk or to provide a strategic alignment such as the vertical integration that may occur with the purchase of the filmmaking company.
2 Problems can occur when projects are indivisible and the strict application of this method can result in misleading decisions. For example, investment X has the highest profitability index but it is clearly preferable to not invest in this project since it will not lead to the maximization of NPV when funds are restricted to £400 000.

(d) See 'Taxation and investment decisions' in Chapter 14 for the answer to this question.

(a) It is assumed that all of the cash flows will increase at the general rate of inflation **Question 14.25** so that estimates in current prices at the time of appraising the investment will be equal to real cash flows. Real cash flows must be discounted at a real discount rate but the question includes a nominal required rate of return (i.e. discount rate). Therefore we must convert the nominal discount rate to a real discount rate using the following formula:

1 + nominal rate = (1 + real rate) × (1 + anticipated rate of inflation)

so that (1 + real rate) = 1 + nominal rate / (1 + anticipated rate of inflation)

giving a real rate of 8% (1.14 / 1.055) = 1.08

Contribution per box sold = £20 – (£8 + £2 + £1.50 + £2) = £6.50

Allocated fixed overheads do not represent incremental cash flows and are therefore not relevant to the decision. The annual cash flows are 150 000 boxes × £6.50 × (1 – corporate tax rate (0.33)) = £653 250. The annual cash flows are constant so the cumulative discount (i.e. annuity tables) in Appendix 2 of the text can be used.

$$NPV = (£653\ 250 \times 3.993) – £2m = £608\ 428$$

IRR = (annual cash flows) × (the cumulative discount factor at $x\%$ for 5 years) – investment outlay = 0

so that IRR is where the cumulative discount factor at $x\%$ for 5 years = Investment outlay (£2m)/£653 250 = 3.062.

If you examine the five year row in Appendix 2 you will find that the figure closest to 3.062 appears under the 19% column. Therefore IRR = 19%.

Because the project has a positive NPV and the IRR exceeds the real cost of capital of 8% the project is acceptable.

(b) See 'Sensitivity analysis' in Chapter 14 for the answer to this question.

(c) (i) *Price (P)*

$$NPV = 0 = 0.15m(P – £13.50)(1 – 0.33)(AF_{8\%,5}) – £2m$$
$$= 0 = (0.15mP – £2025m)\ 2.675 – £2m$$
$$= 0 = £0.401mP – 5.417m – 2m$$
$$0.401mP = 7.417m$$
$$P = £18.50$$

Therefore the price can drop by £1.50 (or 7.5%) before NPV becomes negative.

Note

$AF_{8\%,5}$ = Annuity factor at 8% for 5 years

(c) (ii) *Volume (V)*

$$NPV = 0 = V (£20 – £13.50) (1 – 0.33) (AF_{8\%,5}) – £2m$$
$$= 0 = £6.50V(2.675) – £2m$$
$$= 0 = £17.3875V – £2m$$
$$V = £2m / 17.3875$$
$$V = 115\ 025$$

Therefore volume can drop by 34 975 boxes (150 000 – 115 025) or 23% before NPV becomes negative.

The results suggest that the NPV of the project is more sensitive to price variations than to changes in volume. The company therefore should review the estimated price to ensure that it is confident that prices will not decline by more than 7%. If prices decline by more than 7%, and the other variables remain unchanged, the project will yield a negative NPV. Consideration should be given to advertising to ensure that demand is maintained at the proposed price but it should be noted that NPV will decline by the amount spent on advertising.

Question 14.26

(a) The question indicates that a uniform inflation rate applies to all costs and revenues. Therefore, current prices will be equivalent to real cash flows. The NPV can be calculated either by discounting real cash flows at the real discount rate or discounting nominal cash flows at a nominal discount rate. If the former approach is applied, it is necessary to convert the nominal discount rate (15.5%) to a real discount rate. The calculation is as follows:

(1 + real discount rate) = (1 + nominal discount rate)/(1 + anticipated rate of inflation)
(1 + real discount rate) = (1.155)/(1.05) = 1.10
Real discount rate = 1.10 – 1 = 0.10 = 10%
Expected value of sales = (£800 × 0.25) + (£560 × 0.50) + (£448 × 0.25) = £592 000
Contribution £325 600 (£592 000 × 0.55)
Less fixed costs £ 90 000
Taxable profits £235 600
Tax at 30% £70 680

The calculation of NPV using real cash flows and the real discount rate is as follows:

	Year 1 (£)	Year 2 (£)	Year 3 (£)	Year 4 (£)	Year 5 (£)	Year 6 (£)
Contribution less fixed costs	235 600	235 600	235 600	235 600	235 600	
Scrap value					55 000	
Tax payable	(35 340)	(70 680)	(70 680)	(70 680)	(70 680)	(35 340)
Net cash flow	200 260	164 920	164 920	164 920	219 920	(35 340)
Discount factor	0.909	0.826	0.751	0.683	0.621	0.564
Present value	182 036	136 224	123 855	112 640	136 570	(19 932)

NPV = Total present value £671 393 – investment outlay (£550 000) = £121 393

The question implies that all of the above items will increase with the rate of inflation, but this is unlikely to apply to the time lag in the payment of taxation. As a result the tax payment in real terms for the delayed payment (50% × £70 680) will be slightly less than £35 340, but this will not have a significant effect and it is assumed that it is the examiner's intention for this factor not be taken into account. An alternative approach to answering the question would have been to express all of the above cash flows in nominal terms (that is, inflate them at 5% per annum) and discount them at the nominal rate of 15.5%. Given the positive NPV, the proposed expansion should be undertaken.

(b) Let x = contribution (£) after deduction of fixed costs.

The following expression indicates the point at which NPV will be zero:

$$0.85x(0.909) + 0.7x(0.826) + 0.7x(0.751) + 0.7x(0.683) + 0.7x(0.621) + £55\,000(0.621) - 0.15x(0.564) = £550\,000$$

In year 1 the after tax cash flows will be 85% of the contribution after deduction of fixed costs, for years 2–5 it will be 70% (1 – tax rate) and the final year represents the last instalment of the tax payment (30% × 0.15). The figures in parentheses represent the discount rates for years 1 – 6 and the £55 000 represents the disposal value at the end of year 5. The final item in the expression represents the investment outlay.

The above expression after undertaking the arithmetical calculations equals:

$$2.70475x + £34\,155 = £550\,000$$

$$x = £190\,718$$

To derive the annual contribution we must add back the fixed costs of £90 000 giving £280 718. Thus, annual contribution can fall by £44 882 (£325 600 – £280 718), representing a decline of 13.78% before NPV becomes zero.

(c) Because the annual writing down allowances are fixed and do not increase with inflation they will decline in real terms over the years. In other words, they are already expressed in nominal terms. To express them in real terms it will be necessary to divide them by $(1 + \text{anticipated inflation rate})^n$. An alternative and easier approach to calculate their impact, after taking account of inflation, is to discount them (note they are already expressed in nominal terms) at the nominal discount rate.

The calculation of the present value of the writing down allowances is as follows:

Writing Down Allowances schedule

	(£)	Tax saved @ 30%[a] (£)	Year 1 (£)	Year 2 (£)	Year 3 (£)	Year 4 (£)	Year 5 (£)	Year 6 (£)
Initial expenditure	555 000							
WDA Year 1, 25%	137 500	41 250	20 625	20 625				
	412 500							
WDA Year 2, 25%	103 125	30 938		15 469	15 469			
	309 375							
WDA Year 3, 25%	77 344	23 203			11 602	11 601		
	232 031							
WDA Year 4, 25%	58 008	17 402				8701	8701	
	174 023							
Sale for scrap, year 5	70 195[b]							
Balancing allowance	103 828	31 148					15 574	15 574
Total tax savings			20 625	36 094	27 071	20 302	24 275	15 574
Discount factor (nominal rate)[c]			0.866	0.750	0.649	0.562	0.487	0.421
Present value			17 861	27 071	17 569	11 410	11 822	6557
Total present value		92 290						

The net present value for the investment will increase by £92 290 arising from the tax savings from writing down allowances.

Notes:
[a] Because one half of the tax payment is delayed until the following year, 50% will occur in the current year and 50% in the following year.
[b] The sales value must be adjusted to a nominal value so that the value equals £55 000 $(1.05)^5$ = £70 195.
[c] Discount factors = £$1/(1.155)^n$. For example, the discount factor for year 2 = $1/(1.155)^2$ = 0.750.

Question 14.27

(a) The present value of the cash flows is calculated as follows:

Year	0 (£m)	1 (£m)	2 (£m)	3 (£m)	4 (£m)	5 (£m)
Initial outlay	(1.000)					
EU grant		0.250				
FSL's fee		(0.050)				
Increase in costs		(0.315)	(0.331)	(0.347)	(0.365)	
Tax saving on increased costs at 33%			0.104	0.109	0.115	0.120
Tax savings on WDAs[a]		0.083	0.062	0.047	0.035	0.104
Net cash flows	(1.000)	(0.032)	(0.165)	(0.191)	(0.215)	0.224
Discount factor at 12%	1.000	0.893	0.797	0.712	0.636	0.567
Present value of cash flows at 12%	(1.307)					
Present value of savings in fines[b]	1.250					
NPV of project	(0.057)					

Notes

ᵃ The annual writing down allowances are calculated as follows:

Year	0	1	2	3	4	5
	(£m)	(£m)	(£m)	(£m)	(£m)	(£m)
Opening WDV	1.000	0.750	0.562	0.421	0.316	
Annual WDAs (Balancing allowance in year 4)	(0.250)	(0.188)	(0.141)	(0.105)	(0.316)	
Tax savings at 33% with a 1 year delay		0.083	0.062	0.047	0.035	0.104

ᵇ The expected value of the level of the fines = (£0.5m × 0.3) + (£1.4m × 0.5) + (£2m × 0.2) = £1.25m

(b) The following points should be incorporated in the answer:

(i) The project is not justifiable if only those items that can be expressed in financial terms are incorporated in the analysis.

(ii) The weaknesses of the expected value approach is based on it representing an average outcome. See 'Expected values' in Chapter 12 for an explanation.

(iii) The preference for examining the probability distribution of outcomes. The project has a 70% probability that the savings relating to the fines will exceed the negative present value of the net cash flows of £1.307m from the investment.

(iv) The fact that the company may not be pursuing purely financial objectives and that it may wish to pursue socially responsible objectives. The negative NPV of £0.057m indicates the cost to the shareholders of pursuing other objectives.

(v) Increased sales may result if the company is seen by customers and potential customers as being environmentally friendly.

(vi) The company has a moral responsibility to undertake such projects.

Question 14.28   (a) (i)

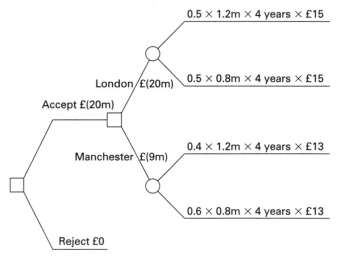

Figure Q14.28a

Note that the amounts of £15 and £13 relate to the contribution per visitor of £15 for London (£25 – service cost of £10) and £13 for Manchester (£23 – £10).

(a) (ii) *Expected NPV of London location*

	(£m)
0.5 × 1.2m × £15 × 3.170 (4 year cumulative discount factor at 10%)	28.53
0.5 × 0.8m × £15 × 3.170	19.02
	47.55
Less investment outlay (£20m dome + £20m land)	40.00
	7.55
Sale of land (£14m × 0.683)	9.56
NPV	17.11

Expected NPV of Manchester location

	(£m)
0.4 × 1.2m × £13 × 3.170 (4 year cumulative discount factor at 10%)	19.78
0.6 × 0.8m × £13 × 3.170	19.78
	39.56
Less investment outlay (£20m dome + £9m land)	29.00
	10.56
Sale of land (£10m × 0.683)	6.83
NPV	17.39

Manchester should be selected because its NPV is £0.28m greater than the London location.

(b) (i)

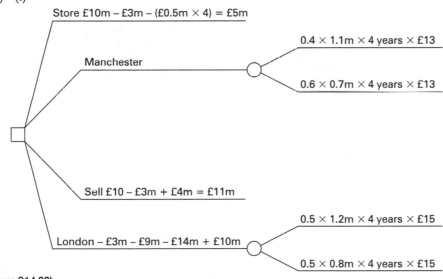

Figure Q14.28b

Note that an explanation of the meaning of each of the above figures is provided in (b) (ii).

(b) (ii) *NPV of storing the dome at Manchester*

	(£m)
Sale of the land in year 4 (£10m at year 4 discount factor of 0.683)	6.83
Dismantling cost in year 4 (£3m at year 4 discount factor of 0.683)	(2.05)
Storage costs (0.5m per annum at a cumulative discount factor of 2.165 for years 5–8)	(1.08)
NPV	3.70

	(£m)
Expected present value of annual contributions:	
(0.4 × 1.1m × £13 × 2.165 cumulative discount factor)	12.38
(0.6 × 0.7m × £13 × 2.165 cumulative discount factor)	11.82
	24.20
Dismantling cost in year 8 (£2m × 0.466)	(0.93)
Sale of land in year 8 (10m × 0.466)	4.66
NPV	27.93

Selling the dome in year 4

Sale of dome (£4m) and land (£10m) less dismantling cost (3m) = £11m
Present value (£11m × year 4 discount factor of 0.683) = £7.51m

Transferring the dome to London

	(£m)
Expected present value of annual contributions:	
(0.5 × 1.2m × £15 × 2.165 cumulative discount factor)	19.49
(0.5 × 0.8m × £15 × 2.165 cumulative discount factor)	12.99
	32.48
Year 4: Sale of land at Manchester (£10m) – purchase of land at London (£14m) – dismantling cost (3m) – moving cost (£9m) = – £16m discounted at 0.683	(10.93)
Sale of land in year 8 (£14m) less dismantling cost (£2m) = £12m × 0.466	5.59
NPV	27.14

The highest NPV is obtained from continuing operations at Manchester.

(c) In parts (a) and (b) the analysis was based on two separate periods rather than a single period and Manchester was the preferred option for both periods. Storing or selling the dome clearly have lower NPV's than the other alternatives over the 8 year period. Therefore the focus should be on comparing siting at London or Manchester. The relevant calculations based on the 8 year time horizon are as follows:

Manchester

	(£m)
First 4 years at Manchester (without the sale of the land)	10.56
Second 4 years	27.93
NPV	38.49

London

	(£m)
First 4 years at London without the sale of the land	7.55
Second 4 years:	
(0.5 × 1.1m × £15 × 2.165 cumulative discount factor)	17.86
(0.5 × 0.7m × £15 × 2.165 cumulative discount factor)	11.37
Dismantling and sale of land in year 8	5.59
NPV	42.37

Focusing on an 8 year horizon indicates that locating the dome and keeping it at London gives the higher expected NPV.

(d) There would appear to be little to gain from trying to assess the profitability of the individual products (i.e. individual rides or individual item of merchandise). Each of the products is likely to be complementary and so there is little point in trying to ascertain their individual profitability. Profitability analysis is likely to be more helpful in terms of customer segments (e.g. families, teenagers, parties, etc). Although insufficient information is given in the question, the data given suggest that costs are mainly direct and variable and facility sustaining. Therefore, the proportion of indirect costs that fluctuate according to the demand for them is likely to be very small. Under such circumstances ABC is unlikely to be justified and it may be preferable to adopt a direct/variable costing system for customer profitability analysis. See 'Types of costing systems' in Chapter 10 and 'Cost-benefit issues and cost systems design' in Chapter 3 for additional points that are relevant to this question.

(a)

Question 14.29

Revised estimate of the project's net present value
Calculation of tax liability

(£000)

Year	1	2	3	4	5	6
Sales	2950	3820	5200	5400	5600	5800
Direct costs	(1499)	(1940)	(2642)	(2743)	(2845)	(2946)
Incremental overheads	(185)	(240)	(315)	(321)	(328)	(330)
Capital allowances	(140)	(480)	(480)	(480)	(480)	(340)
	1824	2660	3437	3544	3653	3616
Taxable profits	1126	1160	1763	1856	1947	2184
Taxation (40%)	450	464	705	742	779	874

Calculation of NPV

Cash flows

Year	0	1	2	3	4	5	6	7
Land and buildings	(500)	(600)						
Plant and machinery	(700)	(1700)						
Working capital[a]	(230)	(340)	(110)	(20)	(20)	(20)	740	
Operating cash flows[b]		1266	1640	2243	2336	2427	2524	
Taxation[c]			(450)	(464)	(705)	(742)	(779)	(874)
Terminal value						8725		
Tax on terminal value[d]								(3050)
	(1430)	(1374)	1080	1759	1611	1665	11 210	(3924)
Disc. Factor (18%)		0.847	0.718	0.609	0.516	0.437	0.370	0.314
Present values	(1430)	(1164)	775	1071	831	728	4148	(1232)

NPV = £3 727 000
The NPV of the project is estimated to be £3 727 000. On the basis of this information, the project should be accepted.

Interest is not deducted in the calculation of the tax liability, because this is already reflected within the after tax interest rate in the weighted average cost of capital calculation. Also, the interest payments are not included in the cash flows, because this is reflected within the discounting process.

Notes

[a] The cumulative amount of working capital is assumed to be released at the end of year 6.

[b] Operating cash inflows = sales − direct costs − incremental overheads.

[c] Terminal value = Year 6 after tax operating cash inflows (£2524 − £779) × 5 = £8725.

[d] The WDV of plant and machinery for taxation purposes at the end of year 6 is zero. It is assumed that the realizable value of plant and machinery at the end of the planning horizon is 7625 (£8725 − £1100 for land and buildings). This would result in a potential balancing taxation charge of £3050 (£7625 × 0.4).

The risk-adjusted cost of equity capital for this project is derived by applying the beta for a company whose major activity is the manufacture of products that are similar to the proposed projects:

$$\frac{\text{cost of}}{\text{equity}} = \frac{\text{risk-free}}{\text{rate (12\%)}} + \left[\frac{\text{return on market}}{\text{portfolio (20\%)}} - \frac{\text{risk-free}}{\text{rate (12\%)}}\right] \times \text{beta (1.5)} = 24\%$$

The after-tax cost of debt is 15% × (1 − tax rate) = 9%

The weighted average cost of capital (WACC) is calculated by assuming a capital structure of 60% equity and 40% debt;

WACC = 0.6 (24%) + 0.4 (9%) = 18%

The estimated discount rate is therefore 18%.

The recommended acceptance is subject to the following reservations:

(i)   The cash flow estimates do not include any adjustments for estimated price level changes.

(ii) It is extremely difficult to estimate discount rates accurately, and there is a need to ascertain how sensitive the NPV calculation is to higher discount rates.

(iii) The project has not been evaluated over its expected life. An unsophisticated approach has been used to estimate the terminal value. Given that the estimate of the terminal value is critical to the NPV calculation, it is important that the estimate be reviewed before recommending acceptance. Ideally, the project ought to be re-evaluated over its expected life.

(b) The 18% discount rate is an observed nominal discount rate, which will include a premium for inflation. If the cash flows have not been adjusted for inflation, the NPV will have been calculated by discounting real cash flows at a nominal discount rate. This approach is incorrect, and it will be necessary to adjust the cash flows for inflation.

The budgeting process

Solutions to Chapter 15 questions

(a) Incremental budgeting uses the previous year's budget as the starting point for the preparation of next year's budget. It is assumed that the basic structure of the budget will remain unchanged and that adjustments will be made to allow for changes in volume, efficiency and price levels. The budget is therefore concerned with increments to operations that will occur during the period and the focus is on existing use of resources rather than considering alternative strategies for the future budget period. Incremental budgeting suffers from the following weaknesses:
   (i)   it perpetuates past inefficiencies;
   (ii) there is insufficient focus on improving efficiency and effectiveness;
   (iii) the resource allocation tends to be based on existing strategies rather than considering future strategies;
   (iv) it tends to focus excessively on the short term and often leads to arbitrary cuts being made in order to achieve short-term financial targets.

(b) See 'Activity-based budgeting' in Chapter 15 for the answer to this question. In particular, the answer should stress that:
   (i)   the focus is on managing activities;
   (ii) the focus is on the resources that are required for undertaking activities and identifying those activity resources that are un-utilized or which are insufficient to meet the requirements specified in the budget;
   (iii) attention is given to eliminating non-value-added activities;
   (iv) the focus is on the control of the causes of costs (i.e. the cost drivers).

For a more detailed discussion of some of the above points you should also refer to 'Activity-based management' in Chapter 22.

(a) *Cumbersome process*
   The answer to the first comment in the question should include a very brief summary of 'Stages in the budgeting process' in Chapter 15. The process involves detailed negotiations between the budget holders and their superiors and the accountancy staff. Because the process is very time consuming it must be started well before the start of the budget year. Subsequent changes in the environment, and the fact that the outcomes reflected in the master budget may not meet financial targets, may necessitate budget revisions and a repeat of the negotiation process. The renegotiating stage may well be omitted because of time constraints. Instead, across the board cost reductions may be imposed to meet the budget targets.

   Concentration on short-term financial control
   Short-term financial targets are normally set for the budget year and the budget is used as the mechanism for achieving the targets. Budget adjustments are made to ensure that the targets are achieved often with little consideration being given to the impact such adjustments will have on the longer-term plans.

   Undesirable motivation effects on managers
   Managers are often rewarded or punished based on their budget performance in terms of achieving or exceeding the budget. There is a danger that the budget will

be viewed as a punitive device rather than as an aid to managers in managing their areas of responsibility. This can result in dysfunctional consequences such as attempting to build slack into the budgeting system by overstating costs and understating revenues. Alternatively, cuts may be made in discretionary expenses which could have adverse long-term consequences. The overriding aim becomes to achieve the budget, even if this is done in a manner that is not in the organization's best interests.

Emphasizing formal organizational structure
Budgets are normally structured around functional responsibility centres, such as departments and business units. A functional structure is likely to encourage bureaucracy and slow responses to environmental and competitive changes. There is a danger that there will be a lack of goal congruence and that managers may focus on their own departments to the detriment of the organization. Also if budgets are extended to the lower levels of the organization employees will focus excessively on meeting the budget and this may constrain their activities in terms of the flexibility that is required when dealing with customers.

(b) *Cumbersome process*
Managers could be given greater flexibility on how they will meet their targets. For example, top management might agree specific targets with the managers and the managers given authority to achieve the targets in their own way. Detailed budgets are not required and the emphasis is placed on managers achieving their overall targets.

Another alternative is to reduce the budget planning period by implementing a system of continuous or rolling budgets.

Concentration on short-term financial control
This might be overcome by placing more stress on a manager's long-term performance and adopting a profit-conscious style of budget evaluation (see 'Side effects from using accounting information for performance evaluation' in Chapter 16) and also placing more emphasis on participative budgeting (see 'Participation in the budget process' in Chapter 16). Attention should also be given to widening the performance measurement system and focusing on key result areas that deal with both short-term and long-term considerations. In particular a balanced scorecard approach (see Chapter 23) might be adopted.

Undesirable motivation effects on managers
The same points as those made above (i.e. profit-conscious style of evaluation, participative budgeting and a broader range of performance measures) also apply here. In addition, the rewards and punishment system must be changed so that it is linked to a range of performance criteria rather than being dominated by short-term financial budget performance. Consideration could also be given to changing the reward system from focusing on responsibility centre performance to rewards being based on overall company performance.

Emphasizing formal organizational structure
Here the answer could discuss activity-based budgeting with the emphasis being on activity centres and business processes, rather than functional responsibility centres that normally consist of departments. For a discussion of these issues you should refer to 'Activity-based budgeting' in Chapter 15 and 'Activity-based cost management' in Chapter 22. Consideration should also given to converting cost centres to profit centres and establishing a system of internal transfer prices. This would encourage managers to focus more widely on profits rather than just costs. Finally, budgets should not be extended to lower levels of the organization and more emphasis should be given to empowering employees to manage their own activities (see 'Employee empowerment' in Chapter 1).

(a) See 'Incremental budgeting' and 'Zero-based budgeting' in Chapter 15 for the answer to this question. Note that incremental budgeting is described within the section on activity-based budgeting. **Question 15.32**

(b) The answer should draw off the material within the section on zero-based budgeting and point out that projects should be identified as decision packages and ranked on a cost versus benefits basis with resources allocated according to the ranking up to the spending cut-off level.

(c) See 'Activity-based budgeting' in Chapter 15 for the answer to this question.

(a) Production budget **Question 15.33**

Product	A	B
Sales	2000	1500
Opening stock	(100)	(200)
Closing stock		
(10% × sales level)	200	150
	2100	1450

(b) Materials usage budget

Material type	X	Y
	Kg	Litres
Usage		
(2100 × 2) + (1450 × 3)	8550	
(2100 × 1) + (1450 × 4)		7900

(c) Materials purchases budget

Usage	8550	7900
Opening stock	(300)	(1000)
Closing stock[a]	850	800
	9100	7700
	× £10	× £7
	£91 000	£53 900

(d) Labour budget

	Skilled hours	Semi skilled hours
(2100 × 4) + (1450 × 2)	11 300	
(2100 × 2) + (1450 × 5)		11 450
	× £12	× £8
	£135 600	£91 600

Note:
[a]Material Closing Stock
Material X (2000 × 2 + 1500 × 3) × 10% = 850
Material Y (2000 × 1 + 1500 × 4) × 10% = 850

Workings **Question 15.34**
Budgeted sales (units and value)

Product	Units	Price	Value (£)
F1	34 000	£50.00	1 700 000
F2	58 000	£30.00	1 740 000
			3 440 000

Budgeted production (units)

Product	Sales	Stock increase	Production
F1	34 000	1000	35 000
F2	58 000	2000	60 000

(i)   Component purchase and usage budget (units and value)

Product	Component C3	Component C4	Total
F1	280 000u	140 000u	
F2	240 000u	180 000u	
	520 000u	320 000u	
Value	£650 000	£576 000	£1 226 000

(ii)   Direct labour budget (hours and value)

Product	Assembly	Finishing	Total
F1	17 500 hours	7000 hours	
F2	15 000 hours	10 000 hours	
	32 500	17 000	
Value	£162 500	£102 000	£264 500

(iii)   Departmental manufacturing overhead recovery rates

	Assembly	Finishing
Total overhead cost per month	£617 500	£204 000
Total direct labour hours	32 500	17 000
Overhead rate (per direct labour hour)	£19.00	£12.00

(iv)   Selling overhead recovery rate

Total overhead cost per month	£344 000
Total sales value (Month 9)	£3 440 000
Selling overhead rate	10%

(v)   Closing stock budget

Product	Units	Cost[a] £	Value £
F1	1000	32.80	32 800
F2	2000	19.40	38 800
			71 600

Note:
[a]See part (b) for the calculation of the cost per unit

(b)   Standard unit costs for month 9

			Product		
			F1 £/unit		F2 £/unit
Material	C3	8 × £1.25	10.00	4 × £1.25	5.00
	C4	4 × £1.80	7.20	3 × £1.80	5.40
Labour	Assembly	30/60 × £5	2.50	15/60 × £5	1.25
	Finishing	12/60 × £6	1.20	10/60 × £6	1.00
M'fg. overhead	Assembly	30/60 × £19	9.50	15/60 × £19	4.75
	Finishing	12/60 × £12	2.40	10/60 × £12	2.00
Manufacturing	cost		32.80		19.40
Selling overhead (10% of selling price)			5.00		3.00
Total cost			37.80		22.40
Selling price			50.00		30.00
Profit			12.20		7.60

(c) Budgeted profit and loss account for month 9

	(£)
Components	1 226 000
Direct labour	264 500
Manufacturing overhead	821 500
Subtotal	2 312 000
Less closing stock	71 600
Cost of sales	2 240 400
Selling overhead	344 000
Total cost	2 584 400
Sales	3 440 000
Net profit	855 600

(d) The company currently uses an absorption costing system but computes predetermined overhead rates on a monthly basis. It is preferable to calculate a predetermined overhead rate at annual intervals. This is because a large amount of overheads are likely to be fixed in the short-term whereas activity will fluctuate from month to month, giving large fluctuations in overhead rates if monthly rates are used. An average, annualized rate based on the relationship of total annual overhead to total annual activity is more representative of typical relationships between total costs and volume/activity than a monthly rate. For a more detailed discussion of these issues you should refer to 'Budgeted overhead rates' in Chapter 3.

Question 15.35

(a)

Product	V	S	T
	(£)	(£)	(£)
Contribution per unit	60	53.75	40.50
Litres of Q per unit	10	8	5
Contribution per litre of Q	6	6.72	8.10
Ranking	3	2	1

The allocation of material Q and the optimum production schedule based on the above ranking is as follows:

Product	V	S	T	Total
Minimum production (units) [a]	24	67	71	
Usage of Q (litres)	240	536	355	1131
Additional production		312.5[c]	1353[b]	
Usage of Q (litres)		2 500	6765	9265
				10 396
Production	24	379.5	1424	

Notes:
[a] Accepted orders less stock decrease.
[b] Maximum demand is 1450 units less stock decrease of 26 units gives a required production of 1424 units comprising of 71 units allocated to minimum production and 1353 units to additional production.
[c] After the allocation of the minimum production and the stock decrease there are 9265 litres unused. Production of 1353 units will require 6765 litres (1353 units × 5 litres) thus leaving 2500 litres to be allocated to S. This will require 312.5 additional units of S (2500/8).

(b)

Product (units)	V	S	T
Production budget	24	379.5	1424
Add stock decrease	10	8	26
Sales	34	387.5	1450

(c) (i) *Marginal costing profit statement*

Product	V	S	T	Total
Sales (units)	34	387.5	1450	
Contribution per unit (£)	60	53.75	40.50	
Contribution (£)	2040	20 828	58 725	81 593
Less fixed overheads (£)				95 000
Loss (£)				13 407

(c) (ii) When stocks are declining, absorption costing will report a lower profit (or higher loss) compared with marginal costing due to the fixed overhead previously deferred in the stock valuation being charged as an expense against the current period. This is represented by the stock decreases for each product multiplied by the fixed overhead rate. The calculations are as follows:

	(£)
V = Stock decrease of 10 units at a fixed overhead rate of £24 per unit	= 240
S = Stock decrease of 8 units at a fixed overhead rate of £30 per unit	= 240
T = Stock decrease of 26 units at a fixed overhead rate of £12 per unit	= 312
	792

Therefore the absorption costing loss will be £14 199 (£13 407 + £792).

For an explanation of the above issues you should refer to 'Variable costing and absorption costing: a comparison of their impact on profits' in Chapter 7.

(d) (i) Profits are based on the accruals concept to meet financial accounting reporting requirements. For example, an investment in a new asset of £100 000 involving an immediate cash payment is a cash flow but it would be recorded as a depreciation expense of £10 000 per annum (assuming a life of 10 years and no scrap value). Therefore profits are reduced by £10 000 per annum but the cash flow is £100 000.

(d) (ii) Marginal costing profits are a better indicator of cash flows because fixed overheads are recorded as an expense in the period that they are incurred whereas absorption costing includes fixed overheads in the stock valuation and records them as an expense in the period when the stocks are sold.

Question 15.36   (a) The following points should be included in the answer:

Budget preparation
A brief discussion of budget participation (see Chapter 16) and an indication that some element of participation is generally considered desirable. The lack of consultation and involvement with the departmental manager should be addressed.

Implication of the increase in volume
A fixed budget is being operated for cost control and performance evaluation but the number of visits were 12 000 compared with a budget of 10 000. For those items of expense that vary with the number of visits (such as wages, travel expenses and consumables), it is inappropriate to compare the actual costs of visiting 12 000 clients compared with a budget of 10 000 clients. The current report draws attention to this invalid comparison. There is a need to implement flexible budgets (see Chapter 16) instead of fixed budgets.

Controllability

Some of the costs in the report are not controllable by the departmental manager. Adopting the controllability principle (see Chapter 16), non-controllable costs should either be excluded from the report or shown in a separate section indicating that they are not directly controllable by the departmental manager. At present the departmental manager appears to be held accountable for expenses (e.g. allocated administrative costs) that he/she cannot directly influence.

Funding allocation

As indicated by the director it is important that the department keeps within its funding allocation to ensure that costs are controlled. For fixed expenses, such as the salary of the supervisor, managers should ensure that costs do not exceed the original (fixed) budget but for variable expenses the costs should not exceed the flexed budget for the actual level of activity. Increased expenditure should only be permitted if more funds are allocated from local or central government.

Social aspects

Social aspects generally cannot be expressed in financial terms but they must not be lost sight of in the pursuit of only those items that are incorporated in the budget. Where budget amounts are allocated to social aspects it is important that managers seek to use these funds, since underspending represents a failure to pursue objectives expressed in the budget. The main difficulty with expenses relating to social aspects is that there is not any clear input–output relationship, so it can be difficult to ascertain whether the funds are being utilized efficiently.

Other aspects

The focus of the report is entirely on financial aspects. Non-financial measures should also be incorporated such as total staff hours worked, feedback on client satisfaction on the service provided and the frequency of visits. These aspects can be vital to the success of the service and the present system does not appear to highlight them. Consideration also should be given to incorporating additional columns in the report that compare the actual against budget for the year to date so that the focus is not only on the most recent period. Also the lack of consultation and the apparent authoritarian manner in the way that the report is being used warrants attention, since this is likely to result in harmful behavioural consequences.

(b) The answer should draw off the material within the section on zero-based budgeting (ZBB), pointing out its claimed advantages. In addition, the answer should draw attention to the weaknesses of conventional budgets in the form of incremental budgets (an explanation can be found at the beginning of the section on activity-based budgeting). Finally, the problems associated with implementing ZBB should be described with an indication that for this organization it may be more appropriate to approximate the principles of ZBB using a more simplistic form of priority-based budgeting.

(a) Cost driver rates:

Question 15.37

$$W \quad \frac{£160\,000}{(20 \times 4) + (30 \times 5) + (15 \times 2) + (40 \times 3) + (25 \times 1)} = £395$$

$$X \quad \frac{£130\,000}{(20 \times 3) + (30 \times 2) + (15 \times 5) + (40 \times 1) + (25 \times 4)} = £388$$

$$Y \quad \frac{£80\,000}{(20 \times 3) + (30 \times 3) + (15 \times 2) + (40 \times 4) + (25 \times 2)} = £205$$

$$Z \quad \frac{£200\,000}{(20 \times 4) + (30 \times 6) + (15 \times 8) + (40 \times 2) + (25 \times 3)} = £374$$

Actual activities during October 2002:

W (18 × 4) + (33 × 5) + (16 × 2) + (35 × 3) + (28 × 1) = 402
X (18 × 3) + (33 × 2) + (16 × 5) + (35 × 1) + (28 × 4) = 347
Y (18 × 3) + (33 × 3) + (16 × 2) + (35 × 4) + (28 × 2) = 381
Z (18 × 4) + (33 × 6) + (16 × 8) + (35 × 2) + (28 × 3) = 552

Budget control statement

Activity	Original budget (£000)	Flexible budget (£000)	Actual costs (£000)	Variance (£000)
W	160	159 (402 × £395)	158	1F
X	130	135 (347 × £388)	139	4A
Y	80	78 (381 × £205)	73	5F
Z	200	206 (552 × £374)	206	0
	570	578	576	2F

(b) For the answer to this question see the points listed at the end of the section on the factors influencing the effectiveness of participation in Chapter 16.

(c) A fixed budget represents the original budget set at the beginning of the period based upon the planned level of activity. A flexible budget represents a budget that is adjusted to reflect what the budget would have been, based on the actual level of activity that occurred during the period. Flexible budgets are appropriate for those costs that are expected to vary with activity. Therefore actual expenditure should be compared with a flexible budget. Fixed budgets are more appropriate for controlling discretionary items of expenditure. Examples include advertising and research and development. These items do not vary with activity and there is no obvious level of optimum spending. Also the budget represents a commitment or policy decision to allocate a specific amount of funds to spend on these items. Thus underspending may be considered undesirable because it represents a failure to pursue management commitments of spending to be incurred during the budget period.

(d) y = Total cost for the period
a = Variable cost per unit of activity
b = Fixed costs for the period
x = Activity level for the period

For a more detailed explanation of the above terms you should refer to the first section in Chapter 24.

Management control systems

Solutions to Chapter 16 questions

(a) See Chapter 16 for the answer to this question. In particular, your answer should stress: **Question 16.32**
   (i) The need for a system of responsibility accounting based on a clear definition of a manager's authority and responsibility.
   (ii) The production of performance reports at frequent intervals comparing actual and budget costs for individual expense items. Variances should be analysed according to whether they are controllable or non-controllable by the manager.
   (iii) The managers should participate in the setting of budgets and standards.
   (iv) The system should ensure that variances are investigated, causes found and remedial action is taken.
   (v) An effective cost control system must not be used as a punitive device, but should be seen as a system that helps managers to control their costs more effectively.
(b) Possible problems include:
   (i) Difficulties in setting standards for non-repetitive work.
   (ii) Non-acceptance by budgetees if they view the system as a punitive device to judge their performance.
   (iii) Isolating variances where interdependencies exist.

(a) See 'Planning', 'Motivation' and 'Performance evaluation' in the section on the **Question 16.33** multiple functions of budgets in Chapter 15 for the answer to this question. The answer should emphasize that the role of motivation is to encourage goal congruence between the company and the employees.
(b) See 'Conflicting roles of budgets' in Chapter 15 for an explanation of how the planning and motivation roles can conflict. Prior to the commencement of the budget period, management should prepare budgets that represent targets to be achieved based upon anticipated environmental variables. It is possible that at the end of the budget period the *actual* environmental variables will be different from those envisaged when the budget was prepared. Therefore actual performance will be determined by the actual environmental variables, but the plans reflected in the budget may be based on different environmental variables. It is inappropriate to compare actual performance based on one set of environmental variables with budgeted performance based on another set of environmental variables. Consequently, a budget that is used for planning purposes will be in conflict with one that is used for performance evaluation.

The conflict between motivation and evaluation is described by Barrett and Fraser (1977) (see Bibliography in main text) as follows:

> In many situations the budget that is most effective in the evaluation role might be called an ex-post facto budget. It is one that considers the impact of uncontrollable or unforeseeable events, and it is constructed or adjusted after the fact.
> The potential role conflict between the motivation and evaluation roles involves the impact on motivation of using an ex-post facto standard in the evaluation process. Managers are unlikely to be totally committed to achieving

the budget's objectives if they know that the performance standards by which they are to be judged may change.

In other words, for evaluation purposes the budget might be adjusted to reflect changes in environmental variables. If a manager expects that the budget will be changed for evaluation purposes, there is a danger that he or she will not be as highly motivated to achieve the original budget.

(c)　(i)　The planning and motivation conflict might be resolved by setting two budgets. A budget based on most likely outcomes could be set for planning purposes and a separate, more demanding budget could be used for motivation purposes.

(ii)　The planning and evaluation role conflict can be resolved by comparing actual performance with an ex-post budget. See 'Ex-post variance analysis' in Chapter 19 for an illustration of how this conflict can be resolved.

(iii)　Barrett and Fraser (1977) suggest the following approach for resolving the motivation and evaluation conflict:

> The conflict between the motivation and evaluation roles can also be reduced by using 'adjustable budgets.' These are operational budgets whose objectives can be modified under predetermined sets of circumstances. Thus revision is possible during the operating period and the performance standard can be changed.
>
> In one company that uses such a budgeting system, managers commit themselves to a budget with the understanding that, if there are substantial changes in any of five key economic or environmental variables, top management will revise the budget and new performance criteria will be set. This company automatically makes budget revisions whenever there are significant changes in any of these five variables. Naturally, the threshold that triggers a new budget will depend on the relative importance of each variable. With this system, managers know they are expected to meet their budgets. The budget retains its motivating characteristics because it represents objectives that are possible to achieve. Uncontrollable events are not allowed to affect budgeted objectives in such a way that they stand little chance of being met. Yet revisions that are made do not have to adversely affect commitment, since revisions are agreed to in advance and procedures for making them are structured into the overall budgeting system.

A more detailed answer to this question can be found in Barrett and Fraser (1977).

Question 16.34

(a)　The answer should include a discussion of the following points:

(i)　Constant pressure from top management for greater production may result in the creation of anti-management work groups and reduced efficiency, so that budgetees can protect themselves against what they consider to be increasingly stringent targets.

(ii)　Non-acceptance of budgets if the budgetees have not been allowed to participate in setting the budgets.

(iii)　Negative attitudes if the budget is considered to be a punitive control device instead of a system to help managers do a better job. The negative attitudes might take the form of reducing cooperation between departments and also with the accounting department. Steps might be taken to ensure that costs do not fall below budget, so that the budget will not be reduced next year. There is a danger that data will be falsified, and more effort will be directed to finding excuses for failing to achieve the budget than trying to control or reduce costs.

(iv) Managers might try and achieve the budget at all costs even if this results in actions that are not in the best interests of the organization, e.g. delaying maintenance costs.

(v) Organizational atmosphere may become one of competition and conflict rather than one of cooperation and conciliation.

(vi) Suspicion and mistrust of top management, resulting in the whole budgeting process being undermined.

(vii) Belief that the system of evaluation is unjust and widespread worry and tension by the budgetees. Tension might be relieved by falsifying information, blaming others or absenteeism.

(b) For the answer to this question see 'Dealing with the distorting effects of uncontrollable factors before (and after) the measurement period' in Chapter 16.

Question 16.35

The answer should include a discussion of the following:
(i) The impact of targets on performance.
(ii) The use of accounting control techniques for performance evaluation.
(iii) Participation in the budgeting and standard setting process.
(iv) Bias in the budget process.
(v) Management use of budgets and the role of the accountant in the education process.
See Chapter 16 for a discussion of each of the above items.

Question 16.36

(a) See Chapter 16 for the answer to this question.

(b) For the answer to this question see 'Dealing with the distorting effects of uncontrollable factors before (and after) the measurement period', 'Participation in the budget and target setting process' and 'Side effects from using accounting information for performance evaluation' in Chapter 16.

(c) Figure 16.1 in Chapter 16 illustrates the importance of feedback (information comparing planned and actual outcomes in the control process). Feedback takes the form of control reports issued by the accountant to the managers responsible for controlling inputs. Effective control requires that corrective action be taken so that actual outputs conform to planned outputs in the future. In order to assist managers in controlling activities, the performance reports should highlight those areas that do not conform to plan. The performance reports should also provide clues as to why the actual outputs differ from the planned outputs. Feedback information is necessary to provoke corrective managerial action.

It should be noted that accounting reports of performance also have a direct effect on motivation by giving the department manager knowledge of performance. Knowledge of results has been shown in various psychological experiments to lead to improved performance. This is partly because it conveys information that can be used for acting more effectively on the next trial; but also partly because knowledge of results motivates through satisfying the achievement need. Stok (1959) investigated the effect of control systems using visual presentation of quality on workers quality performance. He found that visual presentation of quality had both an information and a motivation effect and both were instrumental in improving performance. It appears that communicating knowledge of results acts as a reward or punishment. It can serve either to reinforce or extinguish previous employee behaviours.

(d) The purpose of goal congruence is to encourage an individual manager's goals to be in agreement with the organization's goals. For a description of this process see 'Goal congruence' in Chapter 16.

Reference
Stok, T.L. (1959) *De Arbeider en de Zichbaarmaking van de Kwaliteit*, Leiden, Stenfert Kruese.

Question 16.37   Managers may be reluctant to participate in setting budgets for the following reasons:
   (i) Managers may consider that they do not engage in true participation if they can-
       not influence the budget. They may consider the process to be one of the senior
       managers securing formal acceptance of previously determined target levels.
  (ii) Personality of budgetees may result in authoritarian managers having authori-
       tarian expectations of their superiors. Consequently, authoritarian budgetees
       may be reluctant to participate in the budget process.
 (iii) The degree to which individuals have control over their own destiny (see
       Brownell's (1981) research in Chapter 16) appears to influence the desire for
       participation. Managers may believe that they cannot significantly influence
       results and thus consider participation to be inappropriate.
  (iv) Bad management/superior relationships.
   (v) Lack of understanding of the budget process or a belief by the budgetees that
       they will be engaging in a process that will be used in a recriminatory manner by
       their superiors.
The unwanted side-effects that might arise from the imposition of budgets by senior
management include the following:
   (i) Non-acceptance of budgets.
  (ii) The budgetees might consider the method of performance evaluation to be
       unjust.
 (iii) Creation of anti-management cohesive work groups.
  (iv) Reduced efficiency by work groups so as to protect themselves against what
       they consider to be increasingly stringent targets.
   (v) The budget system will be undermined. The real problem is the way manage-
       ment use the system rather than inadequacies of the budget system itself.
  (vi) An increase in suspicion and mistrust, so undermining the whole budgeting
       process.
 (vii) Encouraging budgetees to falsify and manipulate information presented to
       management.
(viii) Organizational atmosphere may become one of competition and conflict rather
       than one of cooperation and conciliation.
  (ix) Managers might try to achieve the budget at all costs even if this results in
       actions that are not in the best interests of the organization.

Question 16.38   See 'Setting financial performance targets' in Chapter 16 for the answer to this
                      question.

Question 16.39   (a) For the answer to this question see 'Setting financial performance targets' in
                          Chapter 16. In particular, the answer should stress that a tight budget is preferable
                          for motivation purposes, whereas for planning and control purposes an expected
                          target should be set that management believes will be achieved. Consequently, a
                          conflict occurs between the motivational and management reporting objectives.
                      (b) The levels of efficiency that may be incorporated in the standards used in bud-
                          getary control and/or standard costing include the following:
                           (i) *Perfection:* Standards based on perfection are termed 'ideal standards'. Case 6
                               illustrated in Figure 16.4 in Chapter 16 is typical of a standard based on per-
                               fection. Ideal standards have no motivational advantages and are unsatisfac-
                               tory for planning and control purposes.
                          (ii) *Tight standards:* These standards represent targets that are set at a level of
                               performance that is difficult, but not impossible, for budgetees to achieve.
                               Cases 3–5 illustrated in Figure 16.4 represent tight standards. It can be seen
                               from the figure that tight standards should increase aspiration levels and
                               actual performance. Because tight standards may not be achieved, they are
                               unsatisfactory for planning and control purposes.

(iii) *Expected performance:* Expected performance standards are based on the level of efficiency expected to be attained (i.e. Case 2 in Figure 16.4). One advantage of expected standards is that variances indicate deviations from management's expectations. A further advantage is that expected standards can be used for planning purposes. Expected standards are likely to be unsatisfactory for motivational purposes, since they may not provide a challenging target.

(iv) *Loose standards:* With loose standards, the level of efficiency implied by the standard is less than expected. Case 1 illustrated in Figure 16.4 represents a loose standard. Loose standards are poor motivators and are unsatisfactory for planning and control purposes.

(c) See 'Participation in the budgeting and target setting process' in Chapter 16 for the answer to this question.

Question 16.40

(a) For a discussion of feedback and feedforward controls see Chapter 16. The remaining terms are also discussed in Chapter 16.

(b) For the answer to this question see 'Dealing with the distorting effects of uncontrollable factors before (and after) the measurement period', 'Participation in the budget and target setting process' and 'Side effects from using accounting information for performance evaluation' in Chapter 16.

Question 16.41

(a) For an explanation of responsibility accounting you should refer to 'The nature of management accounting control systems' in Chapter 16. Potential difficulties in operating a system of responsibility accounting include:

1   identification of specific areas of responsibility where actions can be influenced by two or more persons resulting in the problem of joint responsibility occurring. It therefore becomes difficult to ascertain which managers should be held accountable for the outcomes;

2   distinguishing between those items which managers can control and for which they should be held accountable and those items over which they have no control and for which they are not held accountable (see 'The controllability principle' in Chapter 16);

3   determining how challenging the targets should be (see 'Setting financial performance targets' in Chapter 16);

4   determining how much influence managers should have in setting financial performance targets (see 'Setting financial performance targets' in Chapter 16);

5   choosing an appropriate mix of financial and non-financial measures to be included in the performance report and seeking to avoid some of the harmful side-effects of controls (see 'Harmful side-effects of controls' in Chapter 16).

(b) See 'Feedback and feedforward controls' in Chapter 16 for the answer to this question. A diagram of feedback control is presented in Figure 16.1. This diagram can be modified to represent a feedforward control system by deleting the arrow from the output box to the regulator box. The feedforward mechanism takes place by comparing the planned inputs with the expected outcomes (the arrow from the process box to the regulator box) and taking appropriate action where plans do not meet expectations (reflected in the arrow from the regulator box to the input box).

(c) (i) The budget acts as a resource allocation device by determining the total resources available for a non-profit organization and allocating these resources within the budget process to the different programmes or activities (e.g. between spending on education, care of the elderly, or leisure provision within a municipal authority). The budget planning process specifies where and how the available funds should be spent during the current period.

(c) (ii) When the master budgets (and thus the budgets making up the master budget) have been reviewed by the appropriate top management committee, they represent the formal approval for each budget manager to carry out the plans contained in his/her budget. At the end of the appropriate budget period, actual expenditure will be compared against the budget authorization. For example, a school may be allocated with a budgeted sum to spend on part-time teaching staff. At the end of the period actual spending will be compared against the budget and the head will be held accountable for any difference.

(c) (iii) For the answer to this question see 'Control' within the section on multiple functions of budgets in Chapter 15. An example of the control process is provided in 'Line item budgets' within the section on the budgeting process in non-profit-making organizations in Chapter 15.

Question 16.42

Task 1
Reclamation Division Performance Report – 4 weeks to 31 May:
Original budget   250 tonnes
Actual output   200 tonnes

	Budget based on 200 tonnes	Actual	Variance	Comments
Controllable expenses:				
Wages and social security costs[a]	43 936	46 133	2197A	
Fuel[b]	15 000	15 500	500A	
Consumables[c]	2 000	2 100	100A	
Power[d]	1 500	1 590	90A	
Directly attributable overheads[e]	20 000	21 000	1000A	
	82 436	86 323	3887A	
Non-controllable expenses:				
Plant maintenance[e]	5 950	6 900	950A	
Central services[e]	6 850	7 300	450A	
	12 800	14 200	1400A	
Total	95 236	100 523	5287A	

Notes:
[a] 6 employees × 4 teams × 42 hours per week × £7.50 per hour × 4 weeks = £30 240.
[b] 200 tonnes × £75
[c] 200 tonnes × £10
[d] £500 + (£5 × 200) = £1500
[e] It is assumed that directly attributable expenses, plant maintenance and central services are non-variable expenses.

Task 2
(a) (i) Past knowledge can provide useful information on future outcomes but ideally budgets ought to be based on the most up-to-date information. Budgeting should be related to the current environment and the use of past information that is two years old can only be justified where the operating conditions and environment are expected to remain unchanged.

(ii) For motivation and planning purposes budgets should represent targets based on what we are proposing to do. For control purposes budgets should be flexed based on what was actually done so that actual costs for actual output can be compared with budgeted costs for the actual output. This ensures that valid comparisons will be made.

(iii) For variable expenses the original budget should be reduced in proportion to reduced output in order to reflect cost behaviour. Fixed costs are not adjusted since they are unaffected in the short-term by output changes. Flexible budgeting ensures that like is being compared with like so that reduced output does not increase the probability that favourable cost variances will be reported. However, if less was produced because of actual sales being less than budget this will result in an adverse sales variance and possibly an adverse profit variance.

(iv) Plant maintenance costs are apportioned on the basis of capital values and therefore newer equipment (with higher written-down values) will be charged with a higher maintenance cost. Such an approach does not provide a meaningful estimate of maintenance resources consumed by departments since older equipment is likely to be more expensive to maintain. The method of recharging should be reviewed and ideally based on estimated usage according to maintenance records. The charging of the overspending by the maintenance department to user departments is questionable since this masks inefficiencies. Ideally, maintenance department costs should be recharged based on actual usage at budgeted cost and the maintenance department made accountable for the adverse spending (price) variance.

(v) The comments do not explain the causes of the variances and are presented in a negative tone. No comments are made, nor is any praise given, for the favourable variances.

(vi) Not all variances should be investigated. The decision to investigate should depend on both their absolute and relative size and the likely benefits arising from an investigation.

(vii) Central service costs are not controllable by divisional managers. However, even though the divisional manager cannot control these costs there is an argument for including them as non-controllable costs in the performance report. The justification for this is that divisional managers are made aware of central service costs and may put pressure on central service staff to control such costs more effectively. It should be made clear to divisional managers that they are not accountable for any non-controllable expenses that are included in their performance reports.

Question 16.43

Task 1

(a)

	Quarter 1 units	Quarter 2 units	Quarter 3 units	Quarter 4 units
Actual sales volume	420 000	450 000	475 000	475 000
Seasonal variation	+25 000	+15 000	—	240 000
Deseasonalized sales volumes	395 000	435 000	475 000	515 000

(b) The trend is for sales volume to increase by 40 000 units each quarter:

Forecast for next year	Quarter 1 units	Quarter 2 units	Quarter 3 units	Quarter 4 units
Trend projection	555 000	595 000	635 000	675 000
Seasonal variation	+25 000	+15 000	—	−40 000
Forecast sales volumes	580 000	610 000	635 000	635 000

Task 2

(a) Seasonal variations represent consistent patterns in sales volume that occur throughout each year. For example, the seasonal variation of +25 000 for Quarter 1 indicates that sales volume in the first quarter tends to be 25 000 units higher than the underlying trend in sales. In contrast, the seasonal variation of $-40\,000$ in Quarter 4 indicates that sales in this quarter tend to be 40 000 units lower than the underlying trend in sales.

To derive the deseasonalized data the seasonal variations must be removed so that a trend can be observed. The above figures indicate an increase of 40 000 units per quarter. This trend is concealed when the actual data is observed because of the distorting effects of seasonal variations. Observations of the actual data suggests that the rate of increase in sales is declining.

(b) Provided that the observed trend in deseasonalized data continues the deseasonalized data can be used to project the trend in future sales. The trend values are adjusted by seasonal variations in each quarter to predict actual sales.

Task 3

(a) A fixed budget is a budget for the planned level of activity and budgeted costs are not adjusted to the actual level of activity. A fixed budget is used at the planning stage because an activity level has to be initially determined so that all department activities can be coordinated to meet the planned level of activity. However, it is most unlikely that actual activity will be the same as the planned level of activity. For example, if the actual level of activity is greater than budgeted level of activity then those costs that vary with the level of activity will be greater than the budgeted costs purely because of changes in activity. It is clearly inappropriate for variable costs to compare actual costs at one level of activity with budgeted costs at another level of activity. The original fixed budget must be adjusted to reflect the budgeted expenditure at the actual level of activity. This procedure is called flexible budgeting. The resulting comparison of actual costs with a flexible budget is more meaningful for cost control because the effect of the change in the activity level has been eliminated.

(b) Possible activity indicators include number of deliveries made, miles travelled and journeys made.

(c) See 'Flexible budgets' in Chapter 16 for the answer to this question.

Task 4

(a) Production budget for product Q

	(units)
Forecast sales for year	18 135
Increase in stock (15% × 1200)	180
Finished units required	18 315
Quality control loss (1/99)	185
Total units input to production	18 500

(b) Direct labour budget for product Q

	(hours)
Active labour hours required (18 500 × 5)	92 500
Idle time allowance (7.5/92.5)	7 500
Total hours to be paid for	100 000
Standard hourly rate	£6
Budgeted labour cost	£600 000

(c) Material usage budget for material M

	(kg)
Material required for processing 18 500 units (× 9 kg)	166 500
Wastage (10/90)	18 500
Material usage for year	185 000

(d) Material purchases budget for material M

	(kg)
Material required for production input	185 000
Increase in material stocks (12%)	960
Expected loss in stores	1 000
Material purchases required	186 960

Task 5

The implications of the shortage is that the budget plans cannot be achieved and the availability of material is the limiting factor. If the limiting factor cannot be removed the materials purchase budget should be the first budget to be prepared and all the other budgets coordinated to ensure the most efficient usage of materials. The following four possible actions could be taken to overcome the problem:

  (i) Seek alternative supplies for material M. Possible problems include the reliability and quality of materials delivered by new suppliers. New suppliers should be carefully vetted prior to entering into any contracts or making company plans dependent on deliveries from new suppliers.
 (ii) Reduce the budgeted sales of product Q. This will lead to loss in profits and the possible permanent loss of customers to competitors if the competitors are able to meet customer demand.
(iii) Reduce the stock levels for product Q and material M. The danger with this course of action is that stocks may not be available when required which could lead to disruptions in production and lost sales.
(iv) Reduce the wastage of material M and the defective output of product Q. This course of action will cause problems if quality standards are reduced resulting in inferior quality output. This could have a harmful effect on future sales. Problems will not be caused if quality standards are maintained and improved working practices result in a reduction of waste and defective output.

Question 16.44

Task 1 (a)

Calculation of unit variable costs

	Original budget	Revised budget	Difference	Variable unit cost[a]
Units	24 000	20 000	4 000	
Variable costs				
Material	216 000	180 000	£36 000	£9
Labour	288 000	240 000	£48 000	£12
Semi-variable costs				
Heat, light and power	31 000	27 000	£4 000	£1
Analysis of heat, light and power				
Variable cost	£24 000	£20 000		
Total cost	£31 000	£27 000		
Fixed cost	£7 000	£7 000		

Note
[a]Unit variable cost = change in total cost/change in volume

Task 1 (b)

Rivermede Ltd – flexible budget statement for the year ended 31 May

	Revised budget	Actual results	Variance	
Production and sales (units)	22 000	22 000		
Variable costs	(£)	(£)		(£)
Material 22 000 × £9	198 000	214 320	(£206 800 + £7520)	6320 (A)

Labour 22 000 × £12	264 000	255 200		8800 (F)
Semi-variable cost				
Heat, light and power				
(22 000 × £1) + £7000	29 000	25 880	(£33 400 − £7520)	3120 (F)
Fixed costs				
Rent, rates and depreciation	40 000	38 000		2000 (F)
	531 000	533 400		2400 (A)

Task 2 (a)

The original statement compares the actual cost of producing 22 000 units with a budget for 20 000 units. This is not comparing like with like. The flexible budget shows what budgeted costs would have been for the actual production level of 22 000 units. Because actual production was greater than budgeted production of 20 000 units variable costs are likely to be higher and this comparison will result in an adverse effect on variable cost variances. The fact that overall variances are smaller when comparisons are made with the flexible budget is due to flexing the budget and not to participative budgeting.

Task 2 (b)

The report should indicate that favourable variances may have arisen for the following reasons:

    (i) Controllable factors due to the more efficient usage of direct labour and heating, light and power.

    (ii) Budget participation may have resulted in the creation of slack through an overstatement of budgeted costs.

    (iii) Uncontrollable factors such as a reduction in the prices charged to Rivermede for rent and rates.

Task 2 (c)

The report should include the following items:

    (i) The increased sales may have been due to a general increase in demand rather than the effort of the salesforce.

    (ii) The original budget of 24 000 units may have been over-estimated or the revised budget of 20 000 units may have been understated due to the sales director creating slack by deliberately understating demand.

Question 16.45

Task 1 (a)

For 2001 x takes on a value of 9.

Therefore annual demand $(y) = 640 + (40 \times 9) = 1000$

weekly demand $= 1\,000/25 = 40$ holidays

Task 1 (b)

Weaknesses of the least squares regression formula include:

    (i) The formula assumes a linear relationship based on time but demand for holidays may not be a linear function of time.

    (ii) Seasonal variations are ignored. Demand may vary throughout the holiday season with some holiday weeks being more popular than others.

    (iii) It ignores changes in holidaymakers' tastes such as a change in demand from short haul to long haul or 10-day holidays to short-break holidays.

    (iv) Cyclical fluctuations are ignored. Demand for holidays is likely to vary depending on the state of the economy, such as boom or recession.

Linear regression is covered in Chapter 24.

Task 2 (a)

Revised cost statement 10 days ended 27 November

Flexed budget	Note	Budget (£)	Actual (£)	Variance (£)
Aircraft seats	1	18 000	18 600	600 A
Coach hire		5 000	4 700	300 F
Hotel rooms	2	14 300	14 200	100 F
Meals	3	4 560	4 600	40 A
Tour guide		1 800	1 700	100 F
Advertising		2 000	1 800	200 F
		45 660	45 600	60 F

Notes

1   £450 × 40 because purchases are in blocks of 20 seats

2   £70 × 10 days × 34 tourists × 0.5   £11 900
    £60 × 10 days × 4 tourists   £2 400
                                          £14 300

3   £12 × 10 days × 38 tourists

Task 2 (b)

The original budget is a fixed budget based on the anticipated demand when the budget was set. If actual demand is different from anticipated demand a fixed budget is inappropriate for control purposes because it does not ensure that like is compared with like. See the answer to Question 16.44 for an explanation of this point. The revised flexible budget shows what costs should have been for the volume of passengers taken on the holiday. This ensures that a more meaningful comparison of budget and actual costs is made.

Task 2 (c)

The factors to be taken into account in deciding whether or not to investigate individual variances is examined in Chapter 19. The following factors should be considered:

  (i)   the absolute amount of the variance;
 (ii)   the relative amount of the variance expressed as a percentage of budgeted costs;
(iii)   the trend in variances by examining the cumulative variances for the period;
 (iv)   whether or not the variance is controllable;
  (v)   the cost and benefits from investigating the variance.

For a more detailed discussion of the above points you should refer to Chapter 19.

Question 16.46

(a) The number of standard deviations by which each regional manager's estimate deviates from the mean of the distribution assumed by the sales director is:

$$\text{Northern } Z = \frac{5.7 - 5.0}{1.0} = 0.7$$

$$\text{Southern } Z = \frac{10.9 - 10.0}{1.0} = 0.9$$

$$\text{Eastern } Z = \frac{7.9 - 8.0}{1.0} = -0.1$$

$$\text{Western } Z = \frac{7.5 - 7.0}{1.0} = 0.5$$

The likelihood of sales being equal or greater than the estimate is obtained by ascertaining the probabilities for the Z scores from a normal distribution table. The probabilities are:

$$\text{Northern} = 0.242$$
$$\text{Southern} = 0.1841$$
$$\text{Eastern} = 1 - 0.4602 = 0.5398$$
$$\text{Western} = 0.3085$$

Note that the negative Z score calculation for the Eastern territory indicates that the probability of sales being less than £7900 is 0.4602. Therefore the probability of sales being £7900 or more is 0.5398.

The standard deviation for the total sales is calculated from the sum of the four variances:

$$\text{Standard deviation} = \sqrt{[4 \times (1\text{ m})^2]} = \text{£2 m}$$

$$Z = \frac{32 - 30}{2} = 1.00 = 0.1587 \text{ probability}$$

Therefore the probability that the total sales will be equal to or greater than £32m is 0.1587.

Otley and Berry (1979) have illustrated the consequences of submitting non-mean (most likely) estimates rather than the expected value of the estimates when they are aggregated at successive levels in the organizational hierarchy. They have demonstrated that estimates that are only slightly optimistic at the unit level (30% probability of achievement) become highly optimistic when nine such units are aggregated at the next level in the hierarchy (16% probability of achievement). This process applies in this question. The aggregation of the budgets results in the overall budget having a relatively low chance of being achieved.

(b) The answer should stress that managers tend to overestimate costs and under-estimate sales in order to obtain slack budgets which can be achieved. In some situations the reverse may apply where managers seek to enhance their position in the short term by submitting optimistic budgets. However, such budgets carry the risk of failure if the budget is not met. Managers may be tempted to overstate budgeted costs in order to preserve previous budget allocations. They will then spend to this limit in order to ensure that future budget allocations are maintained. A superior's budget may also differ from the budget submitted by the manager because they do not have detailed knowledge of the budgetees' activities. Consequently, the superior's budget is unlikely to represent an accurate estimate of future outcomes.

Recommendations for overcoming the above problems include:

(i) Ensure that more emphasis is given to the negotiation and participation process so that differences can be resolved and differing expectations and assumptions clarified.

(ii) Adjusting budgets to the differing aspirations and capabilities of the budgetees (see 'Setting financial performance targets' in Chapter 16).

(iii) Require managers to produce appropriate evidence to justify their budgets.

(iv) Use two sets of budgets – one for planning purposes and a more demanding budget for motivational purposes (see 'Conflicting roles of budgets' in Chapter 15).

(v) Avoid a budget constrained style of evaluation. This approach is likely to encourage substantial bias in the budget process.

(c) The proposed bonus system will encourage budgetees to submit pessimistic budgets so that bonuses can be obtained. Managers will engage in defensive behaviour and put too much effort into trying to justify pessimistic budgets. The process of negotiating budgets will be undermined, and relationships between superior and budgetee may deteriorate. The process might lead to defensive behaviour by the budgetee, and the sales director will find it extremely difficult to negotiate a more demanding budget.

The proposed system will encourage managers merely to achieve the target but not to achieve a performance in excess of standard. Consequently, lost sales orders might result. Where managers are having difficulty in achieving the target, there is a danger that they may seek to stimulate sales by taking on customers with high credit risk. Alternatively, they might be motivated to sell goods with a high probability of subsequently being returned.

Placing too much emphasis on meeting the budget target can undermine the whole budget process, and there are strong arguments for not implementing the proposed system. Possible amendments to the system would be:

(i) Relate the bonuses to a comparison of the growth in market shares for each territory and pay the bonuses according to a 'league table' of market shares.

(ii) Abandon the present bonus system and pay higher wages to competent staff. Bonuses could be paid only for performance significantly in excess of budget.

(iii) Set a series of percentage bonus scales, with the percentage related to a number of ranges in excess of budget. The higher the range achieved, the higher the percentage bonus.

References

Berry, A.J. and Otley, D.T. (1975) The aggregation of estimates in hierarchical organizations, *Journal of Management Studies*, May, 175–93.

See also Otley, D.T. and Berry, A.J. (1979) Risk distribution in the budgetary process, *Accounting and Business Research*, 5, 231–46.

Note

There is no Chapter 17 in the Students Manual, as all the questions in that chapter require essay answers, and none of them are included within the white box to indicate that a sample answer is provided.

Standard costing and variance analysis 1

Solutions to Chapter 18 questions

Question 18.30   See 'Purposes of standard costing' in Chapter 18 for the answer to this question. Additional purposes that could be added include monitoring variances through time to ascertain the need to change the targets or changing the standard to assist in the implementation of a continuous improvement philosophy.

Question 18.31   (a) An explanation of the different uses of standard costing is provided in 'Purposes of standard costing' in Chapter 18. Once standards have been set they cannot be assumed to be valid targets over long periods of time. They should periodically be reviewed to enable the benefits of standard costing to continue. In this respect, standards must change with the changing practices of an organization. Some organizations adopt a continuous improvement philosophy which reflects improvement in methods and more efficient usage of resources. Under these circumstances, standards need to be changed to reflect the planned improvements. The various purposes for which standards are used will be undermined if they are not continually reviewed. Staff will also pay little attention to standards if they do not reflect the current circumstances.

(b) An organization may have non-financial objectives relating to:
- the welfare of employees (e.g. health and safety, the provision of adequate social facilities);
- the environment (e.g. avoiding pollution);
- customer satisfaction (e.g. product/service quality, reliability, on-time delivery and a high quality after-sales service);
- support for community services;
- meeting statutory and regulatory requirements.

Various stakeholders have a non-financial interest in organizations. They include employees, customers, suppliers, competitors, government, regulatory authorities, tax authorities and special interest groups (e.g. environmental protection groups).

Question 18.32   (a) Material price $= (SP - AP)AQ = (AQ \times SP) - (AQ \times AP)$
$= (37\,250\,\text{kg} \times £10) - £345\,000 = £27\,500\text{F}$

Material usage $= (SQ - AQ)SP = (11\,500 \times 3\,\text{kg} = 34\,500\,\text{kg} - 37\,250)£10$
$= £27\,500\text{A}$

Wage rate $= (SP - AP)AH = (AH \times SP) - (AH \times AP)$
$= (45\,350 \times £6 = £272\,100) - £300\,000 = £27\,900\text{A}$

Labour efficiency $= (SH - AH)SP = (11\,500 \times 4\,\text{hours} = 46\,000\,\text{hours} -$
$45\,350\,\text{hours}) \times £6 = £3900\text{F}$

Reconciliation of original budget cost with actual cost

	(£)
Original budgeted total prime cost (12 000 × (£30 +£24))	648 000
Volume prime cost variance (500 units × £54)[a]	(27 000)
Flexed budget (11 500 units × £54)	621 000
Material price variance	27 500
Material usage variance	(27 500)
Wage rate variance	(27 900)
Labour efficiency variance	3 900
Actual prime cost	645 000

Note

[a] Normally cost variances are reconciled with the flexed budget. To reflect the fact that the question requires reconciliation with the original budget, a volume variance must be extracted representing the standard prime cost of the difference between actual and budgeted production.

(b) The wage rate variance indicates that labour was paid a higher rate than the planned rate whereas the labour efficiency indicates that labour was more efficient than the standard, resulting in less hours than those specified in the standard being required for actual production. The increase in wage rate may have increased motivation and thus labour efficiency.

Question 18.33

a) *Standard cost of output produced (18 000 units)*

	(£)
Direct materials	864 000
Direct labour	630 000
Variable production overhead	180 000
Fixed production overhead	900 000
	2 574 000

(b)

	Standard cost of output (£)	Variances (£)	Actual cost (£)
Direct materials	864 000		
Price variance[a]		76 000 (F)	
Usage variance[b]		48 000 (A)	
Actual cost			836 000
Direct labour	630 000		
Rate variance[c]		16 800 (A)	
Efficiency variance[d]		42 000 (F)	
Actual cost			604 800
Variable production overhead	180 000		
Expenditure variance[e]		4 000 (A)	
Efficiency variance[f]		12 000 (F)	
Actual cost			172 000
Fixed production overhead	900 000		
Expenditure variance[g]		30 000 (A)	
Volume variance[h]		100 000 (A)	
Actual cost			1 030 000
	2 574 000	68 800 (A)	2 642 800

Notes

[a] (Standard price − Actual price) × Actual quantity
(£12 − £836 000/76 000) × 76 000 = £76 000 (F)

[b] (Standard quantity − Actual quantity) × Standard price
(18 000 × 4 kg = 72 000 − 76 000) × £12 = £48 000 (A)

[c] (Standard rate − Actual rate) × Actual hours
(£7 − £604 800/84 000) × 84 000 = £16 800 (A)

[d] (Standard hours − Actual hours) × Standard rate
(18 000 × 5 hrs = 90 000 − 84 000) × £7 = £42 000 (F)

[e] (Actual hours × Standard rate) − Actual cost
(84 000 × £2 = £168 000 − £172 000 = £4000 (A)

[f] (Standard hours − Actual hours) × Standard rate
(18 000 × 5 hrs = 90 000 − 84 000) × £2 = £12 000 (F)

[g] Budgeted fixed overheads − Actual fixed overheads
(20 000 × £50 = £1 000 000 − £1 030 000) = £30 000 (A)

[h] (Actual output − Budgeted output) × Standard rate
(18 000 − 20 000) × £50 = £100 000 (A)

(c) The statement in (b) can be used to provide a detailed explanation as to why actual cost exceeded standard cost by £68 800 for the output achieved. The statement provides attention-directing information by highlighting those areas that require further investigation. Thus management can concentrate their scarce time on focusing on those areas that are not proceeding according to plan. By investigating variances, management can pinpoint inefficiencies and take steps to avoid them re-occurring. Alternatively, the investigation may indicate that the current standards are inappropriate and need changing to take account of the changed circumstances. This may result in an alteration in the plans or more up-to-date information for decision-making.

Question 18.34

(a) Budgeted contribution = Standard unit contribution (£1.99 – £1.39 = £0.60) × 50 000 = £30 000

Actual contribution = £96 480 – (£58 450 + £6800 + £3250) = £27 980

(b) Sales margin price = (Actual price – Standard price) × Actual sales volume
= Actual sales (£96 480) – Actual sales volume (49 700) × Standard price (£1.99)
= £2423A (note that the same answer would be obtained using contribution margins in the above formula)

Sales margin volume = (Actual volume – Budgeted volume) × Standard unit contribution
= (49 700 – 50 000) × £0.60 = £180A

Ingredients price = (SP – AP)AQ = (AQ × SP) – (AQ × AP)
= (55 000 × £1.18/1.08 = £60 093) – £58 450 = £1643F

Ingredients usage = (SQ – AQ)SP = (49 700 × 1.08 = 53 676 – 55 000) £1.18/1.08
= £1447A

Wage rate = (SP – AP)AH = (AH × SP) – (AH × AP)
= (1200 × £6 [1] = £7200) – £6800 = £400F

Labour efficiency = (SH – AH)SP = (49 700 × 1.5 minutes = 1242.5 hours –1200hours) × £6 = £255F

Variable conversion price = (SP – AP)AH = (AH × SP) – (AH × AP)
= (1200 × £2.40 [2] = £2880 – £3250 = £370A

Variable conversion efficiency = (SH – AH)SP = (49 700 × 1.5 minutes = 1242.5 hours –1200 hours) × £2.40 = £102F

Notes

[1] Actual price paid for labour = £0.15/1.5 minutes = £0.10 per minute = £6 per hour

[2] Actual variable overhead price = £0.06/1.5 minutes = £0.04 per minute = £2.40 per hour

Reconciliation statement

				(£)	
Budgeted contribution				30 000	
Sales volume contribution variance				180	(A)
Standard contribution on actual sales				29 820	
Sales price variance				2423	(A)
				27 397	

Cost variances		A	F		
Ingredients:	Price		1643		
	Usage	1447			
Labour	Rate		400		
	Efficiency		255		
Conversion cost	Expenditure	370			
	Efficiency		102		
Total		1817	2400	583	(F)
Actual contribution				27 980	

(c) The answer should point out that in any environment fixed overhead volume variances are not particularly helpful for cost control (see 'Volume variance' in Chapter 18 for an explanation of this point). Therefore, a marginal costing variance analysis approach is preferable for most types of environment.

Question 18.35

(a) Because a JIT system is used and production is made to order it is assumed that production equals sales. The difference between marginal and absorption costing sales volume variances is that the former is valued at contribution margins and the latter at profit margins. Thus the difference in margins is due to fixed overheads being assigned to products with the absorption costing system. The budgeted fixed overhead per unit for each product is derived from dividing the difference between marginal costing and absorption costing sales volume variances by the difference between budgeted and actual production.

Alpha = (£24 000 – £18 000)/600 units = £10 per unit
Beta = (£14 175 – £11 925)/300 units = £7.50

Budgeted fixed overheads = Budgeted production × budgeted fixed overhead rate

Alpha = 2400 × £10 = £24 000
Beta = 1800 × £7.50 = £13 500
£37 500

(b) Alpha variable cost = £40 so budgeted selling price = £80 (£40 + £40 × 100%)
Beta variable cost = £47.25 so budgeted selling price = £94.50 (£47.25 + £47.25 × 100%)

Budgeted profit

	(£)
Alpha contribution (2400 × (£80 – £40))	96 000
Beta contribution (1800 × (£94.50 – £47.25))	85 050
Budgeted contribution	181 050
Less fixed overheads	37 500
Budgeted profit	143 550

(c) The £6000 adverse selling price variance is derived from multiplying the difference between the actual selling price and the budgeted price by the actual quantity. In other words, the price variance per unit is derived from dividing the total price variance by the actual sales volume. Therefore the Alpha price variance is £2 per unit adverse (£6000A/3000 units) and Beta is £3 favourable (£4500F/1500units).

Actual profit calculation

	(£)
Sales (Alpha 3000 units at (£80 – £2))	234 000
(Beta 1500 units at (£94.50 + £3))	146 250
Total sales	380 250
Actual costs	277 780
Actual profit	102 470

(d) The labour, material and variable overhead variances have been computed using the same approaches as applied to questions 18.32–18.34. Therefore the variance formulae are not repeated here. For the formulae used to calculate the fixed overhead volume efficiency and capacity variances, you should refer to Chapter 18.

Price/expenditure variances

		(£)	
Direct material:			
X	(10 150 × £5) – £48 890	1860	(F)
Y	(5290 × £8) – £44 760	2440	(A)
Z	(2790 × £10) – £29 850	1950	(A)
Direct labour:	(9140 × £7) – £67 980	4000	(A)
Variable overhead:	(8350 × £1.50) – £14 300	1775	(A)
Fixed overhead:	£37 500 – £72 000	34 500	(A)

Usage/efficiency variances

	(£)		
Direct material:			
X	{[(2 × 3000) + (2.5 × 1500)] – 10 150} @£5	2000	(A)
Y	{[(1 × 3000) + (1.5 × 1500)] – 5290} @£8	320	(A)
Z	{[(0.5 × 3000) + (1 × 1500)] – 2790} @£10	2100	(F)
Direct labour:	Idle time (9140 – 8350) @£7	5530	(A)
	Efficiency{[(2 × 3000) +(1.5 × 1500)] – 8350} @£7	700	(A)
Variable overhead:	{[(2 × 3000) + (1.5 × 1500)] – 8350} @£1.50	150	(A)
Fixed overhead efficiency:	{[(2 × 3000) + (1.5 × 1500)] – 8350} @£5	500	(A)
Fixed overhead capacity:	{[(2 × 2400) + (1.5 × 1800)] – 8350} @£5	4250	(A)

Reconcilliation statement for October 2002

	(£)	(£)	(£)	
Budgeted profit			143 550	
Sales volume variance			6075	(F)
Standard profit on actual sales			149 625	
Selling price variance			1500	(A)
			148 125	
Cost variances:	(A)	(F)		
Price/expenditure:				
Material X		1860		
Material Y	2440			
Material Z	1950			
Direct labour	4000			
Variable overhead	1775			
Fixed overhead	34 500			

Usage/efficiency:

Material X	2000		
Material Y	320		
Material Z		2100	
Labour idle time	5530		
Labour efficiency	700		
Variable overhead	150		
Fixed overhead:			
Efficiency	500		
Capacity		4250	
Total	53 865	8210	45 655 (A)
Actual profit			102 470

(e) Mix and yield variances are appropriate to only those processes where managers have the discretion to vary the mix of materials and deviate from engineered input–output relationships. In this question the materials input consists of metres, litres and kilogrammes which suggests that they are likely to be different and cannot be mixed. Managerial discretion to mix the material is more likely to occur where all of the materials are of a similar type, such as litres of different types of liquids. In addition, yield variances are more likely to be applicable where there is a loss inherent in the process, but managers can influence this loss by a more effective mix or usage of the materials input.

Question 18.36

(a) Wage rate variance $= (SP - AP)AH = (SP \times AH) - (AP \times AH)$
$= (£5 \times 53 \text{ workers} \times 13 \text{ weeks} \times 40 \text{ hrs}) - £138\,500$
$= £700A$

Labour efficiency $= (SH - AH)SP$
SH (Standard hours) $= (35\,000 \times 0.4 \text{ hrs}) + (25\,000 \times 0.56 \text{ hrs})$
$= 28\,000$
AH (Actual hours) $= 53 \text{ workers} \times 13 \text{ weeks} \times 40 \text{ hrs} = 27\,560$
Variance $= (28\,000 - 27\,560) \times £5 = £2200A$

(b) Material price variance $= (SP - AP)AQ$
$= (AQ \times SP) - (AQ \times AP)$
£430F (given) $= 47\,000\,SP - £85\,110$
SP (Standard price) $= \dfrac{£430 + 85\,110}{47\,000}$
$= £1.82$

Material usage variance $= (SQ - AQ)SP$
$= (SQ \times SP) - (AQ \times SP)$
£320.32A (given) $= £1.82\,SQ - (33\,426 \times £1.82)$
$- £320.32A$ $= £1.82\,SQ - £60\,835.32$
£1.82 SQ $= £60\,515$
SQ $= £60\,515/£1.82 = 33\,250$
Note that SQ $=$ Actual production (35 000 units) $\times$ Standard usage
Therefore 35 000 $\times$ Standard usage $= 33\,250$
Standard usage $= 33\,250/35\,000$
$= 0.95$ kg per unit of component X

(c) For the answer to this question you should refer to the detailed illustration of the budget process shown in Chapter 15. In particular, the answer should indicate that if sales are the limiting factor the production budget should be linked to the sales budget. Once the production budget has been established for the two components, the production quantity of each component multiplied by the standard usage of material A per unit of component output determines the required quantity of material to meet the production requirements. The budgeted purchase quantity of material A consists of the quantity to meet the production usage requirements plus or minus an adjustment to take account of any planned change in the level of raw material stock.

Question 18.37

(a) (i) *Sales margin volume variance (Marginal costing):*
(Actual volume − Budgeted volume) × Standard contribution margin per unit
(9500 − 10 000) × Standard margin (SM) = £7500A
500 SM = 7500
Standard margin = £15

(ii) *Sales margin volume variance (Absorption costing):*
(Actual volume − Budgeted volume) × Standard profit margin per unit
(9500 − 10 000) × Standard margin (SM) = £4500A
500 SM = £4500
Standard profit margin per unit = £9

(iii) *Fixed overhead volume variance:*
(Actual production − Budgeted production) × Standard rate
(9700 − 10 000) × Standard rate = £1800A
Standard fixed overhead rate per unit = £6
Budgeted fixed overheads = 10 000 units × £6 = £60 000
Fixed overhead expenditure variance = £2500F
Actual fixed overheads (£60 000 − £2500) = £57 500

(b) Absorption costing unitizes fixed overheads and treats them as product costs whereas marginal costing does not charge fixed overheads to products. Instead, the total amount of fixed overheads is charged as an expense (period cost) for the period. A fixed overhead volume variance only occurs with an absorption costing system. Because marginal costing does not unitize fixed costs product margins are expressed as contribution margins whereas absorption costing expresses margins as profit margins. For a more detailed answer you should refer to the section on standard absorption costing in Chapter 18.

(c) See the section on volume variance in Chapter 18 for the answer to this question.

(d) See an illustration of ABC and traditional product costing systems in Chapter 10 and the section on activity-based cost management in Chapter 22 for the answer to this question.

Question 18.38

(a) (i)

$$\text{Production volume ratio} = \frac{\text{Standard hours of actual output}}{\text{Budgeted hours of output}} \times 100$$

$$= \frac{(400 \times 5) + (300 \times 2.5) + (140 \times 1)}{(400 \times 5) + (400 \times 2.5) + (100 \times 1)} \times 100 = 93.2\%$$

$$\text{Production efficiency ratio} = \frac{\text{Standard hours of output}}{\text{Actual hours worked}} \times 100$$

$$= \frac{(400 \times 5) + (300 \times 2.5) + (140 \times 1)}{2800 \text{ hrs}} \times 100 = 103.2\%$$

(ii) The production volume ratio shows the relationship between the actual output and budgeted output (both measured in standard hours). Therefore the ratio shows the extent to which the budgeted output was met. The fixed overhead volume variance represents the monetary measure equivalent of the production volume ratio.

The production efficiency ratio represents a labour efficiency measure. During the period 2890 hours of output were produced but only 2800 hours were used thus resulting in an efficiency level in excess of 100%. The monetary equivalent variances of this ratio are the labour efficiency, volume efficiency and variable overhead efficiency variances.

(b) Practical capacity is the level of capacity at which a department can normally be expected to operate. It includes an allowance for unavoidable losses in capacity arising from such factors as planned machine maintenance and set-ups.

Budgeted capacity represents the capacity level which is planned to meet the budgeted output for the period. It is based on the budgeted level of efficiency for the period.

Full capacity represents the level of output that could be achieved without any losses or inefficiencies occurring.

Standard costing 2: Further aspects

Solutions to Chapter 19 questions

Question 19.28

(a) The management accountant should consider the following factors when deciding whether or not to investigate variances:

  (i) *The size of the variances*: This may be expressed in terms of percentage variation from standard or budget. Alternatively, statistical techniques can be used to determine the probability of the variance occurring when it is under control. The size of the variance indicates the likelihood that the variance is due to an assignable cause.

  (ii) *Costs and benefits of investigation*: The management accountant should assess whether the costs of investigation are less than the benefits that are expected to result from the investigation.

  (iii) *Nature of the standard*: Are expected or ideal standards used? If ideal standards are used then investigation of the variances is unlikely to result in the variances being eliminated.

  (iv) *Cumulative variances*: A variance showing an increase in size over time may justify an investigation even when the variance for the particular period is not significant. Alternatively, a variance that is significant for a particular period but that is decreasing over time may be under control.

  (v) *Validity of standard or budget*: The validity of the standard will help the accountant to gauge the significance of the variance. A price variance in times of rapidly rising prices is unlikely to be due to an assignable cause.

(b) The management accountant can take the following action to improve the chances of achieving positive results from investigating variances:

  (i) *Speedy identification and reporting of variances*: Significant delays between the occurrence of a variance and its notification to managers will limit the degree of control that managers can achieve. The sooner a variance is identified, the sooner it can be investigated and acted upon.

  (ii) *Analysis of variances*: The accountant should provide clues as to the possible reasons for the variances by pinpointing where the variances have arisen. For example, the accountant might identify the reason for a direct material variance as being due to excessive usage of a certain material in a particular process. This should assist the responsibility manager in quickly identifying the cause of the excessive usage.

  (iii) *Statistical procedures*: Statistical procedures and quality control charts should be used so as to determine the probability that variances are due to an assignable cause. If managers are frequently required to investigate variances that are due to random variations then it is unlikely that they will give detailed attention to the investigation process. However, if the majority of variances reported are significant then managers will attach greater importance to the investigation process.

  (iv) *Develop a team effort approach*: The accountant should be seen by managers as supportive within the control process. If a team effort approach is developed then it is likely that managers will be more actively involved in the investigation process.

(a) The following problems might occur during periods of rapid inflation:

(a) The following problems might occur during periods of rapid inflation:

   (i) The standards will presumably include some assumptions about inflation. If this assumption is not clearly stated then it is difficult to determine how much of a price variance is due to inflation and how much is due to buying efficiency.

   (ii) Price indices tend to reflect average price changes. Consequently, it is difficult for a company to predict future costs and interpret variances if the specific rate of inflation for its inputs is considerably different from the general rate of inflation.

   (iii) Inflation may result in relative changes in the prices of inputs. Therefore standard mixes requiring different inputs may no longer be the most efficient mix.

   (iv) If standard prices are not adjusted then the efficiency variances will be understated.

   (v) The impact of inflation will have an immediate effect on cash flows, but some delay will occur before the full extent of the variances is ascertained. Therefore management may not respond quickly enough to pricing, output and sourcing decisions in order to effectively control cash flows.

   (vi) Sharp rises in prices will raise questions as to whether unadjusted standards can be used in the decision-making process (e.g. pricing decisions).

   (vii) Administrative work in maintaining up-to-date standards when prices are constantly changing.

(b) (i) When establishing standards, the inflation factor that has been assumed should be clearly stated so that variances can be analysed by price and efficiency changes.

   (ii) Internal indices of price changes could be maintained for cost items that do not move in line with the general rate of inflation.

   (iii) Variances should be analysed by their forecasting and operational elements as indicated in Chapter 19.

   (iv) Standard mixes should be established for a range of prices for the material inputs, and management should be prepared to implement changes in the mix immediately price changes dictate that a change is necessary.

(a) The sales volume variance is the difference between budgeted sales volume and actual sales volume. It can be valued at the sales revenue per unit sold, contribution margin per unit sold or the profit margin per unit sold. For an explanation of the weaknesses arising from valuing the variance using sales revenues see 'Sales variances' in Chapter 18. It is preferable to value variances at the unit contribution margin. This is because deviations from budgeted sales will result in profit changing by the amount of the unit contribution multiplied by sales volume, assuming all other factors remain unchanged. Profit margins are derived after deducting unit fixed overheads from the contribution per unit. However, in the short term, fixed overheads will remain unchanged, so changes in sales volume will not result in profit changing by the change sales volume multiplied by the profit margin per unit. As indicated above, profit will be a function of sales volume multiplied by the contribution per unit.

(b) The principle of separating variances into the planning and operational variances is explained in the section on ex post variance analysis in Chapter 19. Note that in this section the terms 'efficiency' or 'controllable variances' are used to describe operational variances. The principles described in this section can be applied to sales price variances. For example, if the original budgeted selling price was £100 and the actual price was £110 the conventional method would report a price variance of £10 per unit sold. However, if the ex post efficient market price for the product is £115, it should represent the revised standard and the price variance can be separated into a favourable planning variance of £15 (£115 – £100) and an unfavourable operational price efficiency variance of £5 (£110 – £115). Future planning should be based on using the £115 standard since it reflects the most up to date standard, and investigations should be made as to why the actual selling price was less than the ex post expected market price.

Question 19.29

Question 19.30

Question 19.31

(a) Because standard costs represent future target costs based on the elimination of avoidable inefficiencies they are preferable for decision-making to estimates based on an adjustment of past costs which may incorporate inefficiencies. For example, where cost-plus pricing is used as an input to pricing decisions, standard costs provide more appropriate information because efficient competitors will also base any price bids on costs where efficiencies have been eliminated. Alternatively, where competitive market prices exist for a firm's products so that they are price takers, it will be necessary for such firms to periodically review the profitability of their products to identify possible loss making activities. In such circumstances product costs for input into the profitability analysis should be extracted from a database of standard costs reviewed periodically. A periodic cost audit should be undertaken to provide a strategic review of the standard costs and profitability of a firm's products. The review provides attention-directing information for signalling the need for more detailed studies to make cost reduction, discontinuation, redesign and outsourcing decisions. Standard costs thus provide the basis for such decisions and avoid the need for the detailed tracking of costs.

Standard costing can also be used with target costing for decision-making. Target costs can be compared with costs derived from the standard costing system to identify the estimated cost. If the estimated/standard cost exceeds the target cost, ways are investigated of driving down the estimated cost to the target cost. You should refer to Chapter 22 for a detailed explanation of target costing.

Finally, trends in variances can be monitored to identify the need for actions for improvement and changes in product design, production methods, etc. Situations where there has been a lack of improvement in the variances can be investigated with a view to introducing alternative designs and improvements in production methods.

(b) See 'The effect of the level of budget difficulty on motivation and performance' in Chapter 16 for the answer to this question. In addition, the following points should be included in the answer.

1 An over-emphasis on achieving standards and reporting variances can have dysfunctional effects. For example, purchasing officers might strive to achieve favourable price variances by purchasing inferior materials or focusing on prices at the expense of reliable and on-time deliveries and generally not fostering long-term supplier relationships.

2 Excessive focus on labour efficiency variances may encourage large production batches to reduce idle and set-up time but such savings may be outweighed by the increased costs associated with the higher stocks and work in progress. Also favourable volume variances may be achieved by producing in excess of demand and maintaining excessive stocks.

3 If overheads are absorbed on the basis of direct labour this can result in an over-emphasis on direct labour efficiency. However, improvements in direct labour will not cause overheads to reduce where there is only a weak cause-and-effect relationship between direct labour hours and overhead spending.

For a more detailed discussion of the above points you should refer to 'Criticisms of standard costing' in Chapter 19.

Question 19.32

(a) *Variance analysis*
Material price = (standard price − actual price) × actual purchases

X	= (£20 − £20.50) × 9000
	= £4500A
Y	= (£6 − £5.50) × 5000
	= £2500F

Material usage = (standard usage − actual usage) × standard price

X	= (800 × 10 kg − 7800 kg) × £20
	= £4000F

$$Y \quad = (800 \times 5 \text{ litres} - 4300 \text{ litres}) \times £6$$
$$= £1800A$$

Wage rate = [standard rate (£6) − actual rate (£24 150/4200)]
$$\times \text{ actual hours (4200)}$$
$$= £1050F$$

Labour efficiency = [standard hours (800 × 5 hrs) − actual hours (4200)]
$$\times \text{ standard rate (£6)}$$
$$= £1200A$$

Fixed overhead expenditure = budgeted cost (10 800/12 × £50)
$$- \text{ actual cost (£47 000)}$$
$$= £2000A$$

Volume efficiency = [standard hours (800 × 5 hrs) − actual hours (4200)]
$$\times \text{ (£50/5 hours)}$$
$$= £2000A$$

Volume capacity[a] = [actual hours (4200) − budgeted hours[b] (4500)]
$$\times \text{ FOAR (£50/5 hours)}$$
$$= £3000A$$

Notes
[a] Note that the CIMA Terminology (at the time of setting the examination) described the volume variance as being equivalent to the volume capacity variance.
[b] Budgeted hours = monthly budgeted output (10 800/12) × 5 hrs

(b)

Stores control

	(£)		(£)
K Ltd: X (AQ × SP)	180 000	WIP: (SQ × SP)	160 000
C Ltd: Y (AQ × SP)	30 000	WIP: (SQ × SP)	24 000
Material usage variance (X)	4 000	Material usage variance (Y)	1 800
		Balance	28 200
	£214 000		£214 000

Wages control account

	(£)		(£)
Cash	20 150	Wages owing b/fwd	6 000
PAYE and NI	5 000	Labour efficiency	1 200
Accrued wages	5 000	WIP (SQ × SP)	24 000
Wage rate variance	1 050		
	£31 200		£31 200

WIP control account

	(£)		(£)
Stores control: X	160 000	Finished goods control a/c	248 000
Y	24 000		
Wages control	24 000		
Fixed overhead	40 000		
	£248 000		£248 000

Fixed overhead control

	(£)		(£)
Expense creditors	33 000	WIP (SQ × SP)	40 000
Depreciation provision	14 000	Expenditure variance	2 000
		Efficiency variance	2 000
		Capacity variance	3 000
	£47 000		£47 000

Finished goods control

	(£)		(£)
WIP control	£248 000	Cost of sales	£248 000

Cost of sales

	(£)		(£)
Finished goods control	£248 000	Profit and loss (P/L)	£248 000

Material price variance

	(£)		(£)
K Ltd: X	4500	C Ltd: Y	2500
		P/L	2000
	£4500		£4500

Material usage variance

	(£)		(£)
Stores control: Y	1800	Stores control: X	4000
P/L	2200		
	£4000		£4000

Labour rate variance

	(£)		(£)
P/L	£1050	Wages control	£1050

Labour efficiency variance

	(£)		(£)
Wages control	1200	P/L	1200

Fixed overhead expenditure variance

	(£)		(£)
Overhead control	2000	P/L	2000

Fixed overhead efficiency variance

	(£)		(£)
Overhead control	2000	P/L	2000

Fixed overhead capacity variance

	(£)		(£)
Overhead control	£3000	P/L	£3000

Sales

	(£)		(£)
P/L	320 000	Debtors	320 000

K Limited

		(£)
	Stores control	180 000
	Price variance account	4 500

C plc

	(£)		(£)
Price variance account	2500	Stores control	30 000

Expense creditors

		(£)
	Fixed overhead control	33 000

Provision for depreciation

		(£)
	Fixed overhead control	14 000

Profit and loss account

	(£)	(£)	(£)
Sales			320 000
Cost of sales			248 000
			72 000
Variances	(F)	(A)	
Material price	—	2 000	
usage	2200	—	
Labour rate	1050	—	
efficiency	—	1 200	
Overhead expenditure	–	2 000	
efficiency	–	2 000	
volume	–	3 000	
	3250	10 200	6 950
Gross profit			65 050

(c) The difference of £250 in the accounts is due to the fact that the material price variance has been calculated on purchases (instead of usage) and written off as a period cost. In the question the raw material stocks are recorded at actual cost, and therefore the £250 is included in the stock valuation and will be recorded as an expense next period.

Question 19.33

(a) *Cost variance calculations*

Material price:

	(£)	(£)
(SP − AP) × AQ		
A(£0.30 − £0.20) × 8000		800 F
B(0.70 − £0.80) × 5000		500 A

Material mix:
(actual wage in standard proportions − actual wage in actual proportions) × SP

A (6500 − 8000) × £0.30	450 A	
B (6500 − 5000) × £0.70	1050 F	600 F

Material yield:[a]
(actual yield − standard yield) × SC per unit of output

(12 000 − 13 000) × £0.50		500 A

Wage rate:
(SR − AR) × AH

Skilled (£3 − £2.95) × 6000		300 F
Semi-skilled (£2.50 − £2.60) × 3150		315 A

Labour mix:[b]
(AQ in standard and proportions − AQ in actual proportions) × SR

Skilled (5799 − 6000) × £3	603 A	
Semi-skilled (3351 − 3150) × £2.50	503 F	100 A

Labour productivity:[c]
(SQ in standard and proportions − AQ in standard proportions) × SR

Skilled (5400 − 5799) × £3	1197A	
Semi-skilled (3120 − 3351) × £2.50	578A	1775A

Fixed overhead spending:
BC − AC

£10 000 − £9010		990F

Variable overhead spending:
flexed budgeted − AC

12 000 × £0.50 = 6000 − £7500		1500A

Fixed overhead volume:
(actual production − budgeted production) × FOAR

(12 000 − 10 000) × £1		2000F
Total cost variances		Nil

Sales margin variance calculations

Sales volume variance: (£)

  (actual sales volume − budgeted volume)

  × standard margin

  $(11\,000 - 10\,000) \times £1$ 1000F

Sales margin price variance:

  (actual selling price − budgeted selling price)

  × actual sales volume

  $(£5 - £5) \times 7000 = 0$

  $(£4.75 - £5) \times 4000 = 1000A$ 1000A

Total sales variances   nil

The question requires the calculation of the material usage variance and the labour efficiency variance. These variances are calculated as follows:

$$\text{direct material usage variance} = \text{mix variance} + \text{yield variance}$$
$$= £600F + £500A = £100F$$

$$\text{labour efficiency variance} = \text{mix variance} + \text{productivity variance}$$

			(£)
Skilled	= £603A + £1197A	=	1800A
Unskilled	= £503F + £578A	=	75A
			1875A

Reconciliation of actual and budgeted profit

The total of the cost variances and the sales variances are zero. Therefore actual profit equals budgeted profit.

Notes

[a] Budgeted usage is 1 kg of materials for 1 unit of output. The standard yield for an input of 13 000 kg is therefore 13 000 units.

The standard material cost per unit of output is:

		(£)
A $(0.5 \times £0.30) =$		0.15
B $(0.5 \times £0.70) =$		0.35
		0.50

[b]
$$\text{Skilled} = 9150 \text{ hrs} \times 4500/7100 = 5799 \text{ hrs}$$
$$\text{Semi-skilled} = 9150 \text{ hrs} \times 2600/7100 = 3351 \text{ hrs}$$

[c] The standard labour quantity is 0.45 skilled hours and 0.26 unskilled hours for each unit of output. For an output of 12 000 units the standard labour hours are:

$$\text{skilled} = 5400 \;(12\,000 \times 0.45 \text{ hrs})$$
$$\text{semi-skilled} = 3120 \;(12\,000 \times 0.26 \text{ hrs})$$

(b) The sales volume variance shows the effect on profit from sales volume being in excess of budget (assuming standard costs remain unchanged). The adverse sales price variance of £1000 indicates the lost profits from selling below the standard price. However, the reduction in the selling price will be partly accounted for by the increase in sales volume. An ex-post budget comparison should be used. For example, a revised target for sales that could have been obtained at the actual selling prices should be used to calculate the volume variance.

The price paid for material A is less than standard and the price paid for B is above standard. This might explain why the company has substituted material A for B during the period. The usage variance is £100 favourable, but £600 of this is due to the change in the materials mix. The difference of £500 represents the excess wage when the mix variance is not taken into account. The analysis does not indicate whether the excess usage is due to using a non-standard mix or to inefficient usage.

The wage rate variances arise because the skilled rate is below standard but the semi-skilled rate is above the standard. There is a significant adverse labour efficiency variance, which should be investigated. The mix and productivity variances are unlikely to provide any helpful clues in explaining the adverse efficiency variance.

The fixed overhead volume variance arises because output is in excess of budget but this variance is not particularly useful (see 'Volume variance' in Chapter 18 for an explanation). The variable overhead expenditure variance is partly a spending variance and a usage variance, and on its own is not very meaningful. Any meaningful analysis of this variance requires a comparison of the actual expenditure with budget for each variable cost item.

Question 19.34

(a) It is assumed that the actual selling price for the period was the same as the budgeted selling price.

Sale volume variance = (Actual sales volume − Budgeted sales volume)
$$\times \text{ Standard contribution}$$
$$= (2850 - 2500) \times £78$$
$$= £27\,300\text{F}$$

Material price variance = (Standard price − Actual price) Actual quantity
$$= (£20 - £18) \times 12\,450$$
$$= £24\,900\text{F}$$

Material usage variance = (Standard quantity − Actual quantity) Standard price
$$= (2850 \times 4\,\text{kg} = 11\,400 - 12\,450) \times £20$$
$$= £21\,000\text{A}$$

Wage rate variance = (Standard rate − Actual rate) Actual hours
$$= (£7 - £8) \times 18\,800$$
$$= £18\,800\text{A}$$

Labour efficiency variance = (Standard hour − Actual hours) Standard rate
$$= (2850 \times 6\,\text{hrs} = 17\,100\,\text{hrs} - 18\,800\,\text{hrs}) \times £7$$
$$= £11\,900\text{A}$$

Reconciliation statement

	(£)	(£)
Budget contribution		195 000
Sales volume variance	27 300F	
Sales price variance	−	
		27 300F
Material usage variance	21 000A	
Material price variance	24 900F	
		3 900F

	Wage rate variance		18 800A	
	Labour efficiency variance		11 900A	30 700A
	Actual contribution			195 500

(b) (i) *Original standard*

			(£)
Materials	2500 × 4 kg × £20	=	200 000
Labour	2500 × 6 hrs × £7	=	105 000
			305 000
Sales	2500 × £200	=	500 000
Contribution			195 000

(ii) *Revised ex post standard*

			(£)
Materials	2500 × 4.5 kg × £16.50	=	185 625
Labour	2500 × 6 hrs × £6.50	=	97 500
			283 125
Sales	2500 × £200	=	500 000
Contribution			216 875

(iii) *Actual*

			(£)
Materials	12 450 kg × £18	=	224 100
Labour	18 800 hrs × £8	=	150 400
			374 500
Sales	2850 × £200	=	570 000
Contribution			195 500

The total variances consist of a favourable planning variance of £21 875 (£216 875 − £195 000) and an adverse operational variance of £21 375 (£216 875 − £195 500). The analysis of these variances is shown below.

Planning variances (1 − 2)	(£)	(£)
Material usage[a] (2500 × 0.5 kg × £20)	25 000A	
Material price[a] (£20 − £16.50) × (2500 × 4 kg)	35 000F	
Joint price/quantity variance		
(2500 × 0.50 kg) × (£20 − £16.50)	4 375F	
		14 375F
Wage rate (2500 × 6 hrs × £0.50)		7 500F
		21 875F

Operational variances		
Material usage		
(2850 × 4.5 kg = 12 825 kg − 12 450) £16.50	6 187.50F	
Material price (£16.50 − £18) × 12 450 kg	18 675.00A	
		12 487.50A
Labour efficiency		
(2850 × 6 hrs = 17 100 hrs − 18 800) × £6.50	11 050.00A	
Wage rate (£6.50 − £8) × 18 800 hrs	28 200.00A	
		39 250.00A
Sales volume (350 units at £86.75 revised unit contribution[b])		30 362.50F
		21 375.00A

[a] It is questionable whether it is meaningful to analyse the materials planning variance into its price and quantity elements because of the joint price/quantity variance. An alternative answer would be to present only the total materials planning variance of £14 375 (£200 000 − £185 625).

[b] Operational variances should be valued at the ex-post standard. The ex post unit contribution is £200 selling price − (6 hrs × £6.50 labour) − 4.5 kg × £16.50 materials) = £86.75.

Reconciliation statement

	(£)	(£)
Budgeted contribution		195 000
Planning variances:		
Materials	14 375F	
Wage rate	7 500F	
		21 875.00F
Operational variances		
Materials usage	6 187.50F	
Materials price	18 675.00A	
		12 487.50A
Labour efficiency	11 050A	
Wage rate	28 200A	
		39 250.00A
Sales volume		30 362.50F
Actual contribution		195 500.00

(c) The answer to this question should explain the meaning of planning and operational variances and why it is preferable to analyse the variances into their planning and operational elements. In particular, the answer should explain why the conventional approach reports an adverse material usage variance and a favourable price variance whereas the ex-post approach highlights a favourable usage and an adverse price variance.

Question 19.35

(a) The question relates to the role of standard costing in a modern manufacturing environment. For the answer to this question see 'The future role of standard costing' and 'The role of standard costing when ABC has been implemented' in Chapter 19.

(b) The expenditure variance is the difference between the budgeted fixed overheads (£100 000) and the actual fixed overheads (£102 300). For more detailed cost control the variance should be disaggregated by the individual categories of fixed overheads.

The budgeted capacity measured in direct labour hours of input were 10 000 but actual hours were 11 000. The extra hours of input should have enabled an extra 1000 hours of overheads to be absorbed at a budgeted rate of £10 per hour. Therefore a favourable variance of £10 000 is reported.

Budgeted standard hours for each unit of output is 0.10 hours (10 000 hours/100 000 units). Therefore for an actual output of 105 000 units the target hours are 10 500 (105 000 × 0.10 hours) but the actual hours were 11 000. This has resulted in a failure to recover £5000 overheads (500 hours × £10).

For a more detailed discussion of the above variances and a discussion of their usefulness you should refer to the sections in Chapter 18 on fixed overhead expenditure, volume capacity and volume efficiency variances.

(c) (i) It is assumed that material handling expenditure fluctuates in the longer term with the number of orders executed. The variance has been derived adopting a flexible budgeting approach using the number of orders as the cost driver as follows:

Budgeted materials handling overheads (5500 orders at a budgeted rate of £30 000/5 000) £33 000

Actual materials handling expenditure £30 800

Variance (favourable) £2 200

The variance therefore indicates that the actual expenditure is £2200 less than expected for the actual level of activity. The same approach is used to calculate the expenditure variance for set ups:

Budgeted set up overheads (2600 production runs at a budgeted rate of £70 000/2800) £65 000

Actual set up expenditure £71 500

Variance (adverse) £6 500

The variance indicates that the actual expenditure is £6500 more than expected for the actual level of activity.

The efficiency variances compare the standard/budgeted cost driver usage for the actual output with the actual usage valued at the standard cost driver rate. The material handling overhead efficiency variance is calculated as follows:

Standard usage for actual output (5000/100 000 × 105 000 units = 5250 orders)

Actual number of orders (5500)

Adverse variance = 250 orders at £30 000/5000 per order = £1500 A

The variance indicates that 250 orders more than expected were executed at £6 per order.

The calculation of the set up efficiency variance is as follows:

Standard usage for actual output (2800/100 000 × 105 000 units = 2940 set ups)

Actual number of set ups (2600)

Favourable variance = 340 set ups at £70 000/2800 = £8500

The variance indicates that 340 less set ups than expected were required at £25 per set up.

(c) (ii) Presumably the company has introduced ABC because there was no cause-and-effect relationship between the previous cost drivers used by the traditional cost system and the overhead expenditure. Hence there is a need for the standard costing system to support the decision-making and cost management applications which would have been instrumental in introducing ABC. Failure to change the standard costing system to be consistent with the ABC system would have undermined the ABC system. Where reported variances prompt actions such as decisions to change the production processes/methods it is important that decisions are based on cost driver rates that are the causes of the overheads being incurred.

For further discussion of aspects relating to (c) (i) and (c) (ii) you should refer to 'The role of standard costing when ABC has been implemented' in Chapter 19.

(a) (i) (£) **Question 19.36**

Material price variance:

(standard price − actual price) × actual quantity

[£0.05 − (£45/1000)] × 105 000 525F

Material usage variance:

(standard quantity − actual quantity) × standard price

(100 000 − 105 000) × £0.05 250A

Total variance 275F

(ii)

	Dr (£)	Cr (£)
Dr Stores ledger control account (AQ × SP)	5250	
Cr Creditors control account (AQ × AP)		4725
Cr Material price variance account		525
Dr Work in progress (SQ × SP)	5000	
Dr Material usage variance account	250	
Cr Stores ledger control account (AQ × SP)		5250

(iii) On the basis of the above calculations, the buyer would receive a bonus of £52.50 (10% × £525) and the production manager would not receive any bonus. It could be argued that the joint price/usage variance should be separated if the variances are to be used as the basis for calculating bonuses. (For a discussion of joint price/usage variances see Chapter 18.) The revised analysis would be as follows:

	(£)
Pure price variance:	
(standard price − actual price) × standard quantity	
(£0.05 − £0.045) × 100 000	500F
Joint price/usage variance:	
(standard price − actual price) × excess usage	
(£0.05 − £0.045) × 5000	25F

Buyer's viewpoint

At the purchasing stage the buyer can influence both quality and price. Consequently, the buyer can obtain favourable price variances by purchasing inferior quality materials at less than standard price. The adverse effects in terms of excess usage, because of the purchase of inferior quality of materials, are passed on to the production manager and the buyer gains from the price reduction. Indeed, if the joint price/usage is not isolated (see above), the buyer gains if production uses materials in excess of standard. Therefore the bonus system might encourage the buyer to purchase inferior quality materials, which results in an overall adverse *total* material cost variance and inferior product quality. In summary, the bonus system appears to be biased in favour of the buyer at the expense of the production manager.

Production manager's viewpoint

The isolation of the joint price/usage variance might encourage the buyer not to purchase inferior quality materials, and this will be to the production manager's advantage. Nevertheless, the problem of the control of material quality still exists. The production manager would need to ensure that the quality of material purchased is in line with the quality built into the standard. Therefore some monitoring device is necessary. If variations do occur, the quantity standard should be adjusted for the purpose of performance reporting and bonus assessment.

Company's viewpoint

The objective of the bonus system is to encourage goal congruence and increase motivation. Interdependencies exist between the two responsibility centres, and it is doubtful that the bonus system encourages goal congruence or improves motivation. If the quality of materials that can be purchased from the various suppliers does not vary then the adverse effects of the bonus system will be reduced. Nevertheless, interdependencies will still exist between the responsibility centres. One solution might be to base the bonuses of both managers on the *total* material cost variance. In addition, standards should be regularly reviewed and participation by both managers in setting the standards encouraged.

(b) (i) The minimum present value of expected savings that would have to be made in future months in order to justify making an investigation is where

$$IC + (P \times CC) = Px$$

where IC = investigation costs, P = probability that process is out of control, CC = correction cost, x = present value of expected savings if process is out of control

Therefore £50 + (0.5 × £100) = 0.5x
$$0.5x = £100$$
$$x = £200$$

Therefore the minimum present value of expected savings that would have to be made is £200.

(ii) The standard cost will probably represent the mean value, and random variations around the mean value can be expected to occur even when the process is under control. Therefore it is unlikely that the £500 variance will be eliminated completely, because a proportion of the variance simply reflects the randomness of the variables affecting the standard. If the process is found to be out of control, the corrective action will only confine variances to the normal acceptable range of standard outcomes. If the £500 is an extreme deviation from the standard then it is likely that the potential savings from investigation will be insignificant.

(iii) Applying the notation used in (i), the firm will be indifferent about whether to conduct an investigation when the expected savings resulting from correction are equal to the expected cost of correction. That is, where

$$IC + (P \times CC) = Px$$

if x = £600 then

$$50 + P \times 100 = P \times 600$$
$$500P = 50$$
$$P = 10\%$$

if x = 250 then

$$50 + P \times 100 = P \times 250$$
$$150P = 50$$
$$P = 33\tfrac{1}{3}\%$$

Divisional financial performance measures

Solutions to Chapter 20 questions

Question 20.25

(a) The following factors should be considered:

(i) *Definition of profit:* The question states that the measure should be used for performance measurement. It is therefore necessary to define 'controllable profit' for the companies. Clearly, apportionment of group headquarters expenditure should be excluded from the calculation of controllable profit. If investment decisions are made by the companies then depreciation should be included as a controllable expense. Otherwise, companies can increase controllable profit by substituting capital equipment for direct labour when this is not in the best interest of the group as a whole.

(ii) *Definition of capital employed:* There are many different definitions of capital employed, and it is important that the same basis of measurement be used for comparing the performance of the different companies. Capital employed might be defined as total assets or net assets. All assets that are controlled by the companies should be included in the valuation. If debtors are controlled by the companies but not included in the capital employed then there is a danger that managers might lengthen the credit period to increase sales even when this is not in the best interests of the group. The benefits from the increased credit period accrue to the companies, but the increased investment is not reflected in the capital employed.

(iii) *Valuation of capital employed:* Capital employed can be valued on an historical cost basis, or an alternative method such as replacement cost might be used. If historical cost is used then assets might be valued at written-down value or gross value. Both approaches can result in misleading comparisons. If written-down value is used then an asset that yields a constant profit will show an annual increase in ROCE because the written-down value will decline over the asset's life. Therefore those companies with old assets and low written-down values might incorrectly show higher ROCE calculations. For a more detailed discussion of this topic see 'The impact of depreciation' in Chapter 20.

(iv) *Alternative accounting methods:* For comparisons, it is important that the same accounting methods be applied to all companies within the group. For example, one company may capitalize major expense items such as advertising, lease rentals, and research and development expenditure, whereas another company might not capitalize these items. For example, if company A capitalizes lease payments and company B does not then the accounting treatment will result in the capital employed of company B being understated and consequently ROCE overstated.

(b) A single ROCE might not be an adequate measure because:

(i) Companies operate in different industries and a single ROCE measure might not give an adequate measure of performance. For example, if companies A and B have ROCEs of 20% and 10%, respectively, one might conclude that company A has produced the better performance. However, the industry ROCEs might be 25% for the industry in which A operates and 5% for the industry in which B operates. Relative to industry performance, company B has performed better than company A. The ROCE should therefore be compared with other companies and supplemented by other measures such as percentage market shares

(ii) Companies with a high existing ROCE might reject projects whose returns are in excess of the cost of capital but less than existing ROCE. Such companies might be reluctant to expand and be content with a high ROCE and low absolute profits. The ROCE should be supplemented with a measure of absolute profits (e.g. residual income) and details of investment in new projects. This would indicate whether or not the companies were restricting growth in order to preserve their existing high ROCE.

(iii) Concentration on short-run ROCE at the expense of long-run profitability. For an illustration of points that could be considered here see 'Addressing the dysfunctional consequences of short-term financial measures' in Chapter 20.

Question 20.26

(a) For cost control and performance measurement purposes it is necessary to measure performance at frequent intervals. Managers tend to be evaluated on short-term (monthly, quarterly or even yearly) performance measures such as residual income (RI) or return on investment (ROI). Such short-term performance measures focus only on the performance for the particular control period. If a great deal of stress is placed on managers meeting short-term performance measure targets, there is a danger that they will take action that will improve short-term performance but that will not maximize long-term profits. For example, by skimping on expenditure on advertising, customer services, maintenance, and training and staff development costs, it is possible to improve short-term performance. However, such actions may not maximize long-term profits.

Ideally, performance measures ought to be based on future results that can be expected from a manager's actions during a period. This would involve a comparison of the present value of future cash flows at the start and end of the period, and a manager's performance would be based on the increase in present value during the period. Such a system is not feasible, given the difficulty in predicting and measuring outcomes from current actions.

ROI and RI represent single summary measures of performance. It is virtually impossible to capture in summary financial measures all the variables that measure the success of a manager. It is therefore important that accountants broaden their reporting systems to include additional non-financial measures of performance that give clues to future outcomes from present actions.

It is probably impossible to design performance measures which will ensure that maximizing the short-run performance measure will also maximize long-term performance. Some steps, however, can be taken to improve the short-term performance measures so that they minimize the potential conflict. For example, during times of rising prices, short-term performance measures can be distorted if no attempt is made to adjust for the changing price levels. ROI has a number of deficiencies. In particular, it encourages managers to accept only those investments that are in excess of the current ROI, and this can lead to the rejection of profitable projects. Such actions can be reduced by replacing ROI with RI as the performance measure. However, merely changing from ROI to RI will not eliminate the short-run versus long-run conflicts.

(b) One suggestion that has been made to overcome the conflict between short-term and long-term measures is for accountants to broaden their reporting systems and include non-financial performance measures in the performance reports. For example, obtaining feedback from customers regarding the quality of service encourages managers not to skimp on reducing the quality of service in order to save costs in the short term. For a discussion of the potential contribution from including non-financial measures in the reporting system see 'Addressing the dysfunctional consequences of short-term financial performance measures' in Chapter 20.

Other suggestions have focused on refining the financial measures so that they will reduce the potential for conflict between actions that improve short-term performance at the expense of long-term performance. For a description of these suggestions see 'The impact of depreciation' and 'The effect of performance measurement on capital investment decisions' in Chapter 20.

Question 20.27

(a) Current budgeted ROCE = 330/(1500 − 720) + 375 = 330/1155   = 28.57%

(A) Profit − 8
Current assets − 30
Revised ROCE = 322/1125   = 28.62%

(B) Profit + 15
Current assets + 40
Revised ROCE = 345/1195   = 28.87%

(C) Loss on sale (60 WDV − 35 sale proceeds) = (25)
Loss of profits = (45)
Reduced depreciation = 60
Net impact on profits = (10)

Note that the above calculation assumes that the £45 000 profit contribution relates to profits before deduction of £60 000 depreciation. If the £45 000 profit is after deduction of depreciation, the £60 000 reduction in depreciation should not be included in the above calculation. It is assumed that capital employed will decline by £60 000 arising from the deletion of the £60 000 WDV of the asset. However, sale proceeds are £35 000, and it could be argued that this will increase capital employed. It is assumed that the £35 000 is remitted to group headquarters, and thus the overall impact of the transaction increases capital employed by £60 000. The revised ROCE is (330 − 10)/(1155 − 60) = 29.22%

(D) Profit (+52.5 − 36 depreciation) = + 16.5
Fixed assets (+ 4/5 × 180) = +144
Revised ROCE = 346.5/1299 = 26.67%

An alternative assumption is that capital employed would be reduced by a further £180 000 to reflect the cash payment for the asset. It is assumed in the above calculations that group headquarters provides the cash for acquiring the asset.

If divisional managers are evaluated on ROCE, the divisional manager would accept transactions A, B and C since they would result in an increase in ROCE. Transaction D would be rejected because it would result in a lower ROCE.

(b) (i) The evaluation should be based on NPV calculations in order to determine whether or not the non-routine transactions are in the best interests of the group as a whole. The NPV calculations are as follows:

Transaction	Year	Cash inflows (£000)	Cash outflows (£000)	Net cash flow (£000)	Discount factor (15%)	NPV (£000)
A	1	30	(8)	22	0.8696	19.131
	2–4		(8)	(8)	1.9854	(15.883)
						+3.248
B	1	15	(40)	(25)	0.8696	(21.74)
	2–4	15		15	1.9854	29.781
						+8.041
C	0	35		35	1.000	35.000
	1		(45)	(45)	0.8696	39.132

D	0		(180)	(180)	1.000	(180.000)
	1–5	52.5		52.5	3.352	175.980

$$-(4.020)$$

Transactions A and B yield positive NPVs and should be undertaken, while transactions C and D should be rejected.

There is goal congruence between G Ltd and GAP Group plc in respect of transactions A, B and D, but there is no goal congruence for transaction C.

(ii) The answer should not support the proposal to substitute a ROCE investment criterion in place of DCF techniques for appraising capital projects. In particular, the answer should stress that ROCE ignores the time value of money and the opportunity cost of capital. For a discussion of the limitations of ROCE of an investment appraisal technique see 'Accounting rate of return' in Chapter 13.

Question 20.28

(a) (i) Return on capital employed, residual income and economic value added (EVA) should be considered as potential measures. The superiority of EVA or residual income over return on capital employed (see Chapter 20) should be discussed. The objective is to select a performance measure that is consistent with the NPV rule. Residual income is the long-run counterpart of the NPV rule, but it may lead to decisions that are not consistent with the NPV rule if managers base their decisions on short-term measures. Problems occur with both return on capital employed and residual income in terms of bases that should be used for asset valuations. Current values are preferable to historical costs.

(ii) Ideally, market performance measures should indicate sales achievement in relation to the market, competitors and previous performance. Target market shares or unit sales should be established for each product or product range. Actual market shares and unit sales should be compared with targets and previous periods. Trends in market shares should be compared with overall market trends and product life cycles.

(iii) Productivity is concerned with the efficiency of converting physical inputs into physical outputs. Therefore the performance measure should be a physical one. Possible performance measures include output per direct labour hour and output per machine hour. Where divisions produce a variety of products, output could be expressed in standard hours. If monetary measures are used then changes in price levels should be eliminated. In addition to *total* measures of output for each division, performance measures should also be computed for individual products. Output measures should be compared with targets, previous periods and with other divisions.

(iv) Possible measures of the ability of divisions to offer up-to-date product ranges include:
1. number of new products launched in previous periods;
2. expenditure on product development.
Quality and reliability might be measured in terms of:
1. percentage of projects rejected;
2. comparison of target and actual market shares;
3. comparisons with competitors' products;
4. customer surveys.
The performance measures should be compared with previous periods, targets and competitors (if this is possible). Some of the measures may be difficult to express in quantitative terms, and a subjective evaluation may be necessary.

(v) Responsibility towards employees might be reflected by the following measures:

     1. rate of labour turnover;

     2. level of absenteeism.

Additional information is also necessary to explain the reasons for high labour turnover and absenteeism. Possible reasons might be identified by regularly undertaking attitude surveys on such issues as:

1. payment systems;

2. management style;

3. degree of participation;

4. working conditions.

Other proxy measures that might be used include:

1. number of promotions to different employee and management grades;

2. number of grievance procedures processed;

3. number of applications received per vacancy;

4. training expenditure per employee;

5. number of accidents reported per period.

The above measures should be compared with previous periods and targets.

(vi) It is extremely difficult to assess whether a firm is considered to be a socially responsible citizen within the community. Possible areas of inter-action between the firm and the local community include:

1. employment;

2. environmental effects;

3. involvement in community affairs;

4. provision of recreational and social facilities.

Surveys should be undertaken locally in order to assess the attitude of the population to each of the above areas. Possible quantitative measures include:

1. amount of financial support given to charities, sports organizations and educational establishments;

2. amounts spent on anti-pollution measures;

3. number of complaints received from members of the local community.

(vii) Possible growth measures include comparisons over time (in absolute terms and percentage changes) of the following:

1. total sales revenue;

2. profit (expressed in terms of residual income);

3. total assets;

4. total employees;

5. total market share.

Price changes should be removed where appropriate. Comparisons should be made with other divisions, comparable firms and the industry as a whole. Survival in the long term depends on an acceptable level of profitability.

Therefore appropriate profitability measures should be used. The degree of divisional autonomy might be measured in terms of an assessment of the central controls imposed by central headquarters. (For example: what are the limits on the amounts of capital expenditure decisions that divisions can determine independently?)

(b) A single performance measure underestimates the multi-faceted nature of organizational goals. It might be claimed that a profitability measure is sufficiently general to incorporate the other goals. For example, maintaining high market shares, increasing productivity, offering an up-to-date product range, being a responsible employee, and growth tend to result in increased profitability. To this extent a profitability measure might best capture the multi-faceted nature of organizational goals. Nevertheless the profitability goal alone cannot be expected to capture the complexity of organizational goals. Firms pursue a variety of goals, and for this reason there are strong arguments for using multiple performance measures when evaluating organizational performance. For a further discussion of organizational goals see 'The decision-making process' in Chapter 1.

(a) *Calculation of written-down values (WDVs) and capital employed*

Year	1	2	3	4	5
	(£m)	(£m)	(£m)	(£m)	(£m)
Opening WDV	1.5	1.2	0.9	0.6	0.3
Depreciation (straight line)	0.3	0.3	0.3	0.3	0.3
Closing WDV	1.2	0.9	0.6	0.3	—
Opening capital employed (opening WDV + WC)	2.0	1.7	1.4	1.1	0.8

Calculation of residual income and ROCE

Year	1	2	3	4	5
	(£m)	(£m)	(£m)	(£m)	(£m)
Sales	2.0				
Operating costs	(1.35)				
Depreciation	(0.30)				
Net profit	0.35	0.35	0.35	0.35	0.35
Imputed interest (20%)	0.40	0.34	0.28	0.22	0.16
Residual income	(0.05)	0.01	0.07	0.13	0.19
ROCE	17.5%	20.6%	25%	31.8%	43.7%

CP's management would be unlikely to undertake the project if they are evaluated on the basis of ROCE, since it yields a return of less than 30% for each of the first three years. Consequently, the total ROCE will be less than 30% during the first three years. Residual income is negative in the first year and positive for the remaining four years. If the management of CP place more emphasis on the impact on the performance measure on the first year, they may reject the project. On the other hand, if they adopt a longer-term perspective, they will accept the project.

(b) *Calculation of annuity depreciation*

Year	(1) Annual repayment (£m)	(2) 20% interest on capital outstanding (£m)	(3) = (1) − (2) Capital repayment (£m)	(4) = (4) − (3) Capital outstanding (£m)
0				1.5
1	0.5016	0.3	0.2016	1.2984
2	0.5016	0.2597	0.2419	1.0565
3	0.5016	0.2113	0.2903	0.7662
4	0.5016	0.1532	0.3484	0.4178
5	0.5016	0.0838	0.4178	—

For an explanation of the calculations see 'Annuity depreciation' in Appendix 20.1. Note that the annual repayment is determined by referring to the capital recovery table in Appendix D of the text for 5 years at 20%. The capital recovery factor is 0.3344, and this is multiplied by the capital outlay to give an annual repayment of £0.5016m.

Calculation of residual income and ROCE

Year	1	2	3	4	5
	(£m)	(£m)	(£m)	(£m)	(£m)
Opening WDV	1.50	1.30	1.06	0.77	0.42
Annuity depreciation	0.20	0.24	0.29	0.35	0.42
Closing WDV	1.30	1.06	0.77	0.42	–
Total opening capital employed	2.0	1.80	1.56	1.27	0.92

Operating earnings	0.65	0.65	0.65	0.65	0.65
Depreciation	0.20	0.24	0.29	0.35	0.42
Net profit	0.45	0.41	0.36	0.30	0.23
Imputed interest	0.40	0.36	0.31	0.25	0.18
Residual income	0.05	0.05	0.05	0.05	0.05
ROCE	22.5%	22.8%	23.1%	23.6%	25%

Since the projected ROCE is less than 30%, CP's management are likely to reject the project if performance is evaluated on the basis of ROCE. If performance is evaluated on the basis of residual income, the project is likely to be accepted, since it has a positive residual income for all five years.

(c) The calculation of NPV is as follows:

	(£m)
PV of net cash inflows (£0.65m × 2.991 discount factor)	1.944
Working capital released at the end of the project (0.5m × 0.4019)	0.201
Initial outlay	(2.000)
NPV	0.145

The project should be accepted, since it has a positive NPV. The objective is to design a performance measurement system that is consistent with the NPV rule. The ROCE measure may not encourage goal congruence, because managers of divisions with a ROCE in excess of the cost of capital may incorrectly reject projects with positive NPVs. Alternatively, managers of divisions with a ROCE that is less than cost of capital may incorrectly accept projects with negative NPVs. This situation arises because managers who are evaluated on the basis of ROCE may base their investment decisions on the impact on ROCE and use the existing ROCE as the cut-off rate.

The project outlined in the question has a positive NPV, but the ROCE is less than 30% for the first three years in (a), where straight-line depreciation is used. If annuity depreciation is used, the project has a ROCE of less than 30% for each year of the project's life. The manager is therefore unlikely to accept the investment, since it will result in a decline in the overall ROCE of the division.

In the long run, the residual income method produces a calculation that is consistent with the NPV rule. The short-term residual income calculation may not, however, motivate managers to select projects that are consistent with applying the NPV rule. In the case of constant cash flows the problem can be resolved by using the annuity method of depreciation, but when annual cash flows fluctuate, this method of depreciation does not ensure that the short-term residual income measure is consistent with the NPV rule. For a discussion of how this problem might be resolved see 'Reconciling short-term and long-term residual income/EVA measures' in Appendix 20.1 to Chapter 20. You can see that, for the project outlined in the question, residual income is positive for all years where the annuity method of depreciation is used, but it is negative in the first year and positive for the remaining years where straight-line depreciation is used.

Question 20.30 (a) *Calculations based on best outcomes*

	Year 1	Year 2	Year 3	Year 4
Additional capacity (standard hours) [a]	1 050	1 365	1 785	2 100
	(£)	(£)	(£)	(£)
Contribution at £1320 per hour	1 386 000	1 801 800	2 356 200	2 772 000
Less training, consultancy and salary costs	97 500	97 500	97 500	97 500

	1 288 500	1 704 300	2 258 700	2 674 500
Less depreciation	1 000 000	1 000 000	1 000 000	1 000 000
Net profit	288 500	704 300	1 258 700	1 674 500
Less imputed interest (8% × WDV)	320 000	240 000	160 000	80 000
Residual income	−31 500	464 300	1 098 700	1 594 500
ROI[b]	7.2%	23.5%	62.9%	167.5%

NPV at 8% = (£1 288 500 × 0.926) + (£1 704 300 × 0.857) + (£2 258 700 × 0.794) +
(£2 674 500 × 0.735) − £4 000 000
= £2 412 901

Notes

[a] Year 1 = 1000(1.05) with increments for years 2–4 being 300(1.05), 400(1.05) and 300(1.05)

[b] Profit/Opening WDV's of £4m, £3m, £2m and £1m.

(b)   *Bonus calculations*

	Year 1 (£)	Year 2 (£)	Year 3 (£)	Year 4 (£)	Total (£)
Net profit[a]	0	3150	10 350	15 750	29 250
Residual income [b]	0	0	9800	19 000	28 800
ROI basis [c]	6000	6000	6000	6000	24 000
NPV basis (£1 233 700 × 2.5%) in year 4				30 843	30 843

Notes

[a] Year 2 bonus = (£460 000 − £250 000) × 1.5% = £3150

[b] Year 3 bonus = (£740 000 − £250 000 = £490 000 = 4.9 × 5% × £40 000 = £9800)

[c] Year 1 bonus = ROI is positive for all years so the bonus is £6000 per year (15% of £40 000)

(c) The manager's choice is likely to be influenced by his/her attitude towards risk, the potential size of the bonus, the timing and ease of obtaining the bonus. The most likely outcome figures shown in (c) indicate a clear preference for (c) over the time horizon, but there is a long delay in payment. If an early receipt of the bonus is important to the manager, then ROI may be preferred since this provides a considerably higher bonus over the first two years. The manager may also find the NPV and residual income basis less attractive because both measures are influenced by the cost of capital, which is beyond the control of the manager. A risk-seeking manager is likely to find the bonus based on NPV very attractive since it yields the highest bonus if the best or most likely outcomes occur. In contrast, a risk-averse manager is likely to favour the bonus based on ROI since it produces the highest bonus for the worst outcome.

(d) The bonus system and any promotion prospects arising from the success of the programme may influence the manager's level of effort and motivation. Also, the manager's attitude to risk and the perceived extent to which he/she can influence the outcomes is likely to influence the level of effort. The level of motivation to achieve the programme will be affected by the expectation that its success will result in some benefits and the strength of preference of the manager for the benefits. The personal expectations are also important. If the manager believes in the programme he/she will be highly motivated to make it a success. Also, the expectations of success will be important. If the manager believes there is little chance of the programme being successful there may be little motivation to make an effort for it to succeed.

Question 20.31

(a) To compute EVA, adjustments must be made to the conventional after tax profit measures of $44m and $55m shown in the question. Normally an adjustment is made to convert conventional financial accounting depreciation to an estimate of economic depreciation, but the question indicates that profits have already been computed using economic depreciation. Non-cash expenses are added back since the adjusted profit attempts to approximate cash flow after taking into account economic depreciation. Net interest is also added back because the returns required by the providers of funds will be reflected in the cost of capital deduction. Note that net interest is added back because interest will have been allowed as an expense in determining the taxation payment.

The capital employed used to calculate EVA should be based on adjustments that seek to approximate book economic value at the start of each period. Because insufficient information is given, the book value of shareholders funds plus medium and long-term loans at the end of 2000 is used as the starting point to determine economic capital employed at the beginning of 2001.

	2000 ($m)	2001 ($m)
Adjusted profit	56.6 (44 + 10 + (4 × 0.65))	68.9 (55 + 10 + (6 × 0.65))
Capital employed	233 (223 + 10)	260 (250 + 10)

The weighted average cost of capital should be based on the target capital structure. The calculation is as follows:

$2000 = (15\% \times 0.6) + (9\% \times 0.65 \times 0.4) = 11.34\%$

$2001 = (17\% \times 0.6) + (10\% \times 0.65 \times 0.4) = 12.8\%$

EVA 2000 = $56.6 - (233 \times 0.1134) = \$30.18m$

EVA 2001 = $68.9 - (260 \times 0.128) = \$35.62$

The EVA measures indicate that the company has added significant value in both years and achieved a satisfactory level of performance.

(b) The present value of EVA from an investment approximates the NPV of the investment. For an explanation of this point you should refer to 'The effect of performance measurement on capital investment decisions' in Chapter 20.

(c) Advantages of EVA include:
1   because some discretionary expenses are capitalized the harmful side-effects of financial measures described in Chapters 16 and 20 are reduced;
2   EVA is consistent with maximizing shareholders funds;
3   EVA is easily understood by managers;
4   EVA can also be linked to managerial bonus schemes and motivate managers to take decisions that increase shareholder value.

Disadvantages of EVA include:
1   the EVA computation can be complicated when many adjustments are required;
2   EVA is difficult to use for inter-firm and inter-divisional comparisons because it is not a ratio measure;
3   if economic depreciation is not used, the short-term measure can conflict with the long-term measure (see 'The effect of performance measurement on capital investment decisions' in Chapter 20).
4   economic depreciation is difficult to estimate and conflicts with generally accepted accounting principles which may hinder its acceptance by financial managers.

Transfer pricing in divisionalized companies

Solutions to Chapter 21 questions

(a) With cost-based transfer price systems, transfers are made either at actual cost or **Question 21.24** standard cost. Where actual costs are used, there is no incentive for the supplying centre to control costs because any inefficiencies arising in the supplying centre will be passed on to the receiving centre. Consequently, the receiving centre will be held accountable for the inefficiencies of the supplying division. Transfers at actual cost are therefore inappropriate for responsibility accounting.

Where cost-based transfer pricing systems are used, transfers should be at standard cost and not actual cost. This will result in the supplying centre being held accountable for the variances arising from the difference between standard and actual cost of the transfers. The managers of the supplying centres are therefore motivated to minimize their costs. When transfers are made at standard cost, any inefficiencies of the supplying centre are not passed on to the receiving centre. The receiving centre should be held accountable for usage of resources at the standard price, thus ensuring that the manager of the receiving centre is held accountable only for excessive usage of resources.

Where cost-based transfer prices are used, there is still a danger that inappropriate transfer prices are set that will not provide an appropriate basis for allocating profits between divisions. Where there is a competitive market for intermediate products, the current market price is the most suitable basis for setting the transfer price. When transfers are recorded at market prices, profit centre performance is likely to represent the real economic contribution of the profit centre to total company profits. If the supplying centre did not exist, the intermediate product would have to be purchased on the outside market at the current market price. Alternatively, if the receiving centre did not exist, the intermediate product would have to be sold on the outside market at the current market price. Responsibility centre profits are therefore likely to be similar to the profits that would be calculated if the centres were separate independent businesses. Therefore transfers based on selling prices will represent a more appropriate basis for meeting the requirements of a responsibility accounting system.

(b) When the supplying division does not have sufficient capacity to meet all the demands placed upon it, linear programming can be used to determine the optimum production level. The transfer price that will induce the supplying division to produce the optimum output level can be derived from the linear programming model. The transfer price is determined by adding the shadow prices of the scarce resources (as indicated by the output from the linear programming model) to the variable cost of the resources consumed by the intermediate product. This transfer price will result in the supplying division being credited with all of the contribution arising from the transfers and the receiving division earning a zero contribution. The allocation of zero contribution to the receiving division will have a negative motivational influence, and result in a loss of divisional autonomy and a reported performance that does not reflect the economic performance of the division.

Question 21.25

(a) (i) See 'The multiple functions of budgets' in Chapter 15 for the answer to this question.

(a) (ii) See 'Participation in the budgeting and target setting process' for the answer to this question.

(b) You should refer to each transfer pricing method in Chapter 21 for the answer to this question. Note that the marginal cost plus opportunity cost approach is the same as the opportunity cost method stated in the question. With this method the resulting transfer price will be the same as a market based transfer price where full capacity exists. Therefore the supplying and receiving divisions would incur the same costs or receive the same revenues compared with purchasing or selling from/to the external market. However, where spare capacity exists, marginal cost would represent the opportunity cost so the impact on the managers would be the same as applying marginal cost transfer prices.

(c) Where cost-based transfer prices are used, standard costs, and not actual costs, per unit of output should be used. If actual costs are used, the supplying divisions will be able to pass on the cost of any inefficiencies to the receiving divisions. Using standard costs ensures that the cost of inefficiencies are allocated to the supplying divisions.

Question 21.26

(a) DP division variable costs for October

	Budget (£)	Actual (£)
Skilled labour	10 000 (£120 000/12)	11 000 (+10%)
Semi-skilled labour	8 000	8 800 (+10%)
Processing	5 000	4 750 (−5%)
Total	23 000	24 550

(i) Actual variable cost per hour = £24 550/(450 hours) = £54.555
(Note 6000/12 × 0.9 = 450)
Total charge for 200 hours = £10 911

(ii) Standard variable cost plus 40% = £23 000/450 = £51.111 × 1.4 = £71.555
Total charge for 200 hours = £14 311

(iii) Market price is based on total cost plus 40% mark-up

	(£)
Standard variable cost	51.111
Budgeted fixed cost per hour	44.444 (£240 000/5400 hours)
Total cost	95.555
Add 40% mark-up	38.222
Transfer price	133.777

Total charge for 200 hours = £26 755

(b) DP division

Transfer pricing method	Actual variable cost (£)	Standard variable cost + 40% (£)	Market price (£)
External sales (250 hours × £133.777)	33 444	33 444	33 444
Internal sales	10 911	14 311	26 755
Total revenue	44 355	47 755	60 199
Variable costs	24 550	24 550	24 550
Contribution	19 805	23 205	35 649
Fixed costs	20 000	20 000	20 000
Profit/(loss)	(195)	3 205	15 649

Consulting division

Consulting costs	2 600	2 600	2 600
Transfer price	10 911	14 311	26 755
Total cost	13 511	16 911	29 355
Project fee	15 500	15 500	15 500
Profit/(loss)	1 989	(1 411)	(13 855)

(c) Only the variable cost transfer price results in the consulting division making a profit on the project. Given that DP division has spare capacity, the opportunity cost is zero and variable cost is the relevant transfer price. Because DP should be accountable for any cost variances, standard variable cost should be used giving a transfer price of £10 222 (£51.111 × 200 hours). At the proposed transfer price, DP division will earn a zero contribution and the consulting division will obtain a contribution of £2678 [£15 500 – (£10 222 + £2600)]. The company as a whole will be better off by £2678 by accepting the project.

Question 21.27

(a) For the answer to this question see 'The role of a cost accumulation system in generating relevant cost information for decision-making' and 'Volume-based and non-volume-based cost drivers' in Chapter 10. In particular, the answer should point out that ABC ought to lead to the reporting of more accurate product costs and thus improved decision-making. In relation to M Ltd. the product profitability analysis based on the traditional costing system may be providing inaccurate information. The profitability analysis indicates that Q makes a loss although it generates a positive short-run contribution to fixed costs. Q Ltd. may choose to discontinue Q if it considers that a large proportion of the fixed costs is avoidable in the long run. However, the introduction of ABC may result in significant changes in reported product profits, such that Q makes a profit, if the traditional system inaccurately measures resources consumed by the different products.

(b) The following difficulties may be encountered:
1 identifying appropriate activity cost pools and cost drivers;
2 lack of trained staff to implement and operate the system;
3 reluctance of the staff to change to a new system;
4 the traditional system may report reasonably accurate product costs resulting in there being little difference between the reported product costs for the two systems. However, the ABC system is likely to be more costly to operate;
5 traditional systems accurately trace direct costs to cost objects and facility sustaining costs are unavoidable unless there is a dramatic change in the scale or scope of activity. Therefore the costs that can be more accurately traced to cost objects with ABC may represent only a small proportion of total costs;

(c) (i) The supplying division has no external market for chips so the situation is very similar to that illustrated in Example 21.1. You will therefore find the criticisms of the current transfer pricing method in 'An illustration of transfer pricing' in Chapter 21. An alternative system would be for the transfer price to be based on marginal cost plus a fixed lump-sum fee. You should refer to Chapter 21 for an explanation of this method.

(c) (ii) With the introduction of an ABC, M Ltd. should continue to use the transfer pricing system recommended in (c) (i) as explained for an ABC system in the section 'Marginal cost plus a lump-sum fee' in Chapter 21.

Question 21.28   (a)

Residual income calculations

	TM division (£000)		FD division (£000)	
Sales: External	7500	(15 000 × £500)	400	(5000 × £80)
Internal			990	(15 000 × (£60 + 10%))
	7500		1390	
Less variable costs:				
Production	5490	(15 000 × £366)	800	(20 000 × £40)
Selling and distribution	375	(15 000 × £25)	20	(5000 × £4)
Contribution	1635		570	
Less: Fixed production costs	900	(15 000 × £60)	400	(20 000 × £20)
Administration costs	375	(15 000 × £25)	80	(20 000 × £4)
Net profit	360		90	
Less cost of capital charge (12%)	180		90	
Residual income	180		0	

The manager of TM has exceeded his/her target and will thus receive a bonus of £9000 whereas the manager of FD division will not receive any bonus. Given that the majority of FD's sales are internal, it is likely that the transfer price, which is currently below the external selling price, is contributing to FD's poor performance. The fact that the manager of TM receives a bonus and the manager of FD does not is likely to have an adverse motivational impact which may affect future performance.

(b) (i) The manager of TM can suffer a decline in residual income of £75 000 (£180 000 – £105 000) without losing the bonus. This represents an increase in the transfer price of £5 (£75 000/15 000 units) per unit; so at a transfer price of £71 or below a bonus will still be awarded to the manager of TM.

(b) (ii) The manager of FD requires additional residual income of £85 000 in order to receive a bonus. This represents an increase in the transfer price of £5.67 (£85 000/15 000 units) giving a minimum transfer price of £71.67.

(c) At the present level of demand, FD has 5000 units unused capacity (25 000 maximum capacity – 15 000 transfers – 5000 external sales). Therefore, transfers to TM have no opportunity cost in terms of foregone contribution as long as external demand is less than 10 000 units. Under these circumstances, theory suggests that the optimal transfer price for decision-making is the marginal/variable production cost of £40 per unit. If sales demand for the external market exceeds 10 000 units, the opportunity cost of any transfers will be represented by the lost contribution of £36 (£80 selling price – £44 variable cost) per unit on external sales. Applying the marginal cost plus opportunity cost approach described in the chapter results in an optimal transfer price of £76 (£40 variable cost of transfers + £36 opportunity cost). This is identical to the external selling price less variable costs that are specifically attributable to external sales.

Although the above transfer price is optimal for decision-making it is unsatisfactory for performance evaluation. The manager of FD will not obtain a contribution on internal sales and will not be motivated to transfer the goods to TM. Also, the transfer prices computed in (b) indicate that a conflict of interests occurs since only one of the managers can obtain the bonus. To resolve the decision-making and performance evaluation conflicts, it is recommended that a dual-rate or marginal cost plus a fixed lump-sum fee transfer pricing system be implemented. The answer should describe these methods (see Chapter 21 for a description) and show how they can resolve the conflicts.

Question 21.29   (a)

Scenario 1

Since South has spare production capacity, the incremental cost to the company as a whole of using the internal consultant is £100 compared with £500 for the external consultant. The transfer price should encourage the use of the internal consultant. Any transfer price above the variable cost of £100 per day will enable South to obtain a contribution. North division will not be prepared to pay in excess of the external charge of £500 per day. Therefore a transfer price in excess of £100 and less than £500 will encourage both managers to make decisions that are in the best interests of the company as a whole.

Scenario 2

For the company as a whole, it is preferable to lose revenue of £400 rather than incur additional costs of £500. Therefore the transfer price should be set to encourage both managers to use the internal consultant. The transfer price should be set above £400 to encourage the manager of South division to undertake the transaction and below £500 to encourage the manager of North division to buy from South.

Scenario 3

For the company as a whole, it is preferable to earn revenues of £700 and incur external costs of £500. The transfer price should discourage the transfer between the two divisions. Therefore it should be set below £700 to encourage the manager of South division to choose to earn £700 per day and above £500 to encourage the manager of North to use the external consultant.

   The above comments are based on a short-term analysis assuming the objective is to maximize short-run contribution and that the company has access to all the decision-making data that the separate divisions use.

(b) See 'The sections relating to the advantages of divisionalization, disadvantages of divisionalization and pre-requisites for successful divisionalization' in Chapter 20 for the answer to this question.

Question 21.30

(a)

	Blackalls			Brownalls	
	(£)	(£)	(£)		(£)
Selling price		45			54
Component costs: Alpha	18 (3 × £6)		12 (2 × £6)		
Beta	8 (2 × £4)		16 (4 × £4)		
Processing cost	12	38	14		42
Contribution		7			12

Group contribution:	(£)
Blackalls 200 × £7	1400
Brownalls 300 × £12	3600
	5000

(b) Transfer price = variable cost + shadow price
   Alpha   = £6   + £0.50   = £6.50
   Beta   = £4   + £2.75   = £6.75

   (i)

	Division A	Division B
	(£)	(£)
Transfer price	6.50	6.75
Variable cost	6.00	4.00
Contribution/unit	0.50	2.75

   (ii)

	Black division		Brown division	
	(£)	(£)	(£)	(£)
Selling price		45		54
Component cost:				
Alpha	19.50 (3 × £6.50)		13.00 (2 × £6.50)	
Beta	13.50 (2 × £6.75)		27.00 (4 × £6.75)	
Processing cost	12.00	45	14.00	54
Contribution/unit		nil		nil

(c) When the supplying division does not have sufficient capacity to meet all the demands placed upon it, linear programming can be used to determine the optimum production level. The transfer price that will induce the supplying division to produce the optimum output level can be derived from the linear programming model. The transfer price is determined by adding the shadow prices of the scarce resources to the variable cost of the resources consumed by the intermediate product. The transfer price that induces the supplying division to transfer the optimum output to the receiving division results in the supplying division being credited with all of the contribution arising from the transfers and the receiving division earning a zero contribution. This is illustrated in part (b) of the answer.

The managers of the receiving divisions will be indifferent about producing the final products, since they yield a zero contribution, but the group as a whole will be worse off if the final products are not produced. To ensure that the optimal output of the final products is produced, it will be necessary for head office to instruct the receiving divisions to convert all the output that the supplying divisions are prepared to transfer (at the transfer prices derived from the linear programming model). This will have a negative motivational influence on the managers of the receiving division, and will result in a loss of divisional autonomy. In addition, the reported performance of the divisions will not reflect their contribution to group profits. Therefore the transfer prices will not be acceptable to the managers of the receiving divisions, whereas the managers of the supplying divisions (A and B) will be satisfied since they will be allocated with the full amount of the contribution.

(d) (i) The transfer price should reflect the opportunity cost of producing the intermediate products. The transfer prices are calculated as follows:

$$\text{variable cost} + \text{opportunity cost}$$
$$\text{Alpha} = £6 + (5\% \times £6) = £6.30$$
$$\text{Beta} = £4 + (£3.50 - £0.50) = £7$$

Note that the above transfer prices reflect the selling prices (or net sales revenue) from using the capacity of the supplying divisions to produce other products (A division) or sell the intermediate product on the external market (B division).

(ii) The contributions per unit for Blackalls and Brownalls are as follows:

| | Black division | | Brown division | |
	(£)	(£)	(£)	(£)
Selling price		45.00		54.00
Component costs:				
Alpha (at £6.30)	18.90		12.60	
Beta (at £7)	14.00		28.00	
Processing cost	12.00	44.90	14.00	54.60
Contribution/unit		0.10		(0.60)

Brown division will not produce Brownalls, because they yield a negative contribution, but Black division will wish to maximize production of Blackalls. The production capacity of Alpha and Beta is as follows:

Alpha 2400 units (restricts maximum production of Blackalls to 800 units)
Beta 3200 units (restricts maximum production of Blackalls to 1600 units)

Production of Blackalls is therefore restricted to 800 units, thus using all of the available Alpha capacity. Production of 800 units of Blackalls requires 1600 units of Beta (800 × 2 units). The unused Beta capacity of 1600 units (3200 −

1600) will be sold on the external intermediate market. Therefore the optimal output is as follows:

Brownalls zero
Blackalls 800 units
Alpha   2400 units transferred to Black division
Beta   3200 units (1600 units transferred to Black division and 1600 units sold externally)

The resulting maximum group contribution is:

		(£)
Blackalls	(800 × £7)	5 600
Beta	[1600 × (£7 − £4)]	4 800
		10 400

Cost management

Solutions to Chapter 22 questions

Question 22.25 Each of the techniques listed in the question is described in Chapter 22. You should therefore refer to Chapter 22 for the answer to this question.

Question 22.26 (a) See 'Benchmarking' in Chapter 22 for an explanation of the aims and operation. External benchmarking involves a comparison of performing activities with external organizations that are recognized as industry leaders whereas internal benchmarking involves a comparison of performing similar activities in different units within the same organization.

Activity-based-costing information can be used to compare the cost of similar activities undertaken in different business units. The information would enable apparently high cost activities that may be inefficient if targeted for benchmarking. Alternatively, a unit may have established a reputation for being a leader for performing a particular activity. This may provide the stimulus for benchmarking the activity against other similar activities performed elsewhere in the organization. External benchmarking differs in that it is more difficult to obtain access to the industry leader and may be impossible where the leader is a competitor.

A major difficulty with benchmarking is identifying a relevant benchmark and ensuring that the activities being compared are similar in terms of their objectives and the constraints that apply. If internal benchmarking is used there is no guarantee that the targeted unit for comparison represents excellent practice. Hence there will be a danger that inefficiencies will be incorporated into the new methods of undertaking the activity. A further problem is that historical data may be used to compare activity costs, inputs and outputs. Such data may be distorted by changes in technology and methods of working.

(b) Possible reasons for similar standard costs in plants with differing technology include:

(i) The investments may have been made to reduce long-term cost savings and these savings may not have been reflected in cost reductions.

(ii) Cost reduction may not have been a primary objective for investing in new technology. Improved quality, delivery and flexibility to provide product variations and obtain the benefits of economies of scope may have been the objectives of the investment. The benefits will be reflected in an increase in customer satisfaction and future sales revenues rather than cost reductions.

(iii) The new technologies may be subject to the learning curve effect that has not been incorporated into the standard costs.

(iv) Standard cost may have been computed using a traditional costing system that has failed to capture the cost benefits of the new technology. Also if the plants with the new technology are initially operating partly with the old and the new technology they will initially be under-utilized. If short-term capacity, rather than practical capacity, is used as the denominator level to set the overhead rates the new technology will be overcosted. For an explanation of this point you should refer to the sections relating to denominator levels in Chapters 7 and 10.

(v) The new technology plants may have had implementation problems and the extra costs arising from such problems may have been initially incorporated into the standard costs.

(vi) Standard costs may be inappropriate benchmarks if significant variances occur. In these circumstances actual costs would be a more appropriate benchmark.

A reduction in unit costs may not have been the primary objective for investing in new technology. Therefore the focus should be on a comparison between plants of physical measures such as defect rates, cycle times, set-up times, machine efficiencies, stock levels and customer response times.

Question 22.27

(a) For an explanation of TQM you should refer to the 'Cost of quality' in Chapter 22. In addition, the answer should draw attention to the need to introduce a TQM training programme and a study of the production process to ensure that methods are in place to minimize defects and avoid scrap and rework. A 'right first time' policy should be implemented. A daily quality reporting system should also be introduced that reports defects, rework and returns from customers. Consideration should also be given to introducing statistical quality control procedures. In addition, a six-monthly or annual cost of quality reporting system should be introduced.

(b) A JIT philosophy aims to eliminate waste and this is enhanced by the adoption of TQM. With the pull system that accompanies a JIT philosophy, defects bring the whole production process to a halt so a 'right first time' policy supports JIT production. Furthermore, the absence of stocks that is a feature of JIT means that safeguards do not exist to cope with defects, rework and returns from customers. The effects of poor quality result in costly production stoppages and a danger that customer commitments will not be met. TQM is therefore an inherent feature of JIT production.

(c) The four quality cost classifications are: prevention costs, appraisal costs, internal failure costs and external failure costs. See 'Cost of quality' in Chapter 22 for an explanation of these terms. Examples include preventive maintenance of food processing machinery (prevention cost), inspection of the output (appraisal cost), scrapping of foods because of inferior quality (external failure cost) and the cost of replacing faulty output delivered to customers and any lost profits on future sales arising from customer dissatisfaction (external failure cost).

Question 22.28

(a) The answer to this question requires a comparison of traditional production flow lines, push manufacturing and purchasing with a JIT manufacturing and purchasing policy. You will find a comparison of traditional and JIT methods in the section on just-in-time systems in Chapter 22.

(b) Cost reduction represents an attempt to reduce costs without affecting the customer's perception of the value of the product or service.

(c) Activity-based management should be introduced. This should involve identifying the product/service attributes that are valued by customers and those that are not valued (i.e. non-value-added activities). The focus should be on eliminating or reducing the cost of non-value-added activities. For a detailed description of this process you should refer to 'Activity-based management' in Chapter 22.

Question 22.29

(a) *Standard costing is a costing system whereas target costing is not a costing sytem*
Standard costing is a costing system whereby a database of estimated costs based on efficient operations is maintained. Target costing represents an approach to deriving a target cost and taking actions to achieve the target cost. It does not represent a costing system. Target costing is applied to new products, whereas

standard costing is concerned with controlling the costs of existing activities. However, where a new product requires some existing operations, the cost of these operations can be derived from the standard costing system. If the estimated/standard cost exceeds the target cost, ways are investigated of driving down the estimated cost to the target cost. Thus, although standard costing is a formal costing system and target costing is not, they may be used together when adopting a target costing approach.

Proactive or not

Standard costing compares the actual cost with the target costs for different operations and provides a detailed analysis of the variances, which are used as clues to identify potential inefficiencies. It is therefore a feedback system that can be viewed as a cost containment mechanism. However, where the variance analysis identifies inefficiencies and steps are taken to avoid them reoccurring in the future, standard costing can be used in a proactive manner. Target costing is a proactive technique. A target cost is identified for a new product and this is compared with the estimated cost. Where the estimated cost exceeds the target cost, intensive efforts are made prior to the production process to drive the estimated cost down to the target cost. The fact that this process takes place before production begins where there is an opportunity for product redesign makes the proactive nature of target costing one of its most attractive features. See 'Target costing' in Chapter 22 for a more detailed discussion of the proactive nature of target costing.

Consultation or not

There is no reason why standard costing should not involve participation of all parties involved, but since it is operated for existing products there is less need for many parties to be involved because operations can be observed when setting the standards. The comment in the question arises because a major feature of target costing is that it involves a team approach. For a description of the team approach see 'Target costing' in Chapter 22. Therefore, although standard costing can allow the same amount of consultation as target costing, in practice it is likely to involve far less participation. This is because standard costing can involve hundreds of products and operations but target costing involves an intensive study of only major new products. Therefore adopting a team approach involving consultation becomes more feasible.

(b) The answer should point out that the company should use standard costing to control the costs of existing operations and products provided that operations are of a repetitive nature to enable standards to be set. For major new products, target costing can be applied as a means of managing costs before production commences. After production commences, standard costing can be used to control the costs.

Question 22.30 (a) (i) See Figure Q22.30 for the answer to this question.

(a) (ii) Product life cycles consist of introductory, growth, maturity and decline stages. Products A and B have similar curves. Instead of an introductory stage they have a period of steady growth, a very short maturity stage followed by a period of rapid decline, but the decline phase is more rapid in B than A. Product A has a life cycle of 8 years compared to 6 years for B. Product C has more of an introductory phase and a slower rate of growth than products A and B. It also appears to have a less rapid decline stage.

(a) (iii)

Profit and loss analysis

| | 2001 | | | | 2002 | | | |
	A (£m)	B (£m)	C (£m)	Total (£m)	A (£m)	B (£m)	C (£m)	Total (£m)
Sales revenue	3.00	9.00	6.50		2.00	3.00	7.50	
Variable costs	0.90	2.25	2.60		0.60	0.75	3.00	
Contribution	2.10	6.75	3.90		1.40	2.25	4.50	
Product specific fixed costs	2.00	4.00	2.80		1.10	1.80	3.00	
Product profits	0.10	2.75	1.10	3.95	0.30	0.45	1.50	2.25
Company fixed costs				2.50				2.50
Net profit/(loss)				1.45				(0.25)

(a) (iv) The forecasted total profit is £1.45m for 2001 and a loss of £0.25m for 2002. The total sales revenue for 2001 is £18.5m which is close to the 100% capacity level of £20m. In 2002 there has been a rapid decline in the sales revenue of product B resulting in total sales of £12.5m which represents only approximately 60% of total productive capacity. There is a need to introduce new products or increase the sales of existing products. All of the products make a positive contribution to company fixed costs.

(b) (i)

NPV calculation for product D

	2002 (£m)	2003 (£m)	2004 (£m)
Contribution at 60%	3.6	4.2	3.6
Less fixed costs	2.5	2.2	1.8
Net cash flows	1.1	2.0	1.8
Discount factor	0.909	0.826	0.751
Present value	0.9999	1.652	1.3518

NPV = Total present value (4.0037) – investment outlay (£4.5m) = –£0.4963m

(b) (ii) For product D to be viable the increase in contribution sales ratio must be sufficient to cover the negative NPV of £0.4963m.

Let x = the change in the contribution sales ratio.

$6x(0.909) + 7x(0.826) + 6x(0.751) = 0.4963$

$15.742x = 0.4963$

$x = 0.0315$

Therefore the required contribution/sales ratio would have to increase from 60% to above 63.15% for the NPV to be positive.

(b) (iii) The target variable cost for the new product exceeds the estimated cost and ways must be found to drive the estimated cost to below the target cost. For a discussion of the actions that can be taken to drive the actual cost down to the target cost, you should refer to target costing in Chapter 22.

(c) The forecasted sales for 2002–04 are respectively £18.5m, £17.5m and £13m. The company has approximately 10% unutilized capacity for the first two years and 35% in the final year. Although there is some scope for seeking methods of utilizing the spare capacity in the first two years, it is the final year where a considerable effort is required. It is important that steps are taken now to address the serious problem in the final year. Potential strategies include:

1   In the short-term make a major effort to extend the sales of products A and B. Consider product redesign to improve its marketability and developing new markets.

2   Seek to extend the maturity phase of product C and increase sales by seeking new markets and making more efforts to retain existing customers. Consider adopting new advertising strategies.

3   Investigate ways of increasing the sales of product D by extending the market and considering alternative pricing and advertising strategies.

4   Introduce a cost management programme that aims to reduce existing costs.

This is particularly applicable in the first two years where only a small amount of unutilized capacity exists.

5   Take steps now to ensure that new products and markets are developed for beyond 2004.

For all of the above strategies cost/benefit principles should be applied to ensure that additional benefits exceed the additional costs.

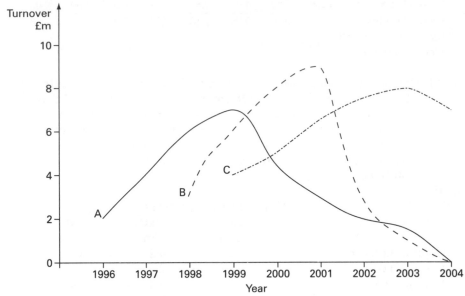

Figure Q22.30

Question 22.31   (a)   (i)   *Total production units (pre-inspection)*

	Existing situation		Revised situation
Total sales requirements	5000		5000
Specification losses (5%)	250	(2.5%)	125
	5250		5125
Downgrading at inspection (12.5/87.5 × 5250)	750	(7.5/92.5 × 5125)	416
Total units before inspection (100/87.5 × 5250)	6000	(100/92.5 × 5125)	5541

(ii)   *Purchase of material X (m²)*

Materials required to meet pre-inspection production requirements (6000 × 8 m²)	48 000	(5541 × 8 m²)	44 328
Processing losses (4/96 × 48 000)	2 000	(2.5/97.5 × 44 328)	1 137
Input to the process (100/96 × 48 000)	50 000		45 465
Scrapped materials (5/95 × 50 000)	2 632	(3/97 × 45 465)	1 406
Total purchases (100/95 × 50 000)	52 632	(100/97 × 45 465)	46 871

(iii)   *Gross machine hours*

Initial requirements (6000 × 0.6)	3600	(5541 × 0.5 hrs)	2771
Rectification units (80% × 250 × 0.2 hrs)	40	(80% × 125 × 0.2 hrs)	20
	3640		2791
Idle time (20/80 × 3640)	910	(12.5/87.5 × 2791)	399
Gross machine hrs (100/80 × 3640)	4550	(100/87.5 × 2791)	3190

Profit and Loss Accounts

	Existing situation (£)		Revised situation (£)
Sales revenue:			
First quality 5000 × £100	500 000	5000 × £100	500 000
Second quality 750 × £70	52 500	416 × £70	29 120
Third quality 200 × £50	10 000	100 × £50	5 000
Scrap sales 50 × £5	250	25 × £5	125
	562 750		534 245
Costs			
Material X (52 632 × £4)	210 528	46 871 × £4	187 484
Insp/storage costs (52 632 × £0.10)	5 263	46 871 × £0.10	4 687
Machine costs (4550 × £40)	182 000	3190 × £40	127 600
Delivery of replacements			
(250 × £8)	2 000	125 × £8	1 000
Inspection and other costs	25 000	60% × £25 000	15 000
Product liability (3% × £500 000)	15 000	1% × 500 000	5 000
Sundry fixed costs	60 000	90% × £60 000	54 000
Prevention programme costs	20 000		60 000
	519 791		454 771
Net profit	42 959		79 474

(c) A cost of quality report is a major feature of a quality control programme. The report should indicate the total cost to the organization of producing products that do not conform to quality requirements. The cost of quality report should analyse costs by prevention costs, appraisal costs, internal failure costs and external failure costs. You should refer to Chapter 22 for a description of each of these cost categories.

The cost of quality report can be used as an attention-directing device to make top management aware of how much is being spent on quality-related costs. The report can be used to draw management's attention to the possibility of reducing total quality costs by a wiser allocation of costs among the four quality categories. For example, by spending more on prevention costs, the amount of spending in the internal and external failure categories can be substantially reduced, and therefore total spending can be lowered.

Examples of each of the four cost categories for Calton Ltd are as follows:

Internal failure costs: Incoming materials scrapped due to poor receipt and storage organization, and downgrading products at the final inspection stage.

External failure costs: Free replacement of goods, product liability claims, loss of customer goodwill.

Appraisal costs: Inspection checks of incoming materials and completed output.

Prevention costs: Training costs in quality prevention and preventative maintenance.

Strategic management accounting

Solutions to Chapter 23 questions

Question 23.22

(a) Physical measures are quantitative measures that do not use monetary measurements as a common denominator. Non-financial indices are ratios that are used to compare the trend in physical measures.

(b) (i)

$$\frac{\text{processing time}}{\text{processing time} + \text{inspection time} + \text{wait time} + \text{move time}}$$

This ratio gives an indication of the proportion of manufacturing cycle time which is engaged on value-added activities. Of the activities outlined above, only processing time adds value.

(ii)

$$\frac{\text{number of deliveries not on time}}{\text{total number of deliveries}}$$

This is a measure of the extent to which a company is failing to meet customer quality requirements in terms of late deliveries.

(iii)

$$\frac{\text{closing stocks}}{\text{average production output per day}}$$

This measure provides an indication of the average number of days production in inventory. This performance measure should be analysed by inventory category and location. It provides an indication of the extent to which the objectives of a just-in-time philosophy of minimizing stock levels is being achieved.

(c) For the answer to this question see 'Criticisms of standard costing' in Chapter 19, and 'Harmful side-effects of controls' in Chapter 16 and 'JIT and management accounting' in Chapter 22.

Question 23.23

For the answer to this question you should refer to 'Benefits and limitations of the balanced scorecard approach' in Chapter 23. In addition to the points included in this section, the answer should also include the following items:

1 it integrates financial and non-financial measures of performance and identifies key performance measures that link the measurements to strategy;

2 it gives top management a fast and comprehensive view of the business unit;

3 each performance measure is part of a cause-and-effect relationship involving a linkage from strategy formulation to financial outcomes.

4 it distinguishes and links both lagging and lead measures.

See the sub-sections that immediately follow the section on establishing objectives and performance measures in Chapter 23 for specific examples of quantitative measures for each aspect of the balanced scorecard.

(a) Firms pursuing a cost leadership strategy aim to be the lowest cost producers or service providers in their industry. Accurate product costing and a strong focus on cost management are required. Accurate product costing is required to ensure that cost management initiatives are reflected in accurate product costs so that companies can have confidence in the bidding process when cost plus pricing is undertaken and also taking on business at prices less than competitors. Cost leadership accompanied by an accurate product costing system provides companies with the ability to lower price and compete effectively in times of severe competition.

Question 23.24

Firms pursuing product differentiation seek to offer products or services that are considered by their customers to be superior and unique relative to their competitors. Product differentiation seeks to add attributes that are valued by the customer and which they are willing to pay for. It is therefore important that the costing system accurately assigns the costs of the resources of providing the attributes to the products requiring them. An appropriate pricing strategy (e.g. price skimming or price penetration) should be followed that ensures that the benefits of providing the attributes are reflected in long-term profits.

(b) You should refer to 'Pricing policies' in Chapter 11 for the answer to the first part of this question. For a discussion of an activity-based approach to pricing see 'A price setting firm facing long-run pricing decisions' in Chapter 11.

(a) (i)

Question 23.25

Profit and Loss Statements
Compuaid Ltd.

	Budget (£)		Actual (£)		Competitors A (£)	B (£)
Revenues						
Home visits	440 000	(22 000 × £20)	464 000	(23 200 × £20)	87 500	810 000
All other advisors	1 168 000	(58 400 × £20)	1 442 000	(72 100 × £20)	756 180	1 266 000
Annual fee customers	584 000	(5840 × £100)	765 000	(7650 × £100)	495 000[a]	1 000 000
	2 192 000		2 671 000		1 338 680	3 076 000
Cost of sales						
Service wages	832 000	(104 000 × £8)	998 400	(124 800 × £8)	720 000	1 099 000
Sundry operating costs	950 000		1 000 000		650 000	1 250 000
Total	1 782 000		1 998 400		1 370 000	2 349 000
Profit/(loss)	410 000		672 600		(31 320)	727 000
Profit/Revenues	18.7%		25.2%		−2.3%	23.6%

Notes
[a] Company A = 6600 agreements at £75, Company B = 10 000 agreements at £100

(a) (ii) The figures show an improvement in net profits and net profits/sales compared with budget. The results also compare favourably with the competitor companies. The main reasons for the improvement and a better performance than the competitors include:
  - Annual fee customers, other advisors and home visits revenues were respectively 30%, 23% and 5% greater than budget.
  - Home visit customers were charged at a rate of £20 per hour. This is lower than the rate charged by competitors A (£87 500/3500 = £25) and B (£810 000/36 000 = £22.50).
  - The rate billed for telephone and written e-mail advice was the same as company B (£1 266 000/63 300) but higher than company A (£756 180/42 010 = £18).
  - The wage rate was £8 per hour compared with £9 per hour for A (£720 000/80 000 hours) and £7 per hour for B (£1 099 000/157 000 hours).
  - Operating costs were budgeted at 43% of sales revenues but the actual percentage was 37%. Companies A and B had, respectively, operating costs as a percentage of sales of 49% and 41%.

- The actual hours taken up by the annual fee customers for Compuaid is significantly less than the competitors:

Compuaid Ltd. = 2.0 Hours (15 300/7650)
Competitor A = 4.5 hours (29 700/6600)
Competitor C = 3.5 hours (35 000/10 000)

Compuaid receives an annual fee of £100 per customer (the same as B but more than A) but significantly less time is required, resulting in this area of the business being far more profitable for Compuaid. This could be reflected in a lower level of customer satisfaction and future growth.

(b) (i) Competitiveness can be measured by market share or sales growth. In terms of sales growth, the annual fee customers, other advisors and home visits revenues were respectively 30%, 23% and 5% greater than budget for Compuaid. Competitiveness can also be measured by the success of the uptake of home visit enquiries received. For Compuaid the budgeted level was 67% and the actual level was 50% compared with 70% and 62% for A and B. However, competitor A had only a small number of visits so competitor B represents a more valid comparison.

(b) (ii) Quality can be measured by remedial work and customer complaints. The budgeted home visits remedial work for Compuaid was 3% but the actual level was 15%. Nevertheless, the actual percentage was significantly less than A (400/1400 = 28%) and B (3400/15 000 = 23%). Customer complaints as a percentage of home visits were 1% for the budget and 2% for actual for Compuaid, compared with 5% for A and 1.5% for B.

(b) (iii) Resource utilization can be measured by the relationship between output to input hours and the percentage of home visit hours that are chargeable and non-chargeable. The budgeted ratio of output hours to input hours is 91.3% [(14 600 + 58 400 + 22 000)/104 000] and the actual ratio is 88.6%. The corresponding figures are 94% for A and 85.5% for B. For home visits the data can be analysed as follows:

	Compuaid (budget) %	Compuaid (actual) %	Company A %	Company B %
Travel	9.3	14.7	5.4	8.7
Re-work	1.8	6.1	8.2	10.1
Idle time	7.4	8.0	38.4	11.6
Chargeable hours	81.5	71.2	48.0	69.6
	100.0	100.0	100.0	100.0

Note
[a] Home visit hours = 2500 + 2000 + 500 + 22 000 = 27 000

The above analysis shows that the percentage of chargeable hours has declined from 81.5% to 71.2% of total home visit hours and there has been a marginal increase in all three categories of non-chargeable hours. However, the actual percentage of chargeable hours is greater than both competitors.

Question 23.26

(a) (i)

Analysis of the total costs of the millennium proposal

	2000 (£m)		2001 (£m)	2002 (£m)
Target cost: variable	6.000	(40% × £15m)	7.200	8.000
fixed	2.000		2.000	2.500
Internal failure cost	1.600	(20% × £8m)	0.920	0.525
External failure cost	2.000	(25% × £8m)	1.104	0.525
Appraisal costs	0.500		0.500	0.500
Prevention costs	2.000		1.000	0.500
Total cost	14.100		12.724	12.550

(a) (ii) Target costs of £8m, £7.2m and £8m in each year are significantly below the expected costs of £14.1m, £12.724m and £12.55m. The target cost represents the cost that will enable the required return on the project to be obtained. The above table shows the analysis of the gap between the target cost and the estimated cost by different categories – internal and external failure costs, appraisal costs and prevention costs. For an explanation and examples of these categories see 'Cost of quality' in Chapter 22. The answer should also point out that there appears to be a step increase in fixed costs in 2002 and a significant decline in internal and external failure costs. This may have arisen because of the large investment in prevention costs in 2000. There has also been a large decline in prevention costs over the three years possibly due to an investment in training costs in 2000 that have diminished over the years.

(b) (i) Corporate vision seeks to define the basis on which the company will compete. The company has indicated that it will seek to identify the key competitors and compete by focusing on close cooperation with its customers by providing products to meet their specific design and quality standards. The aim is to achieve the corporate vision through focusing on internal efficiency and providing an effective after-sales service.

(b) (ii) Appropriate marketing measures indicate a projected increase in sales revenues of 20% in 2001 and 11% in 2002. The market share percentages are 12.5% (£15m/£120m) in 2000, 14.4% in 2001 and 15.4% in 2002. Net profits are expected to increase each year from £0.9m in 2000 (£15m – £14.1m) to £5.28m in 2001 and £7.45m in 2002. Net profits as a percentage of sales are respectively 6%, 29.3% and 37.25%. This may be partly due to the projected fall in quality costs.

(b) (iii) There are several measures in the schedule given in the question that contribute to customer satisfaction. The percentage of production achieving design quality standards improves over the three years from 95% to 98%. Returns from customers also declines from 3% to 0.5% and the cost of after-sales service is predicted to decline from £1.5m to £1m. Sales meeting planned delivery dates increases from 90% to 95% in 2001 and a 99% level is achieved in 2002. The cycle time from customer enquiry to delivery also declines over the three years. Therefore all of the measures support the potential for increased customer satisfaction.

(b) (iv) Decreases in cycle times and levels of waste should contribute to the long-term financial success of the proposal. The average cycle time from customer enquiry to delivery also declines over the three years being 6 weeks in 2000, 5.5 weeks in 2001 and 5 weeks in 2002. Waste, as measured by idle machine capacity, declines from 10% in 2000 to 2% in 2002 and the percentage of components scrapped in production is also expected to fall from 7.5% in 2000 to 2.5% in 2002. The latter may be attributable to the investment in prevention costs. Overall the measures support improved productivity that contribute to the improvement in financial performance.

(b) (v) Measures in (b) (iv) relate to the internal business processes of the balanced scorecard that appear to contribute to improved measures of customer satisfaction shown in (b) (iii), which in turn are assumed to contribute to improved financial performance. The answer should seek to highlight the cause-and-effect relationships that are assumed to occur from adopting a balanced scorecard approach and also show how the performance measures are linked to the mission and strategy of the organization.

Cost estimation and cost behaviour

Solutions to Chapter 24 questions

Question 24.25

(a) The first stage is to convert all costs to a 2002 basis. The calculations are as follows:

	1998 (£000)	1999 (£000)	2000 (£000)	2001 (£000)
Raw materials				
Skilled labour	$242(1.2)^4$	$344(1.2)^3$	$461(1.2)^2$	$477(1.2)$
Unskilled labour				
Factory overheads	$168(1.15)^3(1.2)$	$206(1.15)^2(1.2)$	$246(1.15)(1.2)$	$265(1.2)$
Power	$25(1.1)(1.25)^3$	$33(1.25)^3$	$47(1.25)^2$	$44(1.25)$
Raw materials				
Skilled labour	500.94	595.12	663.84	572.4
Unskilled labour				
Factory overheads	306.432	326.304	339.48	318
Power	53.625	64.35	73.32	55
Total (2002 prices)	861 000	986 000	1 077 000	945 000
Output (units)	160 000	190 000	220 000	180 000

The equation $Y = a + bx$ is calculated from the above schedule of total production costs (2002 prices) and output. The calculations are as follows:

Output in units (000) x	Total cost (£000) y	x^2	xy
160	861	25 600	137 760
190	986	36 100	187 340
220	1077	48 400	236 940
180	945	32 400	170 100
$\Sigma x = 750$	$\Sigma y = 3869$	$\Sigma x^2 = 142\,500$	$\Sigma xy = 732\,140$

We now solve the following simultaneous equations:

$$\Sigma y = Na + b\Sigma x$$
$$\Sigma xy = \Sigma xa + b\Sigma x^2$$

Therefore

$$3869 = 4a + 750b \qquad (1)$$
$$732\,140 = 750a + 142\,500b \qquad (2)$$

Multiply equation (1) by 190 (142 500/750) and equation (2) by 1. Then equation (1) becomes

$$735\,110 = 760a + 142\,500b \qquad (3)$$

Subtract equation (2) from equation (3):

$$2970 = 10a$$
$$a = 297$$

Substitute for a in equation (1):

$$3869 = 4 \times 297 + 750b$$
$$2681 = 750b$$
$$b = 3.57$$

The relationship between total production costs and volume for 2002 is:

$$y = £297\,000 + 3.57x$$

where y = total production costs (at 2002 price) and x = output level.

(b) See pages 1047–1051 in Chapter 24 for the answer to this question.

(c) General company overheads will still continue whether or not product LT is produced. Therefore the output of LT will not affect general production overheads. Consequently, the regression equation should not be calculated from cost data that includes general company overheads. General company overheads will not increase with increments in output of product LT. Hence short-term decisions and cost control should focus on those costs that are relevant to production of LTs. Common and unavoidable general fixed costs are not relevant to the production of LT, and should not be included in the regression equation.

Question 24.26

(a)

$$Y_{1000} = 18 \times 1000^{-0.1520}$$
$$Y_{1000} = 18 \times 0.3499$$
$$Y_{1000} = 6.2990 \text{ minutes}$$

The cumulative average time taken to produce 1000 units is 6.2990 minutes and the time taken to produce a total of 1000 units will therefore be 629.9 minutes (i.e. 104.98 hours).

	(£)
Standard cost of 1000 units:	
Materials (£28/0.95 × 1000)	29 474
Processing cost (104.98 hours at £25)	2625
	32 099

(b)

$$Y_{5000} = 18 \times 5000^{-0.1520}$$
$$Y_{5000} = 18 \times 0.274$$
$$Y_{5000} = 4.9321 \text{ minutes}$$

Therefore the estimated time taken to produce 5000 units is 24 660 minutes (5000 × 4.9321 minutes)

$$Y_{6000} = 18 \times 6000^{-0.1520}$$
$$Y_{6000} = 18 \times 0.2665$$
$$Y_{6000} = 4.7973 \text{ minutes}$$

Therefore the estimated time taken to produce 6000 units is 28 784 minutes (6000 × 4.7973 minutes) so the 1000 units has taken an additional 68.73 hours (28 784 minutes – 24 660 minutes) giving a standard variable processing cost of £1718 (68.73 hours × £25). Adding the direct material cost of £29 474 gives a total standard variable cost of £31 192.

(c) Revised learning curve effect:

$$Y_{1000} = 18 \times 1000^{-0.320}$$
$$Y_{1000} = 18 \times 0.1096$$
$$Y_{1000} = 1.9737 \text{ minutes}$$

The estimated total time to produce 1000 units in April is 32.89 hours (1973.7 minutes/60) giving a total standard variable processing cost of £822 (32.89 hours × £25). The standard direct material cost will remain unchanged at £29 474 giving a total standard cost of £30 296.

Original budgeted profit

	(£)
Sales	60 000
Variable costs	32 099
Contribution	27 901
Fixed costs	20 000
Profit	7 901

Actual profit

		(£)	(£)
Sales (900 × £62)			55 800
Production costs:	Direct materials	31 870	
	Variable processing	1 070	
	Fixed costs	24 840	
		57 780	
Closing stock (100 units at revised standard cost of £30.296 per unit)		3 030	54 750
Profit			1 050

Variance calculations

Processing usage/efficiency variance (original standard of £2625 – revised standard of £822)	£1803F
Selling price variance (£62 actual price – £60 budgeted price) × 900 units	£1800F
Sales volume (900 actual volume – 1000 budgeted volume) × revised stand. contrib. margin[a]	£2970A
Direct material cost (standard cost of 1000 × £29.474 – Actual cost of £31 870)	£2396A
Variable processing expenditure (Flexed budget of 2425 minutes × £25/60 – actual cost)	£60A
Variable processing efficiency (1.9737 minutes revised standard × 1000 units – actual time of 2 425 minutes) × stand. rate (£25 per hour)	£188A
Fixed cost expenditure (Budgeted cost of £20 000 – Actual cost of £24 840)	£4840A
Total variances	£6851A

Notes
[a] revised standard contribution margin = £60 selling price – revised variable cost
(£29.474 + £822/1000)   = £29.704

Reconciliation statement

Original budgeted profit	£7901
Less net variances as shown above	£6851A
Actual profit	£1050

(d) If budgets and standards are set without considering the learning effect, meaningless standards are likely to be set that are easy to attain. Therefore favourable variances would be reported that are not due to operational efficiency. Where learning effects are expected, management should create an environment where improvements are expected.

(a) (i) The learning curve is expressed as:

$$yx = ax^b$$

The exponent b is defined as the ratio of the logarithm of the learning curve improvement rate divided by the logarithm of 2. For an 80% learning curve:

$$b = \log 0.8/\log 2 = -0.322$$

For an output of 14 units:

$y_{14} = 40 \times 14^{-0.322} = 17.1$ hours per unit
Time taken for 14 units $= 14 \times 17.1 = 239.4$ hrs
Actual hours $= 240$

It would therefore appear that an 80% learning effect is a reasonable assumption.

(ii) For an output of 50 units:

$$y_{50} = 40 \times 50^{-0.322} = 11.35 \text{ hours per unit}$$

Hours required for 50 units: $= 50 \times 11.35 = 567.5$ hrs
For an output of 30 units:

$$y_{30} = 40 \times 30^{-0.322} = 13.38 \text{ hours per unit}$$

Hours required for 30 units $= 30 \times 13.38 = 401.4$ hours
The time required for the additional 20 units $= 166.1$ hours $(567.5 - 401.4)$

(iii) *Estimated cost for an order of 30 units*

	(£)
Direct materials (30 × £30)	900.00
Direct labour (401.4 hrs × £6)	2408.40
Variable overhead (401.4 hrs × £0.50)	200.70
Fixed overhead (401.4 × £5)[a]	2007.00
	5516.10

The above product cost has been calculated on an absorption costing basis in accordance with the current standard absorption costing system.

Note
[a]Fixed overhead for the period $= £6000$
Direct labour hours for the period $= 1200$ (75% × 40 hrs × 10 employees
$\qquad\qquad\qquad\qquad$ × 4 weeks)
Fixed overhead hourly rate $= £5$ (£6000/1200)
Where the learning effect is present, unit product costs and labour hours will not be constant per unit of output. Significant variations in product costs and labour hours per unit of output are likely to occur at lower output levels. It is therefore necessary to estimate the extent of the learning effect for standard settings, budgeting and selling price quotations. Failure to take into account the presence of the learning effect can result in significant errors in cost estimates and planned labour requirements. If standards are not adjusted, they will cease to represent meaningful targets and lead to the reporting of erroneous favourable variances.

(b) The statement refers to the fact that, with modern technology, there is a dramatic decrease in the direct labour content of most goods and services. Recent studies suggest that direct labour represents less than 10% of manufacturing cost and that overheads are more closely related to machine hours than direct labour hours. With modern technology, output tends to be determined by machine speeds rather than changes in labour efficiency. Consequently, the presence of the learning effect as workers become more familiar with new operating procedures is of considerably less importance.

The question implies that the learning curve is being replaced by an experience curve. The experience curve relates to the fact that output and efficiency are determined by manufacturing technologists such as engineers and production planners. As these groups of individuals gain experience from a range of applications of the new technology, efficiency improves and costs are minimized. It is therefore claimed that the experience curve has replaced the learning curve. However, the experience curve is extremely difficult to determine, and its impact is likely to take place over a much longer time period. It is therefore extremely difficult to capture the 'experience effect' within short-term standard setting, budgeting and cost estimation activities.

Quantitative models for the planning and control of stocks

Solutions to Chapter 25 questions

Question 25.20

(a) *EOQ*

EOQ = $\sqrt{(2DO/H)}$
where D = demand for period (43 200 units)
       O = ordering cost per unit (£900 + £750)
       H = holding cost per unit (15% × £30 + 2 × £3.25) = £11

Note that, assuming constant demand, the average stock level is one-half of the EOQ. In this question the holding costs applicable to storage space will depend upon maximum (rather than average) stock levels. It is therefore necessary to double the holding cost per unit given in the question.

$$EOQ = \sqrt{[(2 \times 43\,200 \times £1650)/£11]} = 3600 \text{ units}$$

The EOQ is equivalent to one month's sales. Safety stocks equivalent to one month's sales are maintained. Consequently, stock levels will vary between 3600 and 7200 units.

Cash payments to trade creditors
The budgeted stock level of 21 600 units could be reduced to 7200 units. This represents stock reduction of 14 400 units, which is equivalent to 4 months' stocks. In other words, for the next four months, sales demand can be met from stocks. From month 5, purchases would be 3600 units per month.
        Budgeted monthly cost of sales = £108 000 (1296/12)

Trade creditors are therefore equivalent to 2 months' cost of sales. The schedule of payments to trade creditors would be as follows:

July and August 2000	£108 000 per month
September to December 2000	No payments made
January and February 2001	£108 000 per month

(b) (i) *Cash operating cycle at 30 June 2000*

	Months
Stockholding period (£21 600/3600)	6
Debtors average credit period [198/(2376/12)]	1
Creditors average payment period (per (a))	(2)
	5

(ii) *Cash operating cycle at 30 June 2001*

	Months
Stockholding period (7200 units)	2
Debtors (no change)	1
Creditors (no change)	(1)
	1

QUANTITATIVE MODELS FOR THE PLANNING AND CONTROL OF STOCKS ———————————— 197

(c) The answer should include a discussion of the EOQ assumptions and the extent which these may be appropriate in a practical situation. The following points should be included in the answer:

(i) The formula assumes that demand can be accurately estimated and that usage is constant throughout the period. In practice, demand may be uncertain and subject to seasonal variations. Most firms hold safety stocks as a protection against variations in demand.

(ii) The ordering costs are assumed to be constant per order placed. In practice, most of the ordering costs are fixed or subject to step functions. It is therefore difficult to estimate the incremental cost per order.

(iii) Holding costs per unit are assumed to be constant. The financing charge for the investment in stocks is based on the average investment multiplied by the cost of capital. This will result in a reasonable estimate, provided that demand can be accurately estimated and that usage and the purchase price are constant throughout the period. Many holding costs are fixed throughout the period and are not relevant to the model, but other costs (e.g. storekeepers' salaries) are step fixed costs. Opportunity costs of the warehouse space and labour are other relevant holding costs that are included in the model. However, identifying lost opportunities from holding stocks is difficult to determine. Consequently, it is extremely difficult to accurately predict the holding cost for a unit in stock for one year.

(iv) Purchasing cost per unit is assumed to be constant for all purchase quantities. In practice, quantity discounts can result in purchasing economies of scale.

(v) Despite the fact that much of the data in the model represent rough approximations, the EOQ formula is likely to provide a reasonable guide of the EOQ because it is very insensitive to errors in predictions (see 'Effect of approximations' in Chapter 25). The EOQ model can also be adapted to incorporate quantity discounts. For a discussion of other issues relevant to this answer see 'Assumptions of the EOQ formula' in Chapter 25.

(d) The advantages of adopting a JIT approach include:
(i) Substantial savings in stockholding costs.
(ii) Elimination of waste.
(iii) Savings in factory and warehouse space, which can be used for other profitable activities.
(iv) Reduction in obsolete stocks.
(v) Considerable reduction in paperwork arising from a reduction in purchasing, stock and accounting transactions.

The disadvantages include:
(i) Additional investment costs in new machinery, changes in plant layout and goods inwards facilities.
(ii) Difficulty in predicting daily or weekly demand, which is a key feature of the JIT philosophy.
(iii) Increased risk due to the greater probability of stockout costs arising from strikes, or other unforeseen circumstances, that restrict production or supplies.

Question 25.21

(a) Order costs consist of variable purchasing costs (£300) plus transportation costs (£750 or £650). Note that the timing of the payments for 4200 units will be the same irrespective of the order size. Consequently, the cost of capital is omitted from the stockholding costs because it will be the same for all order quantities.

$$\text{EOQ with transportation costs of £750} = \sqrt{\left(\frac{2 \times 1050 \times 4200}{4}\right)}$$

$$= 1485 \text{ units}$$

At this level the company qualifies for the lower transport costs. Therefore the EOQ should be based on ordering costs of £950:

$$EOQ = \sqrt{\left(\frac{2 \times 950 \times 4200}{4}\right)} = 1412 \text{ units}$$

The company should therefore place orders for 1412 units.

Improvement in profit

		(£)
Gross profit (unchanged)		64 000
Purchasing department costs:		
Variable (4200/1412) × £300	(892)	
Fixed	(8400)	(9 292)
Transportation costs:		
(4200/1412) × £650		(1 933)
Insurance costs on average stockholding:		
[200 safety stock + (1412/2)] × £4		(3 624)
Warehouse fixed costs		(43 000)
Revised profit		6 151
Original profit		3 250
Improvement		2 901

(b) The re-order level should be based on the expected usage during the period plus a safety stock to provide a cushion in the event of demand being in excess of the expected usage.

Expected usage = (500 × 0.15) + (600 × 0.20) + (700 × 0.30) + (800 × 0.20)
                 + (900 × 0.15) = 700

Thus it is necessary to consider safety stocks of 0, 100 or 200 units.

Expected usage (units)	Safety stock (units)	Re-order point (units)	Stockout (units)	Annual stockout cost[a] (£18 per unit)	Probability	Annual expected stockout cost (£)	Holding cost[b] (£)	Total expected cost (£)
700	0	700	200	21 600	0.15	3240		
			100	10 800	0.20	2160		
						5400	0	5400
700	100	800	100	10 800	0.15	1620	1800	3420
700	200	900	0	0		0	3600	3600

Notes

[a]Note that expected costs are calculated on an *annual* basis by multiplying 200 units × £18 × 6 (that is, six two-monthly periods).

[b]In the answer to part (a) the interest on the value of the stock was not included, because the timing of the payments for stocks was not affected by the order quantity. Consequently, the interest charge was not relevant in calculating the EOQ. The holding cost in the above calculation consists of £14 interest cost (20% of £70 purchase cost) plus £4 insurance cost. It is assumed that the safety stock represents an investment over and above the annual order quantity of 4200 units. In other words, safety stocks represent an incremental investment, and interest on safety stocks is therefore relevant to the safety stock decision.

Recommendation
Expected costs are minimized at a re-order point of 800 units (this includes a safety stock of 100 units).

(c) The answer to this question should include a discussion of the assumptions of the EOQ model (see 'Assumptions of the EOQ formula' in Chapter 25). The answer should stress that because demand is uncertain and not uniform and lead time is not constant, it is necessary to adjust the EOQ model to take account of these facts. The safety stock model applied in (b) is subject to a number of practical difficulties – for example, the difficulty of producing probability distributions for demand and lead time. In addition, stockout costs are extremely difficult to determine in practice. A further problem is that discrete distributions as estimated in (b) are unlikely to be a representation of reality because they are based on a limited number of outcomes. The answer produced represents the *expected value* of the stockholding costs, and as such represents a long-run average outcome. An alternative is to use continuous distributions, but this requires that the distribution conform to one that can easily be described mathematically (e.g. a normal distribution).

In practice, it is likely that stockout costs will be the most significant cost, and the problem is one of determining the minimum level of stock that is consistent with always satisfying demand. Most small companies are likely to concentrate on frequently reviewing stock levels and use their previous experience to subjectively determine order levels.

Question 25.22

(a) Expected annual demand $= 10\,000$ units $\times 52$ weeks $= 520\,000$ units
Holding cost per unit $= 18\%$ of purchase price (£4.50) $= £0.81$

$$\text{EOQ} = \sqrt{\left(\frac{2 \times 520\,000 \times £311.54}{0.81}\right)}$$
$$= 20\,000 \text{ units}$$

(b) The average usage during the two week lead time is 20 000 units. If sales were always 10 000 units per week, the re-order point would be 20 000 units and stocks would be replenished when the stock level had fallen to zero. No safety stocks would be required. However, if demand is in excess of 20 000 units, stockouts will occur if no safety stocks are maintained. Consideration should therefore be given to holding safety stocks.

Maintaining safety stocks reduces the probability of running out of stock and incurring stockout costs, but this policy also results in additional holding costs. The annual holding cost per unit is £0.81. Over a two-week period, the holding cost per unit is £0.031 15 (£0.81/26 weeks). Stockout costs consist of the costs associated with losing orders. The cost of losing an order is the contribution per unit of £1.50 [£6.30 − (£4.50 + £0.30)]. The lost contribution applies to 25% of the orders in any two-week period. The expected stockout cost is therefore £0.375 (0.25 × £1.50) per unit.

The expected costs for various levels of safety stocks are as follows:

Safety stock (units)	Re-order point (units)	Stockout (units)	Probability of stockout	Expected stockout cost (£)	Holding cost (£)	Total Expected cost (£)
8000	28 000	0	0	0	249[a]	249
4000	24 000	4000	0.05	75[b]	125[a]	200
0	20 000	4000	0.20	300[b]		
		8000	0.05	150[b]	0	450

Expected costs are minimized when safety stocks are 4000 units. Therefore the recommended level of safety stocks is 4000 units.

Notes

[a]Safety stocks of 8000 units = holding cost of 8000 × £0.031 15 = £249

 Safety stocks of 4000 units = holding cost of 4000 × £0.031 15 = £125.

[b]Safety stocks of 4000 units: stockout of 4000 units × £0.375 × 0.05 probability = £75

Safety stocks of zero: if demand is 24 000 units (probability = 0.20), there will be a 4000 units stockout, with an expected cost of 4000 × £0.375 × 0.2 = £300. If demand is 28 000 units (probability = 0.05), there will be a stockout of 8000 units, with an expected cost of 8000 × £0.375 × 0.05 = £150.

(c) If 30 000 units are ordered instead of 20 000 units, there will be an annual purchase cost saving of £23 400 (1% × 520 000 units × £4.50) resulting from the quantity discount. The annual savings in order costs will be as follows:

$$(520\ 000/30\ 000 \times £311.54) - (520\ 000/20\ 000 \times £311.54) = £2700$$

Total annual savings are therefore £26 100 (£23 400 + £2700). The annual holding costs are as follows:

30 000 units = 18% × £4.455 revised purchase price × 15 000 units average
            stock = £12 028
20 000 units = 18% × £4.50 purchase price × 10 000 units average stock = £8100

Therefore the additional holding cost is £3928 (£12 028 – £8100) and the overall net saving is £22 172 (£26 100 – £3928). It would therefore be beneficial to take advantage of the quantity discount.

(d) Total relevant costs would be as follows:

50% higher (30 000 units)   = £0.81 × (30 000/2) + £311.54 × (520 000/30 000)
                                  = £17 550
50% lower (10 000 units)   = £0.81 × (10 000/2) + £311.54 × (520 000/10 000)
                                  = £20 250
Original EOQ (20 000 units) = £0.81 × (20 000/2) + £311.54 × (520 000/20 000)
                                  = £16 200

It is assumed that this part of the question refers to the original data given and that the quantity discount is not available. Total annual costs are 8.3% higher than the original EOQ at the 30 000-units order level and 25% higher at the 10 000-units order level. Therefore stock management costs are relatively insensitive to substantial changes in the EOQ.

(e) It would be necessary to establish seasonal periods where sales are fairly constant throughout each period. A separate EOQ would then be established for each distinct season throughout the year.

(f) The EOQ model is a model that enables the costs of stock management to be minimized. The model is based on the following assumptions.
  (i) Constant purchase price per unit irrespective of the order quantity.
 (ii) Ordering costs are constant for each order placed.
(iii) Constant lead times.
(iv) Constant holding costs per unit.
More sophisticated versions of the above model have been developed that are not dependent on the above assumptions. However, the EOQ is fairly insensitive to changes in the variables used in the model.

Recently, some companies have adopted just-in-time (JIT) purchasing techniques whereby they have been able to negotiate reliable and frequent deliveries. This has been accompanied by the issue of blanket long-term purchase orders and a substantial reduction in ordering costs. The overall effect of applying the EOQ formula in this situation ties in with the JIT philosophy: that is, more frequent purchases of smaller quantities.

The application of linear programming to management accounting

Solutions to Chapter 26 questions

Question 26.16

(a)

	M	F
Contribution per unit	£96	£110
Litres of material P required	8	10
Contribution per litre of material P	£12	£11
Ranking	1	2
Production/sales (units)	1000	2325[a]

Note

[a] 31 250 litres of P less (1000 × 8) for M = 23 250 litres for F giving a total production of 2325 units (23 250 litres/10)

(b)

	M (£000)	F (£000)	Total (£000)
Sales	200	488.250	688.250
Variable costs:			
Material P	20	58.125	78.125
Material Q	40	46.500	86.500
Direct labour	28	81.375	109.375
Overhead	16	46.500	62.500
	104	232.500	336.500
Contribution	96	255.750	351.750
Fixed costs (£150 000 + £57 750)			207.750
Profit			144.000

(c) Maximize Z = 96M + 110F (product contributions) subject to:

8M + 10F ≤ 31 250 (material P constraint)
10M + 5F ≤ 20 000 (material Q constraint)
4M + 5F ≤ 17 500 (direct labour constraint)
M ≤ 1 000 (maximum demand for M)
F ≤ 3 000 (maximum demand for F)

The above constraints are plotted on the graph shown in Figure Q26.16 as follows:

    Material P; Line from M = 3906.25, F = 0 to F = 3125, M = 0
    Material Q; Line from M = 2000, F = 0 to F = 4000, M = 0
    Direct labour; Line from M = 4375, F = 0 to F = 3500, M = 0
    Sales demand of M; Line from M = 1000
    Sales demand of F; Line from F = 3000

The optimal solution occurs where the lines in Figure 26.16 intersect for material P and Q constraints. The point can be determined from the graph or mathematically as follows:

8M + 10F = 31 250 (material P constraint)
10M + 5F = 20 000 (material Q constraint)

multiplying the first equation by 1 and the second equation by 2:

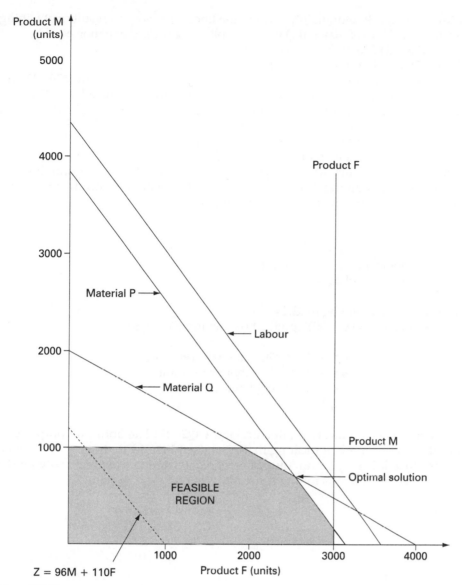

Product M (units)

5000

4000

Product F

3000

Material P →

← Labour

2000

← Material Q

Product M

1000

← Optimal solution

FEASIBLE
REGION

1000   2000   3000   4000

Z = 96M + 110F

Product F (units)

Figure Q26.16

$8M + 10F = 31\ 250$
$20M + 10F = 40\ 000$
subtracting $-12M = -8750$
$M = 729.166$

Substituting for M in the first equation:

$8(729.166) + 10F = 31\ 250$
$F = 2541.667$

(d)

		(£)
Contribution:	(729 units of M at £96)	69 984
	(2542 units of F at £110)	279 620
		349 604
Less fixed costs		207 750
Profit		141 854

Moving from the solution in (c) where the lines intersect as a result of obtaining an additional litre of material Q gives the following revised equations:

8M + 10F = 31 250 (material P constraint)
10M + 5F = 20 001 (material Q constraint)

The values of M and F when the above equations are solved are 729.333 and 2541.533. Therefore, M is increased by 0.167 units and F is reduced by 0.134 units giving an additional total contribution of £1.292 [0.167 × £96) – (0.134 × £110)] per additional litre of Q. Therefore the shadow price of Q is £1.292 per litre.

(e) See Chapter 26 for an explanation of shadow prices.

(f) Other factors to be taken into account include the impact of failing to meet the demand for product M, the need to examine methods of removing the constraints by sourcing different markets for the materials and the possibility of sub-contracting to meet the unfulfilled demand.

Question 26.17

(a) Let X = number of units of XL produced each week
   Y = number of units of YM produced each week
   Z = total contribution

The linear programming model is:
   Maximize $Z = 40X + 30Y$ (product contributions) subject to

$$4X + 4Y \leq 120 \text{ (materials constraint)}$$
$$4X + 2Y \leq 100 \text{ (labour constraint)}$$
$$X + 2Y \leq 50 \text{ (plating constraint)}$$
$$X, Y \geq 0$$

The above constraints are plotted on Figure Q26.17. The optimum output is at point C on the graph, indicating that 20 units of XL and 10 units of YM should be produced. The optimum output can be determined exactly by solving the simultaneous equations for the constraints that intersect at point C:

$$4X + 4Y = 120$$
$$4X + 2Y = 100$$
Subtracting $\quad 2Y = 20$
$$Y = 10$$

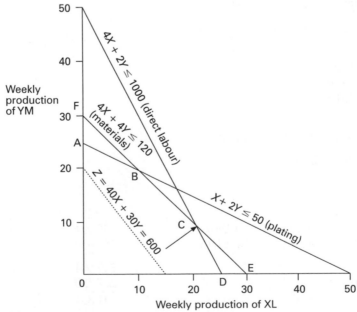

Figure Q26.17

Substituting for Y:

$$4X + 40 = 120$$
$$X = 20$$

The maximum weekly profit is:

$$(20 \times £40) + (10 \times £30) - £700 \text{ fixed costs} = £400$$

(b) The present objective function is $40X + 30Y$ and the gradient of this line is $-40/30$. If the selling price of YM were increased, the contribution of YM would increase and the gradient of the line ($-40/30$) would decrease. The current optimal point is C because the gradient of the objective function line is greater than the gradient of the line for the constraint of materials (the line on which the optimal point C falls). If the gradient of the objective function line were equal to the gradient of the line for the materials constraint, the optimal solution would be any point on FC. The gradient for the materials constraint line is -1. If the gradient for the objective function line were less than -1, the optimal solution would change from point C to point B. The gradient of the line for the current objective function of $40X + 30Y$ will be greater than -1 as long as the contribution from YM is less than £40. If the contribution from YM is £40 or more, the optimum solution will change. Therefore the maximum selling price for YM is £190 (£150 variable cost + £40 contribution).

(c) If plating time can be sold for £16 per hour then any hour devoted to XLs and YMs loses £16 sales revenue. The relevant cost per plating hour is now £16 opportunity cost. The contributions used in the objective function should be changed to reflect this opportunity cost. The contribution should be reduced by £4 (1 hour at £16 − £12) for XL and by £8 (2 hours at £16 −£12) for YL. The revised objective function is:

$$Z = 36X + 22Y$$

(d) The scarce resources are materials and labour. This is because these two constraints intersect at the optimal point C. Plating is not a scarce resource, and the shadow price is zero.

If we obtain an additional unit of materials the revised constraints will be:

$$4X + 4Y = 121 \text{ (materials)}$$
$$4X + 2Y = 100 \text{ (labour)}$$

The values of X and Y when the above equations are solved at 10.5 for Y and 19.75 for X. Therefore YM is increased by 0.5 units and XL is reduced by 0.25 units and the change in contribution will be as follows:

	(£)
Increase in contribution of YM (0.5 × £30)	15
Decrease in contribution of XL (0.25 × £40)	10
Increase in contribution (shadow price)	5

If we obtain one additional labour hour, the revised constraints will be:

$$4X + 4Y = 120 \text{ (materials)}$$
$$4X + 2Y = 101 \text{ (labour)}$$

The values of X and Y when the above equations are solved are 9.5 for Y and 20.5 for X. Therefore XL is increased by 0.5 units and YM is reduced by 0.5 units, and the change in contribution will be as follows:

	(£)
Increase in contribution from XL (0.5 × £40)	20
Decrease in contribution from YM (0.5 × £30)	15
Increase in contribution (shadow price)	5

The relevant cost of resources used in producing ZN consists of the acquisition cost plus the shadow price (opportunity cost). The relevant cost calculation is:

		(£)
Material A [5 kg at (£10 + £5)]		75
Labour [5 hours at (£8 + £5)]		65
Plating (1 hour at £12)		12
Other variable costs		90
		242

The selling price is less than the relevant cost. Therefore product ZN is not a profitable addition to the product range.

(e) The shadow price of labour is £5 per hour. Therefore the company should be prepared to pay up to £5 in excess of the current rate of £8 in order to remove the constraint. An overtime payment involves an extra £4 per hour, and therefore overtime working is worthwhile.

Increasing direct labour hours will result in the labour constraint shifting to the right. However, when the labour constraint line reaches point E, further increases in labour will not enable output to be expanded (this is because other constraints will be binding). The new optimal product mix will be at point E, with an output of 30 units of XL and zero of YM. This product mix requires 120 hours (30 × 4 hrs). Therefore 120 labour hours will be worked each week. Note that profit will increase by £20 [20 × (£5 – £4)].

(f) The limitations are as follows:

(i) It is assumed that the objective function and the constraints are linear functions of the two variables. In practice, stepped fixed costs might exist or resources might not be used at a constant rate throughout the entire output range. Selling prices might have to be reduced to increase sales volume.

(ii) Constraints are unlikely to be completely fixed and as precise as implied in the mathematical model. Some constraints can be removed at an additional cost.

(iii) The output of the model is dependent on the accuracy of the estimates used. In practice, it is difficult to segregate costs accurately into their fixed and variable elements.

(iv) Divisibility of output is not realistic in practice (fractions of products cannot be produced). This problem can be overcome by the use of integer programming.

(v) The graphical approach requires that only two variables (products) be considered. If several products compete for scarce resources, it will be necessary to use the Simplex method.

(vi) Qualitative factors are not considered. For example, if overtime is paid, the optimum solution is to produce zero of product YM. This will result in the demand from regular customers for YM (who might also buy XM) not being met. This harmful effect on customer goodwill is not reflected in the model.

Question 26.18   (a) The calculation of the contributions for each product is:

	X1	X2	X3
	(£)	(£)	(£)
Selling price	83	81	81
Materials[a]	(51)	(45)	(54)
Manufacturing costs[b]	(11)	(11)	(11)
Contribution	21	25	16

Notes
[a]The material cost per tonne for each product is:

$$X1 = (0.1 \times £150) + (0.1 \times £60) + (0.2 \times £120) + (0.6 \times £10) = £51$$
$$X2 = (0.1 \times £150) + (0.2 \times £60) + (0.1 \times £120) + (0.6 \times £10) = £45$$
$$X3 = (0.2 \times £150) + (0.1 \times £60) + (0.1 \times £120) + (0.6 \times £10) = £54$$

[b]It is assumed that manufacturing costs do not include any fixed costs. The initial linear programming model is as follows:

$$\text{Maximize } Z = 21X1 + 25X2 + 16X3$$
$$\text{subject to } 0.1X1 + 0.1X2 + 0.2X3 \leqslant 1200 \text{ (nitrate)}$$
$$0.1X1 + 0.2X2 + 0.1X3 \leqslant 2000 \text{ (phosphate)}$$
$$0.2X1 + 0.1X2 + 0.1X3 \leqslant 2200 \text{ (potash)}$$
$$X1, X2, X3 \geqslant 0$$

(b) The slack variables are introduced to represent the amount of each of the scarce resources unused at the point of optimality. This enables the constraints to be expressed in equalities. The initial Simplex tableau is:

	$X1$	$X2$	$X3$
$X4$ (nitrate) = 1200	-0.1	-0.1	-0.2
$X5$ (phosphate) = 2000	-0.1	-0.2	-0.1
$X6$ (potash) = 2200	-0.2	-0.1	-0.1
Z (contribution) = 0	21	25	16

(c) The starting point for the first iteration is to select the product with the highest contribution (that is, $X2$), but production of $X2$ is limited because of the input constraints. Nitrate ($X4$) limits us to a maximum production of 12 000 tonnes (1200/0.1), $X5$ to a maximum production of 10 000 tonnes (2000/0.2) and $X6$ to a maximum production of 22 000 tonnes (2200/0.1). We are therefore restricted to a maximum production of 10 000 tonnes of product $X2$ because of the $X5$ constraint. The procedure which we should follow is to rearrange the equation that results in the constraint (that is, $X5$) in terms of the product we have chosen to make (that is, $X2$). Therefore the $X5$ equation is re-expressed in terms of $X2$, and $X5$ will be replaced in the second iteration by $X2$. (Refer to 'Choosing the product' in Chapter 26 if you are unsure of this procedure.) Thus $X2$ is the entering variable and $X5$ is the leaving variable.

(d) Following the procedure outlined in Chapter 26, the final tableau given in the question can be reproduced as follow:

	Quantity	$X3$	$X4$	$X5$
$X1$	4 000	-3	-20	$+10$
$X2$	8 000	$+1$	$+10$	-10
$X6$	600	$+0.4$	$+3$	-1
Z	284 000	-22	-170	-40

In Chapter 26 the approach adopted was to formulate the first tableau with positive contribution signs and negative signs for the slack variable equations. The optimal solution occurs when the signs in the contribution row are all negative. The opposite procedure has been applied with the tableau presented in the question. Therefore the signs have been reversed in the above tableau to ensure it is in the same format as that presented in Chapter 26. Note that when an entry of 1 is shown in a row or column for a particular product or slack variable then the entry does not appear in the above tableau. For example, $X1$ has an entry of 1 for the $X1$ row and $X1$ column. These cancel out and the entry is not made in the above tableau. Similarly, an entry of 1 is omitted in respect of $X2$ and $X6$.

The optimum solution is to produce 4000 tonnes of $X1$, 8000 tonnes of $X2$ and zero $X3$ each month. This gives a monthly contribution of £284 000, uses all the nitrate ($X4$) and phosphate ($X5$), but leaves 600 tonnes of potash ($X6$) unused.

The opportunity costs of the scarce resources are:

Nitrate ($X4$)	£170 per tonne
Phosphate ($X5$)	£40 per tonne

If we can obtain an additional tonne of nitrate then output of $X1$ should be increased by 20 tonnes and output of $X2$ should be reduced by 10 tonnes.

Note that we reverse the signs when additional resources are obtained. The effect of this substitution process on each of the resources and contribution is as follows:

	Nitrate ($X4$) (tonnes)	Phosphate ($X5$) (tonnes)	Potash ($X6$) (tonnes)	Contribution (£)
Increase $X1$ by 20 tonnes	$-2(20 \times 0.1)$	-2	-4	$+420$
Reduce $X2$ by 10 tonnes	$+1(10 \times 0.1)$	$+2$	$+1$	-250
Net effect	-1	0	-3	$+170$

The net effect agrees with the $X4$ column in the final tableau. That is, the substitution process will use up exactly the one additional tonne of nitrate, 3 tonnes of unused resources of potash and increase contribution by £170.

To sell one unit of $X3$, we obtain the resources by reducing the output of $X1$ by 3 tonnes and increasing the output of $X2$ by 1 tonne. (Note the signs are not reversed, because we are not obtaining additional scarce resources.) The effect of this substitution process is to reduce contribution by £22 for each tonne of $X3$ produced. The calculation is as follows:

$$\text{Increase } X3 \text{ by 1 tonne} = +£16 \text{ contribution}$$
$$\text{Increase } X2 \text{ by 1 tonne} = +£25 \text{ contribution}$$

$$\underline{\text{Reduce } X1 \text{ by 3 tonnes} = -£63}$$
$$\underline{\text{Loss of contribution} \quad = -£22}$$

(e) (i) Using the substitution process outlined in (d), the new values if 100 extra tonnes of nitrate are obtained will be:

$$X1 \ 4000 + (20 \times 100) = 6000$$
$$X2 \ 8000 - (10 \times 100) = 7000$$
$$X6 \ 600 - (3 \times 100) = 300$$
$$\text{Contribution } 284\,000 + (£170 \times 100) = £301\,000$$

Hence the new optimal solution is to make 6000 tonnes of $X1$ and 7000 tonnes of $X2$ per month, and this output will yield a contribution of £301 000.

(ii) Using the substitution process outlined in (d), the new values if 200 tonnes per month of $X3$ are supplied will be:

$$X1 \ 4000 - (3 \times 200) = 3400$$
$$X2 \ 8000 + (1 \times 200) = 8200$$
$$X6 \ 600 + (0.4 \times 200) = 680$$
$$X3 \ 0 + (1 \times 200) = 200$$
$$\text{Contribution } £284\,000 - (£22 \times 200) = 279\,600$$

Hence the new optimal solution is to produce 3400 tonnes of $X1$, 8200 tonnes of $X2$ and 200 tonnes of $X3$, and this output will yield a contribution of £279 600. (Note that the signs in the final tableau are only reversed when *additional* scarce *resources* are obtained.)

THE APPLICATION OF LINEAR PROGRAMMING TO MANAGEMENT ACCOUNTING

(a) The company should invest in companies A, C and D since they yield positive **Question 26.19**
NPVs. The company should be indifferent about investing in B since it yields a
zero NPV.

(b) (i)

	A ($000)	B ($000)	C ($000)	D ($000)
Present value	60	0	77	80
Investment at time 0	500	250	475	800
NPV per $1 invested at time 0	0.12	0	0.162	0.10
Ranking	2	4	1	3

The company should invest $475 000 in C and the balance of the funds
($225 000) in A.

(b) (ii) Other factors that should be considered are:

1   The risk of the cash flows of each company. A single cost of capital has
been applied to all investments, but the riskier the investment the higher
should be the cost of capital.

2   Are the cash flows of the companies highly correlated? If the cash flows
for two of the companies are not highly correlated, the total risk of the
two investments will be lower than the sum of the individual
investments (see 'Portfolio analysis' in Chapter 12 for an explanation).

3   The experience of the staff in the individual companies and the extent to
which they are dependent on a small number of key staff. Where the
success of a company is dependent on a small number of key staff,
obtaining the returns on the investment will be at risk should the staff
leave.

4   The speed of the payback period if the cash flows can be used to reinvest
in new projects. This is mainly applicable to when funds in future
periods are restricted.

(c)

Let X1 = Proportion of funds invested in company A
Let X2 = Proportion of funds invested in company B
Let X3 = Proportion of funds invested in company C
Let X4 = Proportion of funds invested in company D

Maximize 60X1 + 0X2 + 77X3 + 80X4

Subject to:

500X1 + 250X2 + 475X3 + 80X4 + S1 = 700 (period 0 constraint)
75X1 + 30X2 + 100X3 + 150X4 + S2 = 89.6[1] (period 1 constraint)
40X1 + 20X2 + 30X3 + 50X4 + S3 = 43.91[1] (period 2 constraint)
$0 \le X_j \le 1$ (j = 1, ... 3)

Note
[1] The constraints are expressed in present values, but it is assumed that
constraints applying will be expressed in period 1 and period 2 cash flows so
period 1 = $80 (1.12) and period 2 = $35 (1.12)^2.

The objective function specifies that NPV is to be maximized subject to the investment constraints for the three periods. The terms S1, S2, etc. represent the slack
variables in the form of any unused funds for each period. The final term in the
model indicates that any project (signified by X_j) cannot be undertaken more than
once, but allows for a project to be partially undertaken. For a more detailed
explanation of the meaning of the terms in a capital budgeting model you should
refer to Appendix 26.1.

(d) The benefits from using linear programming in this situation are:
1   Complex investment problems and constraints can be modelled and solved
using computer programs.

2 The model generates opportunity costs and marginal rates of substitution which can be useful for decision-making and control.

3 The model is flexible and can be applied to where fractional projects can be undertaken or modified to exclude fractional investments.

Question 26.20

(a) Let a, b, c, d, e, f and g represent the proportion of projects A, B, C, D, E, F and G accepted and X represent the amount of money placed on deposit in 2001 in £000. The NPV of £1000 placed on deposit is:

$$\frac{£1000(1.08)}{1.10} - £1000 = -£18 = £-0.018 \text{ (in £000)}$$

Maximize $Z = 39a + 35b + 5c + 15d + 14e + 32f + 24g - 0.018X$

subject to $80a + 70b + 55c + 60d + X + \text{DIV0} \leq 250$ (2001 constraint in £000)

$30a + 140e + 80f + 100g + \text{DIV1} \leq 150 + 20b + 40c + 30d + 1.08X$

(2002 constraint in £000)

$$\text{DIV0} \geq 100$$
$$\text{DIV1} \geq 1.05 \text{ DIV0}$$
$$a, b, c, d, e, fg \geq 0$$
$$a, b, c, d, e, fg \leq 1$$

Note that surplus funds are placed on deposit only for 2001. After 2003, capital is available without limit. Consequently, it is assumed at 2002 that it is unnecessary to maintain funds for future periods by placing funds on deposit to yield a negative NPV. It is assumed that capital constraints can be eased by project generated cash flows.

(b) The dual or shadow prices indicate the opportunity costs of the budget constraints for 2001 and 2002. The dual values indicate the NPV that can be gained from obtaining an additional £1 cash for investment in 2001 and 2002. The zero dual value for 2002 indicates that the availability of cash is not a binding constraint in 2002, whereas in 2001 the dual value indicates that £1 additional cash for investment in 2001 will yield an increase in total NPV of £0.25.

The dual values also indicate how much it is worth paying over and above the existing cost of funds. In this question it is worth paying up to £0.25 over and above the existing cost of capital for each £1 invested in 2001. In other words, the company should be prepared to pay up to 35% (10% acquisition cost + 25% opportunity cost) to raise additional finance in 2001.

Dual values can also be used to appraise any investments that might be suggested as substitutes for projects A to G. If the company identifies another project with a life of one year and a cash outflow of £130 000 at t_0 and an inflow of £150 000 at t_1, the NPV would be £3364 at a cost of capital of 10%. However, acceptance of the project would result in a reduction in NPVs from diverting funds from other projects of £32 500 (£130 000 × £0.25). The project should therefore be rejected.

Dual values are not constant for an infinite range of resources. They apply only over a certain range. The question indicates that the values apply over a range between £120 000 and £180 000. Outside this range, it will be necessary to develop a revised model to ascertain the dual values that would be applicable. If resources continued to be increased, a point would be reached at which all potential projects with positive NPVs would have been accepted. Beyond this point, there would be no binding constraints and capital rationing would cease to exist.

(c) Capital rationing can be defined as a situation where there are insufficient funds available to undertake all those projects that yield a positive NPV. The literature distinguishes between hard and soft capital rationing. Hard capital rationing refers to those situations where firms do not have access to investment funds and are therefore unable to raise any additional finance at any price. It is most unlikely that firms will be subject to hard capital rationing.

Soft capital rationing refers to those situations where capital rationing is internally imposed. For various reasons, top management may pursue a policy of limiting the amount of funds available for investment in any one period. Such policies may apply to firms that restrict their financing of new investments to internal funds. Alternatively, in a large divisionalized company, top management may limit the funds available to divisional managers for investment. Such restrictions on available funds may be for various reasons. For example, a company may impose its own restrictions on borrowing limits or avoid new equity issues because of a fear of outsiders gaining control of the business.

Where capital rationing exists, the NPV rule of accepting *all* positive NPV projects must be modified. Where capital is rationed for a single period, the approach outlined in Chapter 14 (see 'Capital rationing') should be applied. Where capital is rationed for more than one period, the optimal investment plan requires the use of mathematical programming (see Chapter 26). The application of the latter is based on a number of underlying assumptions that are unlikely to hold in the real world. For a discussion of these assumptions see the Appendix to Chapter 26.